'As our discipline undertakes the collective responsibility imposed upon it by its method—what good are we as analysts if we cannot face ourselves?—we could have no finer accompaniment than this volume. Braiding personal reflection (some searing), theoretical elaboration, clinical work and social activism, the text becomes a place where we meet ourselves beyond the facile comforts of binary thinking. If this book leads more deeply into the knotty racial labyrinths of our historically shadowed present, it is in the belief that there is no way out but through. Psychoanalysis needs such tools for staying with the good trouble it is in.'

**Francisco J. González**, *personal and supervising analyst; co-chair of Community Psychoanalysis Track, Psychoanalytic Institute of Northern California; staff psychiatrist, Instituto Familiar de la Raza*

'This is a book for our moment. Rachel Kabasakalian-McKay and David Mark and their colleagues have put together a collection of essays that are deeply and sensitively engaged with the myriad crises that define us—especially the crisis of racism, in the context of contemporary relational psychoanalysis. While diverse in their perspectives, the essays are united in taking up both sociopolitical injustices and intimate psychic dynamics: they powerfully combine emotional vulnerability and theoretical savvy. Whether focused on geopolitical conflicts or familial trauma, structural racism or the structures of educational and psychoanalytic institutions, this book helps us understand what it feels like to live in—and think through—complex forms of personal and political responsibility.'

**Michael Rothberg**, *author of* The Implicated Subject: Beyond Victims and Perpetrators

'This is a powerful and exceptional collection of essays and articles that the editors, Rachel Kabasakalian-McKay and David Mark, have astutely assembled and one that I highly recommend. In inviting their authors to address and integrate Michael Rothberg's lens of the "implicated subject and complex implication," they have assembled what will be an indispensable text for the field, both for training in psychoanalysis and for clinicians before and after their training. These authors, who write from a myriad of subject positions, advance how the social, historical/political, racial, cultural, class/caste, and gender/sexuality aspects necessarily can and must be fully integrated into psychoanalytic theories and praxis. These writers offer compelling examples and experiences that prove that no one is outside of regimes of oppression and privilege, and neither is psychoanalysis nor the training institutes. After reading each chapter, I am left with immense gratitude for the deep and thoughtful work that has been done and inspired to make sure this work continues.'

**Jill Salberg**, *faculty and supervisor at the NYU Postdoctoral Program in Psychotherapy and Psychoanalysis*

# Inhabiting Implication in Racial Oppression and in Relational Psychoanalysis

What does it feel like to encounter ourselves and one another as *implicated subjects*, both in our everyday lives and in the context of our work as clinicians, and how does this matter?

With contributions from a diverse group of relational psychoanalytic thinkers, this book reads Michael Rothberg's concept of the *implicated subject*—the notion that we are continuously implicated in injustices even when not perpetrators—as calling us to elaborate on what it feels like to inhabit such subjectivities in relation to others both similarly and differently situated. Implication and anti-Black racism are central to many chapters, with attention given to the unique vulnerability of racial minority immigrants, to Native American genocide, and to the implication of ordinary Israelis in the oppression of Palestinians. The book makes the case that the therapist's ongoing openness to learning of our own implication in enactments is central to a relational sensibility and to a progressive psychoanalysis.

As a contribution to the necessary and long-overdue conversation within the psychoanalytic field about racism, social injustice, and ways to move toward a just society, this book will be essential for all relational psychoanalysts and psychotherapists.

**Rachel Kabasakalian-McKay** (she/her) is a founding board member and the co-director of the Institute for Relational Psychoanalysis of Philadelphia and is on the faculty of the Stephen Mitchell Relational Study Center in New York. Her work has appeared in *Psychoanalytic Dialogues*, *Psychoanalytic Inquiry*, and *Psychoanalytic Perspectives*.

**David Mark** is co-director of the Institute for Relational Psychoanalysis of Philadelphia. With Jeffrey Faude, he is the author of *Psychotherapy of Cocaine Addiction: Entering the Interpersonal World of the Cocaine Addict* (1997). Other works of his have appeared in *Contemporary Psychoanalysis*, *Psychoanalytic Dialogues*, and *Psychoanalytic Perspectives*.

Relational Perspectives Book Series

ADRIENNE HARRIS & EYAL ROZMARIN
Series Editors

STEPHEN MITCHELL
Founding Editor

LEWIS ARON
Editor Emeritus

The Relational Perspectives Book Series (RPBS) publishes books that grow out of or contribute to the relational tradition in contemporary psychoanalysis. The term *relational psychoanalysis* was first used by Greenberg and Mitchell[1] to bridge the traditions of interpersonal relations, as developed within interpersonal psychoanalysis and object relations, as developed within contemporary British theory. But, under the seminal work of the late Stephen A. Mitchell, the term *relational psychoanalysis* grew and began to accrue to itself many other influences and developments. Various tributaries—interpersonal psychoanalysis, object relations theory, self psychology, empirical infancy research, feminism, queer theory, sociocultural studies and elements of contemporary Freudian and Kleinian thought—flow into this tradition, which understands relational configurations between self and others, both real and fantasied, as the primary subject of psychoanalytic investigation.

We refer to the relational tradition, rather than to a relational school, to highlight that we are identifying a trend, a tendency within contemporary psychoanalysis, not a more formally organized or coherent school or system of beliefs. Our use of the term *relational* signifies a dimension of theory and practice that has become salient across the wide spectrum of contemporary psychoanalysis. Now under the editorial supervision of Adrienne Harris and Eyal Rozmarin, the Relational Perspectives Book Series originated in 1990 under the editorial eye of the late Stephen A. Mitchell. Mitchell was the most prolific and influential of the originators of the relational tradition. Committed to dialogue among psychoanalysts, he abhorred the authoritarianism that dictated adherence to a rigid set of beliefs or technical restrictions. He championed open discussion, comparative and integrative approaches, and promoted new voices across the generations. Mitchell was later joined by the late Lewis Aron, also a visionary and influential writer, teacher and leading thinker in relational psychoanalysis.

Included in the Relational Perspectives Book Series are authors and works that come from within the relational tradition, those that extend and develop that tradition, and works that critique relational approaches or compare and contrast them with alternative points of view. The series includes our most distinguished senior psychoanalysts, along with younger contributors who bring fresh vision. Our aim is to enable a deepening of relational thinking while reaching across disciplinary and social boundaries in order to foster an inclusive and international literature.

A full list of titles in this series is available at www.routledge.com/Relational-Perspectives-Book-Series/book-series/LEARPBS.

## Note

1 Greenberg, J., & Mitchell, S. (1983). *Object Relations in Psychoanalytic Theory*. Cambridge, MA: Harvard University Press.

# Inhabiting Implication in Racial Oppression and in Relational Psychoanalysis

Edited by
Rachel Kabasakalian-McKay
and David Mark

Routledge
Taylor & Francis Group
LONDON AND NEW YORK

Cover image: Cover artwork painted by university students Annabelle Sloan, Jared Mar, Sierra Ratcliff, and Benjamin Cahoon as part of a large mural in Newberg, Oregon. Painted in 2018, the mural symbolizes ideals of service, justice, and connection to our broader community.

First published 2023
by Routledge
4 Park Square, Milton Park, Abingdon, Oxon OX14 4RN

and by Routledge
605 Third Avenue, New York, NY 10158

Routledge is an imprint of the Taylor & Francis Group, an informa business

British Library Cataloguing-in-Publication Data
A catalogue record for this book is available from the British Library

Publisher's Note

References within each chapter are as they appear in the original complete work

ISBN: 978-1-032-20768-1 (hbk)
ISBN: 978-1-032-20770-4 (pbk)
ISBN: 978-1-003-26514-6 (ebk)

DOI: 10.4324/9781003265146

Typeset in Times New Roman
by Apex CoVantage, LLC

# Contents

# Acknowledgments

This book has been a deeply collaborative project. We had no idea, when we began, how powerful the interactions would be around working with our colleagues to shape what it has become. Our gratitude is felt first in relation to the authors whose writings compose the book and who engaged us in meaningful, at times challenging, moving, and ultimately transformative ways; to Carnella Gordon-Brown, Natasha Holmes, Beth Kita, and Lynne Layton; Michelle Stephens; Jessica Benjamin; Cynthia Chalker; Sue Grand; Ofra Bloch; Usha Tummala-Narra; Billie Pivnick and Jane Hassinger; Matt Aibel; and Laurel Silber: it is an honor to be able to include your work in this volume. Much gratitude to our colleagues at the Institute for Relational Psychoanalysis of Philadelphia, who have been our home base. We can't name everyone here, but we want to thank especially Dennis Debiak, Audre Jarmas, Denise Lensky, Laura Lipkin, Joe Schaller, Tim Wright, Donna Harris, Marjorie Bosk, Robin Risler, Dana Sinopoli, and Matthew Whitehead. A particular thanks to Heejin Kim, who challenged us in crucial ways to clarify our thinking and teaching regarding implication. Thank you to the participants in the Mitchell Relational Study Center seminar on implication and relational thought in November 2020. A number of colleagues have been enormously supportive of this project since its inception, and their encouragement has been crucial; thank you especially to Francisco J. González, Lauren Levine, Jill Salberg, and Melanie Suchet. Thank you to our friend Steven Kuchuck, co-editor of the Relational Perspectives Book Series, who shepherded us with warmth, openness, and humor.

From Rachel: To the memory of my parents, Rita and Levon Kabasakalian; I have carried them with me throughout this process. Thanks and love to my family—to Jim, who has been unwaveringly supportive and engaged in countless conversations about this project as it took shape; and to Maddi and Nina—I am in awe of all you each bring to your work to make the world a more just place. Thank you to Maddi for your thoughtful read of the introduction and to Nina for your immeasurable help in putting together the final manuscript. Appreciation to Natalie and Ani for their patience as I completed this project before we could finish settling on what to do with that kitchen table and other belongings of our parents. To David, my co-editor, co-author, and all-around collaborator—for thinking and working side by side with me throughout all the parts of this project and for our conversations, which have been a beacon during this time.

From David: I wish to express my love and gratitude to Beth—for encouraging me to write and making it (relatively) easy to find the space to do so—and to Ben and Sam, whose interest, not to mention affectionate teasing, has helped me throughout this process. To Rachel, whose imagination and creativity are responsible for transforming our original paper into this edited book and who has helped me in multiple ways inhabit my implication.

# Credits List

The authors also gratefully acknowledge the permission provided to reprint the following materials:

- Stephens, M. "Getting Next to Ourselves: The Interpersonal Dimensions of Double-Consciousness," *Contemporary Psychoanalysis*, 56:2–3, 201–225 © 2020 William Alanson White Institute of Psychiatry, Psychoanalysis & Psychology and the William Alanson White Psychoanalytic Society, reprinted by permission of Taylor & Francis Ltd on behalf of the William Alanson White Psychoanalytic Society.
- Grand, S. "The Other Within: White Shame, Native-American Genocide," *Contemporary Psychoanalysis*, 54:1, 84–102 © 2018 William Alanson White Institute of Psychiatry, Psychoanalysis & Psychology and the William Alanson White Psychoanalytic Society, reprinted by permission of Taylor & Francis Ltd on behalf of the William Alanson White Psychoanalytic Society.

# Contributors

**Matt Aibel** is a faculty member, supervisor and training analyst at the National Institute for the Psychotherapies (NIP) and elsewhere, submissions editor of *Psychoanalytic Perspectives*, and editor of *The IARPP Bulletin*, the International Association for Relational Psychotherapy and Psychoanalysis newsletter, which reaches over 2000 analysts worldwide. He chairs NIP's Recruitment Committee and serves on IARPP's Colloquium Committee. His writing has been published in *Psychoanalytic Psychology, Psychoanalytic Inquiry, Contemporary Psychoanalysis, Psychoanalytic Perspectives, Attachment: New Directions in Psychotherapy and Relational Psychoanalysis*, and *The IARPP Bulletin*. His student paper, "Being Railroaded: A Candidate's Struggle to Stay on Track," was nominated for a Gradiva Award (2012). His curiosity about psychoanalysis' relationship to political discourse led to his writing "The Personal is Political is Psychoanalytic: Politics in the Consulting Room" (2018), which has received national and international attention and serves as a springboard for his chapter in this volume. He practices in New York City and on Long Island.

**Jessica Benjamin** is best known as the author of *The Bonds of Love* (1988), which has been translated into many languages, and of the article "Beyond Doer and Done To: An Intersubjective View of Thirdness" (2004), the basis for her recent book *Beyond Doer and Done To: Recognition Theory, Intersubjectivity and the Third* (2018). In addition, she is the author of *Like Subjects, Love Objects* (1995) and *Shadow of the Other* (1998). She is a supervisor and faculty member of the New York University Postdoctoral Psychology Program in Psychotherapy and

Psychoanalysis and the Stephen Mitchell Relational Studies Center, where she is a founder and board member. In addition to her private practice in New York City, she lectures, teaches, and supervises at numerous institutes throughout the United States and throughout the world. In 2015 she was awarded the Hans Kilian Award at the University of the Ruhr in Bochum, Germany, the largest European award for work that joins psychoanalysis with the humanities. From 2004 to 2010 she initiated and directed the Acknowledgment Project involving Israeli and Palestinian mental health practitioners and international dialogue leaders.

**Ofra Bloch** is a psychoanalyst and supervisor in private practice in New York City, where she works with individuals and couples. She has a particular clinical interest in intergenerational trauma and the narrative it generates in the private and public sphere. She grew up in Israel, where her deep interest in the short- and long-term consequences of trauma originated. She is an unschooled filmmaker and began experimenting with making documentaries during her analytic training at the National Institute for the Psychotherapies (NIP). Her recent documentary, *Afterward*, premiered at the DOC NYC festival in 2018 and went on to win the 2019 Greenwich International Film Festival Award for the Best Social Impact Film and the 2020 Jonathan Daniels Award for Social Responsibility at the Monadnock International Film Festival. It had its theatrical premiere in NYC and LA in January of 2020.

**Cynthia Chalker** is a Black queer clinical social worker and psychoanalyst who lives and works in New York City. Her research interests include the intersection of race, culture, and identity in psychoanalysis. Cynthia is an associate editor of *Psychoanalytic Dialogues*. She is on the faculty at the South Bay Community for Psychoanalytic Study/Psychoanalytic Institute of Northern California (CA) and the National Institute for the Psychotherapies (NY). She is a board member of the Manhattan Institute of Psychoanalysis, where she completed her psychoanalytic training. Cynthia is published in several psychoanalytic journals and has presented at conferences in the United States and internationally.

**Carnella Gordon-Brown** is a licensed clinical social worker. A black-woman feminist. She is a great-great-great-granddaughter of escaped enslaved Africans who fought in the US civil war for Lincoln, for the preservation of the Union, for the promise of their freedom, and for a better life. Carnella is both amazed and aware of holding great privilege, both literally and figuratively, because finding her voice has been a journey through hell and back. That she has an independent clinical practice is a precious gift, rooted in the deep wisdom and relational work experiences shared with the incredibly generous and resilient consumers of community mental health.

**Sue Grand** is a faculty member and supervisor at the NYU postdoctoral program in psychotherapy and psychoanalysis, a faculty member at the National Institute for the Psychotherapies, a faculty member for the Mitchell Center for Relational Psychoanalysis, a visiting scholar at the Psychoanalytic Institute for Northern California, and a fellow of the Institute for Psychology and the Other. She is an associate editor of *Psychoanalytic Dialogues* and on the board of *Psychoanalysis, Culture & Society*. She is the author of *The Reproduction of Evil: A Clinical and Cultural Perspective* and *The Hero in the Mirror: From Fear to Fortitude*. She has co-edited books on the transgenerational transmission of trauma and on relational theory. She is in private practice in NYC and Teaneck, NJ.

**Jane A. Hassinger** is a psychoanalyst in Ann Arbor, Michigan, and a retired University of Michigan faculty member in women's and gender studies. She is a member of the Michigan Psychoanalytic Society and on the faculty of the Psychoanalytic Institute of Northern California's Group Process Program. Jane's interdisciplinary projects address significant global challenges, including Global Providers Share Program (with Lisa H. Harris, 2007–2021); Community Responses to Survivors of Gender-based Violence in the Democratic Republic of Congo (with Denis Mukwege, MD; 2010–2013); and Women on Purpose: Ending Silence around HIV/AIDS in South Africa (2005–2012, with Kim Berman, MFA, PhD). Her published works include "The Community Turn: Relational Citizenship in the Psychoanalytic Community" (2022, with Billie Pivnick) and "Twentieth Century Living Color: Racialized Enactments in Psychoanalysis" (2014). Her book *Women On Purpose: Resilience and Creativity of the Women of Phumani Paper* (with Kim Berman) was published in 2012. In 2014, she and Billie Pivnick, PhD, founded the Psychoanalytic Community Collaboratory.

**Natasha Holmes** is a licensed psychologist who works from a psychoanalytically and trauma-informed black feminist and womanist perspective while integrating cognitive behavioral and dialectical behavioral theories. She is also the founder and CEO of And Still We Rise, LLC, a mental health company located in Massachusetts and Washington state that is dedicated to dismantling oppressive systems, liberating marginalized people, and providing culturally affirming psychotherapy, consultation, and life-coaching services.

**Rachel Kabasakalian-McKay** (she/her) is a founding board member and the co-director of the Institute for Relational Psychoanalysis of Philadelphia, where she is on the teaching and supervisory faculty. A primary focus of her work has been to expand the reach and responsiveness of relational training, and she has initiated and participated in several community service initiatives and programs in this regard. She is also on the faculty of the Stephen Mitchell Relational Study Center in New York, where she has taught a seminar on implication and relational thought. Rachel has published in *Psychoanalytic Dialogues*, *Psychoanalytic Inquiry*, and *Psychoanalytic Perspectives* on topics including the nature of empathy and recognition in relational clinical work and, with David Mark, attending to intersubjective truths in navigating clinical interactions. She maintains a practice in psychotherapy, psychoanalysis, and supervision in Philadelphia and New York.

**Elizabeth (Beth) Kita** is a clinical social worker in public/private practice in San Francisco, California. In her private practice, she works primarily with people contending with the effects of complex post-traumatic stress and vicarious traumatization; her work in a public clinic is with people who have returned to the community following lengthy periods of incarceration. She obtained her MSW from UC Berkeley and her PhD from Smith College, School for Social Work. In addition to her clinical work, Beth teaches in the MSW program at UC Berkeley and is the co-chair of the Coalition for Clinical Social Work at the San Francisco Center for Psychoanalysis. She thinks, writes, presents, and consults on the intersections of race/racism, trauma, violence, incarceration, and psychodynamic social work praxis in the United States.

**Lynne Layton** is a member of the Massachusetts Institute for Psychoanalysis, where she has taught and supervised. From 2015 to 2021, she taught social psychoanalysis at Pacifica Graduate Institute. She is the author of *Who's That Girl? Who's That Boy? Clinical Practice Meets Postmodern Gender Theory* and co-editor of *Bringing the Plague: Toward a Postmodern Psychoanalysis* and *Psychoanalysis, Class and Politics: Encounters in the Clinical Setting*. From 2004 to 2017, she was the co-editor of the journal *Psychoanalysis, Culture & Society*. She is a past president of Section IX (Psychoanalysis for Social Responsibility) of Division 39, APA, and founder of Reflective Spaces/Material Places-Boston, a group of psychodynamic therapists committed to community mental health and social justice. She is on the steering committee of the Grassroots Reparations Campaign and is the author of *Toward a Social Psychoanalysis: Culture, Character, and Normative Unconscious Processes*, winner of a 2021 book award from the American Academy and Board of Psychoanalysis.

**David Mark** is the founding director and current co-director of the Institute for Relational Psychoanalysis of Philadelphia. He is the former co-director of training for the University of Pennsylvania's Psychotherapy Research Center. He is the author (with Jeffrey Faude) of *The Psychotherapy of Cocaine Addiction: Entering the Interpersonal World of the Cocaine Addict* (Aronson, 1997). His two most recent publications are "Forms of Equality in Relational Psychoanalysis," in *De-Idealizing Relational Theory* (eds. L. Aron, S. Grand, and J. Slochower; Routledge, 2018) and (with Rachel Kabasakalian-McKay) "'The Truth of the Session' and Varieties of Intersubjective Experience: Discussion of Atlas and Aron's *Dramatic Dialogue*" in *Psychoanalytic Perspectives* (2019). David is a psychoanalyst who practices in Philadelphia and Narberth, PA.

**Laurel Moldawsky Silber** is a clinical psychologist in private practice in Bryn Mawr, PA, working with children, adolescents, and their families. She is a faculty member and director of the Child Relational Psychotherapy Program at the Institute for Relational Psychoanalysis of Philadelphia. Her publications and presentations have been focused on clinical work in the subject area of intergenerational transmission of trauma, childism, gender dysphoria, and play. She is on the board of the Section of Children and Adolescents of the Division of Psychoanalysis of APA. Laurel is pleased to be inhabiting a chapter in a volume on the subject of implication.

**Billie A. Pivnick** is a psychoanalytic psychologist in private practice in NYC. She is a faculty member and supervisor at the William Alanson White Institute Child/Adolescent Psychotherapy Program. She is the co-chair of the Humanities and Psychoanalysis Committee of APA's Society for Psychoanalysis and Psychoanalytic Psychotherapy. She is the co-host (with Dr. Romy Reading) of the podcast *Couched*, which features conversations between analysts and influential cultural figures. She is also the co-founder (with Dr. Jane Hassinger) of the Psychoanalytic Community Collaboratory, a web-based seminar and project incubator for psychoanalytically informed projects focused on innovative interdisciplinary responses to significant community problems. Additionally, she is the consulting psychologist for Thinc Design, she partnered with the National September 11 Memorial Museum and the Museum of Science and Industry, and she is the winner of the SPPP's 2015 Schillinger Memorial Essay Award for her essay "Spaces to Stand In: Applying Clinical Psychoanalysis to the Relational Design of the National September 11 Memorial Museum" and IPTAR's 1992 Stanley Berger Award for her contribution to psychoanalysis.

**Michelle Ann Stephens** is a psychoanalyst, a professor of English and Latino and Caribbean Studies, and the founding executive director of the Institute for the Study of Global Racial Justice at Rutgers University. Her recent authored and co-edited works include *Skin Acts: Race, Psychoanalysis and the Black Male Performer* (Duke 2014) and *Contemporary Archipelagic Thinking: Towards New Comparative Methodologies and Disciplinary Formations* (with Yolanda Martínez-San Miguel; Rowman and Littlefield International 2020). Her essays on race and psychoanalysis appear in several edited collections and journals, including *Breaking Boundaries: The Interdisciplinary Foundation of Interpersonal Psychoanalysis* (Frie and Sauvayre), *Lacan and Race* (George and Hook), *History of the Present*, *Studies in Gender and Sexuality*, *Journal of the American Psychoanalytic Association* (*JAPA*), *Psychoanalytic Quarterly*, *Contemporary Psychoanalysis*, and *Psychoanalysis, Culture & Society*. In 2015 she co-founded the Study Group in Race and Psychoanalysis (SGORAP) at the William Alanson White Institute of Psychiatry, Psychoanalysis, and Psychotherapy.

**Pratyusha Tummala-Narra** is a clinical psychologist, the director of community-based education at the Albert and Jessie Danielsen Institute, and a research professor in the Department of Psychological and Brain Sciences at Boston University. Her research and scholarship focus on immigration, trauma, race, and culturally informed psychoanalytic psychotherapy. Her published works include over 90 peer-reviewed articles and chapters in books. She is also in independent practice and works primarily with survivors of trauma from diverse sociocultural backgrounds. Dr. Tummala-Narra is an associate editor of *Psychoanalytic Dialogues* and the *Asian American Journal of Psychology*. She is the author of *Psychoanalytic Theory and Cultural Competence in Psychotherapy* (2016) and the editor of *Trauma and Racial Minority Immigrants: Turmoil, Uncertainty, and Resistance* (2021), both published by the American Psychological Association Books.

# Chapter 1

# Introduction

*Rachel Kabasakalian-McKay and David Mark*

We write within a historical moment of devastation breathtaking in scope and form but also in which calls to reckon with past and present violence and injustice offer a path forward. Such calls confront us with the necessity for acknowledgment and the urgency for repair, processes infinitely more painstaking and complex than the brute force of destructiveness, pushing us up to the limits of what we may already understand and know how to do. How any of us respond to these challenges is shaped by the communities and shared points of reference through which we make meaning. As relational psychoanalysts, who have found community and shared values within this field, we searched for ways to expand our thinking that would both perturb and resonate with these values. Michael Rothberg's theorizing of "the implicated subject" struck us, as soon as we first read it, as offering a promising path forward. Rothberg's position as a theorist of the social realm spoke to the heart of what was unfolding in the global moment, while his focus on the "subject" suggested to us ways that relational psychoanalytic writers might elaborate on what this looks and feels like from the inside.

Along with some of our local Philadelphia colleagues, we began reading *The Implicated Subject* in late 2019, in tandem with the first installment of Nikole Hannah-Jones's culture-shifting *1619 Project*, thus linking these sources in our minds from the start. Where the latter shook and unsettled us, bringing us to reflect more searchingly on the foundational racism that shaped the United States and our own involvement in its continued corrosive forms, the former offered a conceptual tool that helped us name the nature of our involvement in the historical and ongoing destruction, especially of Black lives. Our hope for this volume was to bring together

DOI: 10.4324/9781003265146-1

colleagues who would write from and to the subjectivity and intersubjectivity of what it means to be implicated subjects, to pull back the dissociative curtain that has kept us from seeing and grappling with what this means in the circumstances both intimate and global.

As relational psychoanalysts and global citizens, we are motivated to try to understand the psychic experience more fully and to use such understanding not only for individual growth but for collective safety, dignity, and care. Reading Rothberg's work, we were struck by his insights regarding how people who do not see themselves/ourselves as perpetrators may nonetheless be in the position of beneficiary, perpetuator, or otherwise *implicated* in ongoing oppression, violence, and inequity. While his explicit intent is to interrogate and elaborate on the social positions beyond those of victim and perpetrator, he is equally clear that he is not negating the salience of either of those categories. One of the most compelling examples of implication in our contemporary context involves the ongoing trauma of racism: to be a white person living in the United States is to be implicated in the "foundational crimes of genocide and slavery" (p. 17–18). The past lives on into the present, as insidious forms of structural racism have continued to proliferate in the centuries beyond the original monstrosities of legal slavery, so that even recent immigrants, especially as they are or are read as white, become implicated as they participate, with varying degrees of consciousness, in the perpetuation of ongoing racial injustice.

In Rothberg's conception, the implicated subject is not a fixed identity but a position occupied "in particular, dynamic, and at times clashing structures and histories" (p. 8). Thus, shifting and overlapping modes of implication frame the multiplicity of our entanglements in past and present injustices. Rothberg uses the term "complex implication" to denote the coexistence of different positions in relation to past and current violence and oppression; one may be in an implicated subject position with respect to one historical trauma while being a victim, or the descendant of a victim, in relation to another trauma. Too often, awareness of being a victim or descendant of a victim in one historical trauma works to close off a person (or group) from accepting their (our) position as implicated subjects in other instances of injustice and violence. This defensive "dissociation," as we are thinking of it, results in political rigidity—in much the way dissociation of self-states creates a thinned-out or brittle mode of experience. As a kind of social therapy, Rothberg's theory enables the reader to bear conflict and hold two contrasting positions (the victim or the descendant of a victim in one context, implicated subject in another) simultaneously. Ultimately, he is advocating for self-conscious awareness of and grappling with one's position as implicated subject, opening into "transfiguring implication," and joining with others in collective action for justice (p. 200).

Rothberg's theory orients toward the social realm as a site of both oppression and transformation, with the implicated subject situated within these larger forces. We believe that a relational psychoanalytic perspective can complement this emphasis by exploring and elaborating the dynamics of implicated subjectivity within and between specific persons. How do we find our way into recognizing our own implication and then grappling with what this entails, holding awareness both of complexities of position and vulnerabilities specific to each of us? We see relational theorizing and clinical work as having the potential to deepen our capacities to work our way into and through these questions while helping to make meaningful the inevitable intersubjective collisions as differently and similarly situated subjects engage one another.

At its best, relational work helps us to hold multiple registers at once, such as knowing that while we are shaped as social beings, subjects, and agents by historical and current social forces, we are simultaneously forged within the intimate forces of our families and other "ensembles" (González, 2020) that hold us, the intense pulls for loyalty and fears of betraying those we love, and traumas and "errands" (Apprey, 2014) inherited and largely unspoken. And in yet another (always overlapping and intertwining) register, we are individual subjects marked with traumas, longings, and creative aspirations that are unique to us. The implicated subject is thus infinitely complex; relational psychoanalysis may be particularly useful in facilitating the elaboration and holding of such complexity without shrinking from the challenges of implication. Our hope with this project has been to bring multiple voices to engage with the implication from differing vantage points within our field. In doing so, we hope to advance efforts to meet the implication head-on, elaborate on subjective experiences of coming to grips with this position in specific contexts or relational moments, and navigate through choppy waters toward ethical and responsive actions.

As relational analysts, we work daily to expand, deepen, and elaborate subjectivity and, together with others, create the conditions for intersubjective engagement. Part of what we hope to encourage here is the integration of Rothberg's idea of implication into how we think about what shapes individual subjective experiences and what forces animate various inter-subjective encounters; how do we bring "implication" into our elaboration of this already dense weave? How do we, individually and collectively, grapple with and find ourselves within this subject position—if in fluid, shifting, and complex ways?

As we view the ways the analyst actively engages with their/our own struggles as central to how we can hear and participate with others in mutually influencing relationships, we begin with portions of our own stories, our differing pathways into inhabiting the identities of implicated subjects. We then follow that with an example of implication unfolding in real time as we worked on this book with our colleagues.

## Rachel

The eldest of three daughters, I sat to my mother's left at the kitchen table. My mom wanted me to sit up straight, and so she would reach over and nudge me in the back to remind me to do so. One summer evening, when I was about eight years old, she and my father went into the city to meet friends for a concert at Lincoln Center. Although my father loved classi-cal music and kept it on the radio in our home all the time, they didn't go to such things often. The concert was part of a series called *Promenade*; there was a buffet dinner beforehand, which you ate outside, in the plaza—the Metropolitan Opera House in view and excitement all around you. As my mother told me about it the next day, I asked if I could ever go. She smiled—yes, if I could sit up straight between now and next summer's concert. Whatever she did, my mother was dogged about it, and for the ensuing months, dinnertime was punctuated by the prods from her index finger near my mid-spine and her reminder *"Promenade!"* Instantly, I'd correct my posture. I was rewarded the following summer. Lincoln Center seemed, for a child who had moved from Brooklyn—which felt full of life and potential for a surprise on every block, to a suburb that was greener but lonelier—a magical place.

In my first job after college, I was working as an organizer at the Ameri-can Friends Service Committee in Cambridge. Reagan's early budgets had been passed, and with these had begun the systematic, catastrophic dis-mantling of the programs the War on Poverty had brought less than two decades earlier: slashing funds for vitally needed social services—housing, food stamps, Medicaid, Aid to Families with Dependent Children. My job was to work with community advocacy groups protesting against these cuts and elaborating on the implications for real people who relied on these programs. My closest colleague, G., worked with communities of color in Boston, collaborating with neighborhood organizations to make use of tools like Community Development Block Grants to bring financial resources to support initiatives in these communities. One day as we sat talking, G., a Black man, told me he was from Manhattan. Where in the city? I asked. He had grown up, he told me in his quiet voice, in an apartment in the West 60s—in one of the buildings that were torn down to make room for Lincoln Center.

I didn't have a name for what I felt at that moment, but I can now name it as an implication. I had not torn down the buildings, but the place I loved—where aspects of culture with which I was deeply identified were celebrated—was suddenly shaded. They had demolished homes where families had lived to build Lincoln Center. Many of these families were Black.

How do we grapple with implication when the fabric of the memories and longings that make us who we are, are associated with injury to others, not only accidental but viewed as acceptable or deliberately made invisible?

Reading Rothberg for the first time, I felt an immediate resonance, as his elaboration of the concept of implication seemed to allow for facing one's own participation in the perpetuation of harm without losing hold of complexity. This felt meaningful, even necessary to me in holding my responsibility in the present alongside the strands of my own transgenerational traumas. Rothberg makes clear that people can be victims or descendants of victims in some contexts and *are implicated in ongoing injustices* that oppress, torture, and condemn others. One particularly enormous, consequential, and urgent example of this is that those of us descended from victims of violence and persecution both bear the psychic scars of these histories and—especially to the extent that we carry whiteness—are called to recognize how we participate in ongoing manifestations of racism, especially anti-Black racism, that continues to savage people of color, to mark their lives as mattering less.

González (2020) writes of the "ensembles" we carry within us—the groups to which we feel intense if sometimes unconscious fealty. In the wake of the deaths of both of my parents, I am aware of the power of these ties in a new, deeper, and sometimes unsettling way—I feel myself as the carrier of both their intergenerationally transmitted traumas and their personal efforts and injuries. This creates in me a sharper awareness of how I feel. I do not only speak for myself but for those who brought me here, to the social location from which I write.

My father was born in 1923 to Armenian parents who had just emigrated to the US from Anatolia in what is now Eastern Turkey, via Beirut. They were both survivors of the genocide in what had been their ancestral homeland. Eight years earlier, my grandmother was a nine-year-old child who was hidden by a Turkish family, a fact that spared her from the massacre that left her mother and younger siblings slaughtered in their nearby home. At 13, she was married to my grandfather, then in his late 20s. All the members of his family had been murdered or, in the case of his sister, "carried off." In New York, the family lived in tenement apartments in the east 20s. My father attended Stuyvesant High School and City College, where he learned to love classical music and European literature. In going through his writings since his death, I'm struck by his lifelong efforts to reconcile belonging to a family and group with individual subjectivity, especially regarding creativity, and a unique personal trajectory. Reading González's (2020) description of this kind of psychic struggle resonated with me deeply.

My mother was from the Bronx, an aspect of her identity she held with pride. In her work as a middle school math teacher, she spent much of her career in the South Bronx. She believed in the liberating power of structural understanding of math concepts, seeing equality of access to these foundational understandings as an essential part of equity in education. She was a Jew who married a Christian in 1954, when this was uncommon. The transgenerational historical traumas from her family would emerge in moments and then disappear again into the background. On a trip to Paris she and I made for my 40th birthday, she walked somberly into the old Jewish neighborhood in the Marais: here, she said, was where her Romanian maternal grandmother's sisters had all been taken by the Nazis during the occupation. On the other side of her family, her father emigrated as a child with his brother from Belarus after their father was killed in a pogrom. A few years into their time in the US, this brother was found hung in a jail in Virginia, an obviously Jewish-looking man arrested for vagrancy where he'd gone looking for work. In later life, my mother became increasingly distraught by the Israeli oppression of Palestinians so that when she died with no funeral plans in place, I found myself on the phone late at night, making sure the rabbi who agreed to perform the service understood and respected how central this feeling of implication was to how she was a Jew.

These are the strands that make up my own whiteness—a whiteness that is both Jewish and West Asian Armenian, that involves both inherited traumas and feelings of otherness, and that entails enormous privilege. This privilege has included a sense of entitlement to endless higher education and access to the tools to achieve in this arena, to choose a non-traditional professional path because it feels most authentic, to insist that my voice be heard. And it includes feeling welcomed in the spaces where classical music is played—often beautiful spaces and impressive structures that convey that if you belong here, what moves you matters.

Implication opens a space for the complexity of history and position; Rothberg cites the influence of both Kimberlé Crenshaw (1989) and the Combahee River Collective Statement (Smith et al., 1977), originators of the idea of intersectionality, on his work. In his formulation, implication describes a site within which "the dynamic interplay between subjectivity, structural inequality, and historical violence" takes place, reinscribing hierarchies of power and privilege in multiple and complex ways. One distinction he makes is between genealogical and structural implication with regard to the American history of slavery. Direct descendants of slaveholders bear the former; others of us live as beneficiaries of not only past but ongoing structural racism. Glaude (2020) writes of the perniciousness of what he calls "the value gap"; the unspoken but powerfully destructive belief that "in America white lives have always mattered more than the lives of others" (2020, p. 7). Exploring the writing of James Baldwin, Glaude comes to name as "the lie": that "broad and powerful architecture of false assumptions" (2020, p. 7) that maintains this value gap; that continually, often wordlessly, grinds the engine of this insidious and corrosive force.

That the "powerful architecture" of Lincoln Center and all it contained was an embodiment of liveliness, hope, and possibility for me is inextricable from a system in which Black families were displaced to construct it—because their lives and longings, their community, attachment to home, and sense of place, all presumably mattered less. And in this, as in other similar situations too numerous to name, I am implicated.

## David

I write this as a 66-year-old white, cisgender, heterosexual man. I grew up with enormous educational privilege, told that I could be anything I wanted and I didn't need to hurry to get there. In short, I'm implicated, implicated in the racial hierarchy that accorded great advantage, especially to men of my race and age. As I read Rachel's section (immediately before this section), I marveled at the difference in our experience of identification with, of love and connection to, the larger groups (groups larger than dyads and the conventional triad of child and two-parent figures) that make us up. This difference in our experience of group connection is highlighted by many surface similarities, only some of which will shortly be apparent. Rothberg's "complex implication" helped Rachel hold a painful awareness of participating in manifestations of racism alongside her own transgenerational traumas—traumas with which, out of love and loyalty to her family and ancestors, she is intensely identified with. In contrast, it was Rothberg's implication and his idea of the "implicated subject" as a third category, between victims and perpetrators, that spoke most directly to me with respect to my being a white person, with all the benefits that entails, in a pervasively anti-Black society.

With the important exception of friend groups, I have always felt outside, or on the borders of, most every grouping I can imagine. As best I can tell, there are many reasons for this. My father's mother died in childbirth. After this, his father returned to Romania, abandoning my father at birth on the steps of a Jewish orphanage, where he lived until he was eight. An only child, my father never felt securely attached to, or adequate for, his adoptive parents. While they are not at all malevolent, he felt too ashamed and too deprived of "family feeling" to feel like having a legitimate parent in one. My mother, also an only child, grew up Italian Catholic. Her mother and one aunt were the only children of seven not to spend significant time growing up in an orphanage after their father died young in an industrial accident, and their mother, who did not speak English, was unable to feed her many children. With two crucial exceptions, we did not see a great deal of my mother's large extended family, despite the fact that they continued to live in the Bronx, just miles from the village in which I grew up. At least in part, this was due to the fact that my mother converted to Judaism. My mother's parents lived with us, and her closest cousin lived with her husband and children a block from us. Both my maternal grandmother and my mother's cousin died within a few years of each other when I was a young child and my mother was a young woman. I had the sense that my mother's "family feeling" existed primarily in the form of grief and an unspoken rejection. All of these things contributed to the fact that, while I had strong dyadic relationships, particularly with my mother, I didn't have an attachment to my family as a unit. And whatever "family feeling" I might've had when I was younger dissipated when my parents divorced when I was a teenager.

Neither did I have strong religious, class, or ethnic attachments. I grew up on the outskirts of a working-class village that was largely Italian, but unlike some of the neighborhood kids, I didn't feel I belonged to the working class (both my parents were schoolteachers), nor did I feel culturally Italian. While we nominally identified as Jewish, I never felt "legitimately Jewish"; neither of my parents was a religious Jew, and they lacked a felt sense of its history and traditions. A large estate separated my house from the neighboring town, which was nearly entirely Jewish and very wealthy. To my childhood eyes, the distance between my house and this neighboring town was vast. Nevertheless, through some oddity of school districting, I did not attend the mediocre public school in the village in which I lived but attended the academically rigorous school in the neighboring town. While I developed an intense friend group among my school friends (and an equally close, separate one in my neighborhood), I felt alienated from this school community, not quite Jewish and definitely not from the same economic class.

Politics was very much in the air in my childhood and community; the civil rights movement, the Vietnam War, and the Arab-Israeli conflicts in the years following the Six-Day War significantly impressed themselves in my mind. My self-state around politics, the "political state of mind" (González, 2020) in which, throughout life, I most frequently find myself, replicates something of my position in my family. Both my parents, not to mention my ancestors, had their traumas. But I identified less with my relatives and their traumas than as a privileged outsider to them. Similarly, despite strong feelings of moral outrage and sympathy for the oppressed in the major political conflicts over the past half century, I felt like an outsider here too. I suppose, at my best, I maintained a kind of respectful distance as a witness to injustice and violence. But the sort of witness I was instantiated my privilege and my sense of invulnerability; empathy and solidarity were cut short because I was unable to sustain an identification without feeling illegitimate.

Racism and the wars in Vietnam and the Middle East also left me with a confusing sense of guilt and shame—confusing because, while as a white American Jew, I felt myself to be on the side of the perpetrator, I did not really believe I was one, and confusing because, not really feeling part of the relevant groups, collective guilt and shame were not natural emotions to me. I could not ask "who are *we*?" (González, 2020) without feeling false—not a critic from within, much less a loving one, but an interloper. In this tangle—one moment, a somewhat isolated and distant "witness" to injustice and violence; the next moment, finding myself guilty, ashamed, and confused by it all, only to then irritably reject those feelings—I was unable to find a relatively stable landing pad for myself. It is here that the implicated subject came to my rescue, even if the place it landed me is in the uncomfortable realm of the "un-good" (Benjamin, 2018). Neither "good" nor "bad" in the Kleinian, psychoanalytic sense of these terms— that is, "really, really good" and "really, really bad, truly awful"—in the realm of the "un-good," I'm implicated, not isolated. The concept helped move me from a haunted, albeit irrational, perpetrator guilt to a person with real culpability who has profited in specific and often tangibly material ways from racial terror and injustice. To be clear, to be implicated in perpetuating terrible crimes is not comfortable; to benefit from injustice is sickening. But it is easier to live with being implicated, "un-good," than being a perpetrator, truly "bad" (Medria Connolly, on the *Couched* podcast [April 22, 2021], makes the point that reparations for slavery are more palatable to whites who feel implicated rather than when reparations are framed within the perpetrator/victim binary). Implication transports me from a state of alienation "into proximity" to both victim and perpetrator "without stepping into the shoes of either" (Rothberg, 2019; p. 6).

## Implication in Real Time

We can't opt out of implication, though we can certainly act in ways that implicate us more deeply, more sharply. We are born and interpellated into structures not of our making, but we are shaped by those same structures in countless and often unconscious ways, including what we see as "natural" or fail to see at all. In coming to grips with our own myriad dissociations, or more profoundly with the ways these dissociations have consequences in the present for other people, we both reveal and, in the same moment, can take responsibility for our own parts in the perpetuation of harms (Stephens, personal communication, 1/20/22).

Despite the ways we "know" that we are prone to dissociate the harms we have learned not to see, we felt initial surprise when some of our colleagues challenged us to directly confront our own implication in this book. This surprise was a reminder of how we see situations from within our own structural positions and the ongoing challenges this represents.

Shortly after we sent the letter welcoming all of the prospective contributors to the book, we received an email from a group of authors calling us in to recognize and respond to our own implication as the volume's editors. Carnella Gordon-Brown, Natasha Holmes, Beth Kita, and Lynne Layton pointed out that we are implicated in a history in which editors directly benefit from the labor of contributors, with the former getting both greater professional recognition and any financial remuneration. When the editors are white, as has been overwhelmingly the case, and the contributors BIPoC persons, including Black authors, this hierarchy positions us to re-instantiate a history of harm, including the exploitation of Black labor and the muting of BIPoC voices. One particular concern our colleagues expressed was with regard to visibility and, by extension, recognition. Unlike journal articles that can be easily searched, cited, and accessed individually, book chapters tend to be lost to anyone who doesn't buy the book. Carnella, Natasha, Beth, and Lynne challenged us to consider ways to highlight the contributions of BIPoC authors that would also make these chapters easily available to a wide audience, explicitly inclusive of BIPoC readers. A second request had to do with financial profits the book might garner, asking that we consider donating a portion of any profits toward projects advancing BIPoC and LGBTQ justice.

Admittedly, we felt initially defensive. We had envisioned this book from the start as a collaboration, and we had already planned to channel a good part of any royalties toward racial and economic justice projects. Staying with these initial feelings, we recognized their familiarity—the pain of feeling our individual intentions and efforts were unseen. And as we stayed with this, more emerged within us. We are trying to repair harms done, and we are also beneficiaries of the inequities that rendered the harm. Our colleagues had insisted we see ourselves as operating within an established system, and here we discovered something of Rothberg's assertion that implicated subjects form "the transmission belt" of domination (2019, p. 23; Rothberg credits Simona Forti, 2014, with the origin of this term). If we did not name history that has made us beneficiaries and harmed our colleagues and allowed it to continue to serve as an invisible cloak around us, we would be continuing the harm.

A major hope of this project of marrying Rothberg's "implicated subject" with a contemporary relational sensibility is to try to elaborate aspects of the felt experience of implication as it emerges within and between people so as to work with it in responsible and reparative ways. In this spirit, we want to share more of our own process in this encounter—both with our colleagues and within ourselves. We quickly saw what we needed to do, as the ethical and political position was compelling and in keeping with our intent in this project, and we have enormous respect for our colleagues. At the same time, we felt an initial sting of misrecognition; it felt bad, in that awful and familiar way of being seen as white and culpable despite one's intentions.

We knew we needed to stay with this discomfort and see what emerged. We were enormously grateful, at that moment, that we were working through a careful reread of Michelle Stephens's (2020) crucial and consequential paper "Getting Next to Ourselves: The Interpersonal Dimensions of Double Consciousness," which we are honored to republish in this volume. Through our interaction with her paper, Stephens helped us not only to bear but to make meaning of what was happening in us as we engaged with what our colleagues were calling us to do.

Stephens brings together seminal thinkers on race and experiences of self and other with contemporary relational theories,[1] forging an integration that is not only deeply compelling and creative but both necessary and immediately *usable*. Drawing on insights from Du Bois, Fanon, and Sartre alongside those of Benjamin, Bromberg, and Hart, Stephens answers what she cites as Lynne Layton's (Layton with Leavy-Sperounis, 2020) echoing of George Yancy's (2012) call for the elaboration of a theory of *White* double-consciousness. This call is itself a response to W.E.B. Du Bois's groundbreaking theory regarding the effects of colonialism, slavery, and entrenched racism on Black psyches, including the formation of a double-consciousness. Du Bois coined this term to describe a splitting that operates to preserve the integrity of self while making adaptations necessary for survival in conditions of ongoing oppression and relentless projection, the anti-Black racism transmitted via "the other's projective gaze" (Stephens, p. 212). Black persons are forced to develop the capacity to know the image of themselves as distorted through this projective gaze—knowing how one is being seen as and by the racialized other while working to hold a parallel sense of one's authentic and valued self, embedded within one's community. Fanon, reflecting on this conception by Du

Bois, suggests that something related happens to Whites in an encounter with postcolonial Blackness, in this latter case a fragmenting that comes with imagining what lies behind the gaze of the racialized other whom one feels complicit in harming.

Stephens writes of hearing echoes of Du Bois while listening to Bromberg, as he spoke of the challenge of being able "to see ourselves as others see us" (Bromberg, 2011) without losing touch with other dimensions of ourselves, other truths about who we are. This connection she makes between Du Bois's double-consciousness and this aspect of Bromberg struck us as being so powerful as to seem paradigm-shifting. Stephens also draws on writing by Anton Hart (2017) on the importance of the analyst's really trying on the other's projections—including and especially in racialized enactments where such projections are likely calling forth and joining with disavowed parts of the self. Joining Hart, she advocates for our working to stay with, to take in, and to be willing to engage with what the racialized other is attributing to us, rather than retreating into guilt or shame. To do this entails "a deeper acceptance of these self-alienating projections of the other as tied to, even if not identical with, parts of ourselves . . . holding a both/and position, holding two racialized positions simultaneously" (216). Stephens challenges us to work to get next to ourselves as we are engaged in racial dialogues, both dyadic and beyond; she cites the ideal offered in the work of Benjamin (2004), that of intersubjectivity understood as two-way streets of reciprocal mutual interaction between subjects, and imagines this "expanded now to include a 'twoness' inflected specifically by racial difference" (218–219).

In reading Stephens's paper, we saw a compelling connection possible between the ideas she puts forward regarding White double-consciousness and Rothberg's formulations regarding "complex implication." White double-consciousness seems a compelling way to imagine what some forms of complex implication may feel like from the inside. We hear Stephens urging us to push more deeply into this subjective and intersubjective terrain with one another and thus to move forward.

Holding this ideal in mind, we sat with the attributions of our colleagues: ourselves as the editors whose names will be associated with this work, who were awarded this book contract through the ways we are accepted and at ease in the particular whiteness of American psychoanalysis. These things are true, and they sit uneasily alongside our voices of protest, that want to argue that we have worked so hard to get this right. Then, gradually, we can start to see in ourselves the very self-righteous sense of entitlement we want to tell our colleagues that we are not feeling, and we work to see ourselves as others see us. As we open to the ways we are seen as structurally implicated, something else starts to happen: a deepening of our awareness of our specific implication—what is ours in a more personal way and interpersonal in relation to our colleagues. We see how we are poised to enact an exploitation of our own as we realize we *are*, in fact, dependent upon the labor and creativity of our colleagues in order to keep this book from devolving into a racially segregated project—which would render it a failure in the most profound sense. Realizing this, we were able to inhabit the reality of our implication in a fuller way. We are implicated, and part of what that demands is to hold the racialized attributions that at first feel unfair and hold them until we can find ourselves in them while still maintaining our sense of self-worth that does not require absolution to feel whole. And as we do this, we are more able, we hope, to move closer to our colleagues, to engage in a mutuality that is meaningful, consequential, and transformative—even as it demands the ongoing hard work of examining our own implication.

In this instance, we investigated how we might take action that would respond to what Carnella, Natasha, Beth, and Lynne pointed out—the structural inequities that perpetuate unequal access to shaping psychoanalytic ideas and spaces and the right to engage in dialogue. Finding that we could pay a fee to make an individual chapter available through online Open Access (in which a copyedited and typeset version of the chapter is searchable and available free of charge to anyone), we proposed to our colleagues that we would offer this option for all chapters written in whole or in part by BIPoC contributors, as long as they are original to his volume (this option is not available to us for chapters we are reprinting with permission). Our colleagues agreed to this plan. Subsequently, we wrote to all of the contributors, both offering this option and also inviting others to contribute to funding this effort as a way to make this more of a community process. We had follow-up conversations with a number of the authors, clarifying how this process came about. This process itself felt crucial. Ultimately we are able to place on Open Access the two chapters whose authors elected to do so, funded by the emergent community of the book's authors and supported also with a substantial donation from the Routledge/Taylor & Francis's Relational Perspectives Book Series, of which this volume is a part. We are aware that this solution represents only one small step, but we are moved by the way in which the community of this volume worked together to grapple with implication. And we are especially grateful to our colleagues who raised this issue in the first place.

The most generative concepts are those that not only make an impact on initial landing but catalyze new processes both within and between people and can be elaborated across disciplines and made use of, in Winnicott's sense. They are not flat or static but have more of the properties of a living thing: they grow and change as they come in contact with human minds and collectivities. As a social theorist, Rothberg's focus is political, concerned with collective responsibility and collective action. In keeping with this, his elaboration of the implicated subject has a sociopolitical more than an individual, psychological focus. We see enormous potential in expanding his ideas within the relational psychoanalytic world, enriching the ways we understand subjectivity and intersubjectivity, and infusing implication with the inner and outer worlds of specific subjects. Here is where we saw the potential for this book, bringing together voices from within our field to engage with this concept.

## Overview of Chapters

Michelle Stephens's paper, " 'Getting Next to Ourselves': The Interpersonal Dimensions of Double-Consciousness" first appeared in late 2020, in a special issue of *Contemporary Psychoanalysis*. Addressing race and theorizing the intrapsychic, interpersonal, and intersubjective elements of racial impasse, Stephens engages her readers on both intellectual and affective plains and adds what Mitchell (1993) saw as the crucial ingredient the analyst brings—imagination, or perhaps more precisely, empathically infused imagination. Here, Stephens uses her imagination as a theorist and analyst to invite us, her readers, into precisely the territory where we need to go. She starts with the moment in which, listening to Phillip Bromberg speak of an elusive intersubjective goal—to see ourselves as others see us (while not losing hold of other cherished aspects of self, Bromberg, 2011)—she hears echoes of double-consciousness as theorized by Du Bois (1903/1994), Fanon (1986/1967) and Sartre (1964-1965). Weaving together elements of these two rich bodies of theory, incorporating alongside Bromberg the ideas of Anton Hart and Jessica Benjamin, and citing Lynne Layton's echoing of George Yancy's call for the elaboration of the terrain of White double-consciousness, Stephens tacks both inward (to experiences of the self in the face of the real and projected or otherwise imagined gaze of the other) and outward (to ways in which racial enactments in impasse snag participants in real time). All the while, she keeps moving us forward, to a place we haven't yet gotten but where she believes we could go: As Bromberg envisions an ideal in which private, valued aspects of self-experience and the self as seen by the other can be held alongside one another, without collapse or negation, what if in cross-racial dialogue, we, 21st-century racialized subjects, could strive toward "a deeper understanding and acceptance of . . . self-alienating projections of the other as tied to, even if not identical with, parts of ourselves— maybe sitting next to or alongside them?" (Stephens, 2020, p. 216). While this paper was not written for this volume, as soon as we read it, we were struck by the deep resonance with Rothberg's idea of the implicated subject as we understand it. Stephens's work speaks directly to the project of a relational psychoanalytic elaboration of what implication feels like and how it might be inhabited. More than that, she evokes an ideal of complex, racialized implicated subjects in relation—an implicated *intersubjectivity* that could allow us to get next to multiple parts of ourselves, to one another, and to surrender to the mutual transformations this could bring.

Building on her decades of work developing recognition theory, Jessica Benjamin offers, in her paper, "Recognition in the Face of Harm: Implicated Subjectivity and the Need for Acknowledgment," an extension and elaboration that moves more deeply into our intersubjective engagement with a fundamentally unjust social order. In her earlier work, she has emphasized the necessity for acknowledgment in the process of relational repair; acknowledgment is in response to the harm done by omission or commission, with our own hand (to borrow Ferenczi's phrase), as well as in the form of witnessing the harm caused by another. To disavow the responsibility for providing acknowledgment is to become a *failed witness* to those who are suffering. Benjamin evokes "the moral Third, which emphasizes not the reciprocal recognition of the other, but the specific acknowledgment of relational and social violations." In the face of such violation, acknowledgment entails "admission of wrong, affirmation of how things ought to be, putting things right." In considering Rothberg's implicated subject, Benjamin engages and then deepens her understanding of the role of "failed witness" as she considers the ongoing failures to reckon with and change systems of oppression and violation. What keeps us from seeing the ongoing harm, acknowledging, witnessing, and working to dismantle what perpetuates these harms? One answer she suggests has to do with the fear and insecurity neoliberalism engenders. In her words, "self-protection manifests as the psychological position of the subject who benefits from and identifies with the system of injustice and thereby dissociates his own vulnerability, need and dependency." In dissociating from his own vulnerability, he is driven by the unconscious credo that "only one can live" and then disavows responsibility for—and implication in—the suffering of those in more vulnerable positions. This process of denying vulnerability while being motivated by fear grows more insidious in interaction with the racialized nature of inequity. Benjamin asks, trenchantly, whether "the aim of identifying with Whiteness is to free oneself of fear by embracing the order that subjugates the other while remaining innocent of such actual deeds?"

Throughout the paper, Benjamin engages with a series of partners in thought: Rothberg and Baldwin, especially with Eddie Glaude (2020) serving as interlocutor, as well as recent writings of psychoanalysts Beverly Stoute (2021) and Sally Swartz (2019). In reflecting on Stoute's writing regarding the psychic function of Black rage, which enables the holding of dignity and self-worth in the face of assault, Benjamin concludes that we both are witnesses to and identify with that rage as we are part of the system being raged against. She continues, "I believe we must hold the tension of being alienated from the system we nevertheless participate in and benefit from." In considering Swartz's work, Benjamin extends her own earlier theorizing of Winnicott's survival of destruction: to survive requires not only acknowledgment of one's own responsibility for the past but also "breaking through illusory goodness and myths to an authentic desire to restore social bonds of recognition."

Cynthia Chalker's contribution to this volume, "He's My Brother," is not the one she had intended but one thrust upon her. In the face of sudden, shattering personal loss, what she offers here is the deeply anguished elegy for her younger brother. Her brother was a successful Black man and, as such, "shouldered everyone's expectations and dreams of what a Black man in America could be." The insidious ways in which racism operates, the ways in which it contributed to Cynthia's brother's suffering, and the fear of having this seen are etched sharply into what she writes, from her grief. This calls upon us to try to bear witness to *her* pain as we grapple with these forces and our own implication in relation to them (this piece is available via Open Access online).

In "Psychoanalytic Spaces, Implicated Places," a quartet of writers, two white and two Black African American women of different generations, come together in a deeply anguished but also forward-looking conversation about what psychoanalytic spaces have been and what they might be. Each of the four authors, Carnella Gordon-Brown, Natasha Holmes, Beth Kita, and Lynne Layton, speaks of the harm each has borne, and the white authors speak of the ways they have been implicated in harming despite their intentions to do otherwise. The injuries they name include piercingly painful interactions within psychoanalytic spaces, experiences about which Gordon-Brown is left to conclude, "If I am being honest. To be authentic. I lost faith in there. Inside of that white psychoanalytic institute, I lost faith in myself." Holmes writes of having to split off parts of herself that could trigger white discomfort. Such deep, personal experience of loss is created, the authors make clear, not only by individual sharply painful interactions but by the larger context of the institutions themselves and all of us who are implicated in them. Kita evokes the early years of her own professional development and how she "wanted something that analysts seemed to have: this capacity to think, and to feel, and to think and to feel with such depth and precision and nuance," but then she writes of the ways in which she feels betrayed and simultaneously implicated by the failures of the field to engage with how much whiteness goes unexamined with such destructive effects.

Layton reflects on her experience over decades of working to deepen the appreciation for the role of the social in psychological experience as thoroughgoing, deep, and woven throughout. But what became clearer to her in recent years, she writes, is how the failures to do so not only decontextualize psychic experience but reproduce an institutional culture in which an unreflected-upon upper-middle-class whiteness works to make psychoanalysis a cold and inhospitable, unyielding space to those who are either closed out entirely or pay far too dear a price for entry. Throughout, the authors speak of silences, disavowal, and keeping context, especially whiteness, outside the space of exploration.

The authors write about the extensive harm done by this status quo but also write of many ways they imagine healing. Holmes writes, "the psychoanalytic space I fantasize not only accounts for the socio-political, but it requires the analysts to do their own 'work' of unpacking their socio-political location." This unpacking, as evoked by Holmes, entails the willingness to grapple with implication individually and collectively, as an essential part of moving forward (this chapter is available via Open Access online).

At the beginning of her paper (reprinted with permission from *Contemporary Psychoanalysis*), "The Other Within: White Shame, Native-American Genocide," Sue Grand takes us on her trip to Prague. She is in a Spanish synagogue filled with artifacts plundered by Nazis from European Jews, with whom she is identified. Suddenly, there is a shift in perspective—memory, history, and feeling seep in, and she recalls, as a young child, staring at the dioramas of "still-life Indians" with artifacts—"loin cloths, beaded leather, feather headdresses, peace pipes"—plundered by white men—a whiteness, she realizes, that forms a constituent of her "collective self." Written before Rothberg's complex implication and Stephens's white double-consciousness, Grand seems to anticipate these paradigms: movingly inhabiting the one while engaging in the other: "Imagining Aryan eyes on *my* bones, I discover myself, looking through *Aryan* eyes *at* Native-American bones. My persecuted *Jewishness* flips into a predatory American *whiteness*, and there is an all-seeing Native-American eye on that whiteness. I am suffused with shame. *On whose soil have I made my home?*"

Enacting the myth of the "vanished Indian"—perhaps the originating myth for white American "violent innocence" (Bollas)—in which Native Americans are regarded by white America as if their "disappearance" were a natural evolution, unrelated to human (white) agency, Grand notes, "U.S. psychoanalysis has been silent about this atrocity and its traumatic legacies." Of course, it isn't only psychoanalysis that has been silent here. Grand's thoughts on how "psychopathic regimes often construct seamless insularity for the dominant" race could have been written in response to today's news; consider, for example, the reactionary efforts to suppress the facts of our (white America's) ongoing racial crimes—its violence and inequities—in the name of "protecting" (white) children's self-esteem.

Disrupting this "seamless insularity" surrounding Native American genocide, Grand argues that in order to meaningfully absorb the reality of our history and to begin to offer whatever forms of recognition and reparation are possible, we must first engage in "creative racial shame." In her words, "Repair cannot begin with depressive concern and reparative guilt. It must begin with the rupturing gaze of wounded otherness." Here, she offers a view of shame that not only encompasses a Kleinian perspective but moves beyond it in that she understands shame as "affect, intersubjective process, and cultural commentary." In her words, "[w]hen we are exposed to the eye of the vanished Other, when we allow ourselves to experience our own 'deserved shame' (Watkins, 2016) about cultural evil, that shame allows 'our moral sense to tune in to the beacon of goodness and justice' (Lebron, 2013, p. 7)."

In "Don't Blame the Mirror for Your Ugly Face," Ofra Bloch, an Israeli-born therapist working in New York, opens her paper with an admission of the ways she has allowed herself to feel contentment when her Black patients do not see her as white. And then, "awakening to [her] white skin," the shift—the realization that she is implicated in American racism despite her sense of being an outsider—"unhomed" here even after four decades. From a different social location, she comes to much the same conclusion as David (noted earlier), insofar as her "continued feeling of not belonging" protected her against unwanted implication. Owning her whiteness in the context of American racism is possible only as the result of a long journey to more fully inhabit her implication in the context of being raised as a Jew in Israel.

Bloch came to make the documentary *Afterward*, after years spent immersed in grappling with the experiences of second-generation Holocaust survivors and coming to wonder about the others—the descendants of the Germans whose parents were directly implicated. Unexpectedly, she writes, this project brought her back to the world of her childhood and a protracted (ongoing) search into the roots of her own implication in the oppression of the Palestinian people. Moving between the descendants of German perpetrators and her own personal context and history, the work on the film becomes for Bloch a site for "navigating the complexity of the transgenerational victim-victimizer matrix." She directly takes on the ways in which the horrors of the Holocaust can be invoked to silence others in their pain and oppression and, even more urgently, the ways that history can be used to justify the oppression of others; in her words, the ways that those in power may make cynical use of the Holocaust "to justify unchecked oppression and silence criticism or to provide an excuse for what is done to the Palestinians."

Bloch's approach is both wide in scope and deeply personal, even raw, as she returns to vividly depict moments from her own childhood as an Israeli Jew growing up during the '50s and '60s. As a psychoanalyst, she examines the role of both fear and shame, and especially defenses against shame, that underlie the construction of the narratives within which oppression of the Palestinians is framed. As a relational analyst, she does not move away from acknowledging psychic paradox and complexity; she feels ambiguity and ambivalence, and she tries "not to fight it." Bloch notes that her story of growing up as an Israeli Jewish child is ordinary, which makes it interesting. It is what she does with her reflections on this story that move it out of the ordinary.

In "The Complexity of Implication for Racial Minority Immigrants," Pratyusha Tummala-Narra animates Rothberg's idea of "complex implication," the position of those who have experienced, even still are experiencing, shattering trauma or victimization in some contexts while holding relative privilege in others. Attending to multiple dimensions of this painful, confusing, and at times alienating social and psychic experience, she elaborates on the aspects of the multifaceted subjectivity of racial minority immigrants to the US. She shares moments sitting both with clients and students who hold different forms of marginalization and privilege simultaneously, who feel in many ways unseen with regard to crucial aspects of their own and their communities' experience. The anguish that attends such complex positioning is illustrated with several examples, including a layered consideration of challenges faced by Asian American immigrants and their children. In her words, "when Asian-Americans' racism-related distress is minimized or ignored, their sense of belonging is diminished." Tummala-Narra makes a powerful link between such minimization of harm suffered, profound lack of recognition of this harm, and the ways this impedes seeing implication in other contexts. She writes, "it is . . . challenging to see one's own implication in injustice against other racial minorities when you are not seen as a real American." Another area she considers is the complex positioning of many Black immigrants to this country, for whom the particular racist legacy of the United States contributes to an utter failure of recognition regarding distinctive cultural and immigration experiences.

Tummala-Narra also turns to our training institutions. Moving beyond binary thinking, she argues, means getting past the now-settled question of *whether* race matters in psychotherapy but to the complex lived dynamics of *how* it matters—to the therapist, the patient, and between them and within the institution itself. Crucially, she also addresses our collective implication in mental health systems that are failing to meet the needs, especially of marginalized communities and youth. Invoking Judith Herman's (in press) idea of a *moral community* for healing from trauma,

Tummala-Narra presents this as a compelling way to reimagine our institutions. To people of color who have been made to feel invisible, a moral community is essential; it is also the moral community that allows us to own our implication. Citing concurrent work of her own, Tummala-Narra offers specific suggestions for creating a framework for a decolonizing psychoanalysis. Among these are a capacity and commitment to humanizing cultural narratives through seeing whole, complex persons and "to confront one's own painful affect associated with privilege and marginalization and approach therapeutic work with humility." In this way, she envisions, we can move together toward inhabiting what Rothberg terms "transfiguring implication."

In "The Relational Citizen as Implicated Subject: Emergent Unconscious Processes in the Psychoanalytic Community Collaboratory," Billie Pivnick and Jane Hassinger write of the creation of "ethical communities." Such communities are desperately needed in our times—times in which fear, helplessness, nihilism, and hatred so frequently define our relationship to the body politic. Toward this end, Pivnick and Hassinger are interested in drawing out and cultivating a particular self-state, that of a "relational citizen." Rooted in a sense of belonging, this entails "the intersubjective experience of oneself as a responsible and generative citizen among citizens." As an idea, it links one's specific identities and group identifications, including the very particular trauma histories of one's various ancestors, with Fromm's universalistic ethic, an identification with "humanity at large" (in this age of climate crisis, we might now add, an identification with all living beings). The inhabiting implication, one might say, creates such linkages between the specific and the universal. Not surprisingly, then, there is an overlap between the aims Rothberg set out to achieve and Pivnick and Hassinger's "relational citizen." Both are concerned with the "psychological exploration of the tensions baked into our multiple group identifications, [as well as the] cultivation of an ethos of mutual aid, and community engagement."

Since 2014, Pivnick and Hassinger have launched five different 12-to-14-week online groups, an "experiential laboratory," tasked with serving as a "project incubator" for approaches to community work by psychodynamically oriented practitioners. In describing their experience and observation during two "critical incidents," they movingly illustrate the emergence of "relational citizenship" where members came "to feel themselves to be 'citizens of the group' with benefits, responsibilities, and leadership functions." Catastrophic large-scale events—the Parkland school shootings and the pandemic—which inevitably affected individual participants differently depending on race and social (and even geographic) location, played a central role in igniting enactments reflecting "racial and existential anxieties" and "the return of traumatic histories."

Pivnick and Hassinger write of how cross-cultural and intergenerational differences, even collisions, provided, albeit "slowly and painfully" at times, an opening through which participants—crucially, including themselves—discovered how they "enact[ed] or defend[ed] against acknowledging . . . implication in the suffering of others." In addition to this kind of reckoning with implication, the development of relational citizenship was facilitated by a "democratic" model of group work whereby much space is made for "shared responsibility and role flexibility in which members take on leadership." Just as Rothberg's implicated subject is not a fixed identity, Pivnick and Hassinger write that

> being a citizen, like being a leader of a group, is not a reified identity or single state but an engagement in a constantly shifting dynamic process in which our internal worlds interact with the external world in a way that often reveals the psychological complexity of our multiple identities.

In his chapter, "Awakening to the Political—or Is It All an Undream?" Matt Aibel describes contemporary efforts to establish a home for politics within psychoanalytic theory and treatment. His personal journey, with respect to the place of the political within his thinking and practice, reflects the profession's relationship to politics. During the years of Aibel's psychoanalytic training, politics exists in a separate space. While it matters to individual practitioners—Aibel describes the reaction of candidates and faculty to Barack Obama's election, reactions carefully kept out of classroom, supervision, and treatment—politics is excluded from psychoanalytic theory and praxis; as Aibel writes, "identification with marginality and cultural trauma was largely suppressed (Tummala-Narra, 2016), and due consideration of the impacts of the political surround were disavowed and dissociated." As politics has increasingly entered the field over the past 20 years, we hear of Aibel's increasing immersion in this literature. During this phase, the place of politics in psychoanalysis, as well as the place of it in Aibel's development as a psychoanalyst, was largely from an outside perspective. For Aibel, it was a matter of "research," an intellectual interest; for the field as a whole, the focus was primarily on matters of power and oppression outside of psychoanalysis itself. Culminating with the election of Trump, the field has begun to question itself, question its own implication in perpetuating injustice. At the same time, Aibel feels himself to be personally implicated: "My questions about the place of political discourse in psychoanalytic treatment no longer stemmed just from intellectual curiosity but now from felt necessity."

While Aibel addresses many aspects of the political in psychoanalysis, one senses throughout that his primary concern involves working, as a progressive analyst, with a Trump supporter. How, he wonders, does one maintain genuine curiosity or an analytic sense of playfulness when the other's politics are abhorrent and the circumstances so dire? He offers several suggestions, including counteracting numerous ways the analyst is implicated in collapsing potential space (e.g., by attending to Doñas's, 2021, "microfascist within" or imagining how one's own self-righteousness lands for the other). Ultimately, though, Aibel leaves us with the observation that "many case reports traversing sociopolitical themes sooner or later recruit the notion of impossibility." Ending his chapter on a personal note, we learn of Aibel's lifelong yearning to heal and bring together his rancorously divorced parents. Suddenly, Doñas's "experience of impossibility" while attempting to bridge painfully and deeply divergent points of view gains added resonance.

As a society and as a field—in the US and in psychoanalysis—we are implicated in childism, writes Laurel Moldawsky Silber in "Parental Implication and the Expansion of the Child Relational Therapist's Clinical Imagination." In both arenas, despite rhetoric to the contrary, ideology has mattered more than the rights, not to mention needs, of children. Quoting Kristof (2021), "[f]amilies desperately need help. In other countries, they get it. In the United States, they get empty homilies about the importance of family." In our field, Silber asserts, it had long been sacrosanct to treat parents, actual parents, their subjectivity, as outside of the field of child treatment. In this way, she concludes, psychoanalysis has been "implicated...in maintaining a non-reflective stance regarding [parents'] accountability."

For many years, Silber has advocated for a model of child relational therapy in which engagement of parents—to borrow from a title of Bromberg's—is not only *permissible* in the treatment of children but a vitally *necessary* part of it. Why does she think that? In this paper, she develops the idea that parents are "complexly implicated subjects"; "both fright-ened and frightening," both traumatized and traumatizing, both victim and perpetrator. Parental trauma, transmitted procedurally to the child, often indecipherable without the parent's subjectivity in the room, is "hidden in plain sight." For both parent and child—the one dissociating and the other receiving incomprehensible fragments—individuality and time (the sense of past, present, and future) are flattened. Into this flattened, two-dimen-sional space, the child therapist, imagining the subjectivity of each, is the "nexus" from which a "triadic expansion of consciousness" emerges. In her approach to the work, one hears a tolerance of an extraordinary degree of complexity, even chaos, as the therapist holds in mind the minds of child and parent, of past, present, and future.

Bringing about this "triadic expansion of consciousness" requires more than the clinician's expanded imagination in a search for meaning; a vari-ety of love, a deep affirmation, is needed. Refusing to split responsibility and vulnerability neatly between parent and child, Silber embodies this affirmative stance that, one can sense from her clinical examples, forti-fies both child and parent. The former is enabled to "resist" becoming swallowed up by parental trauma in a bid for recognition; the latter is enabled to tolerate the shame and grief from their own traumatization as they "see themselves through the eyes of their child, a present way into a past otherwise unavailable to consciousness." Holding in mind parental responsibility and vulnerability, she writes, "[a]ccountability for parental implication involves retrieving painful disorganized non-conscious mem-ories. In accomplishing this psychologically courageous feat, forgiveness can potentially emerge in the wake."

Finally, in our chapter, "Implication as Central to a Relational Stance: Vulnerability, Responsibility, and Racial Enactment," we suggest that both the concept and felt experience of implication are central to what is distinctively essential to a relational clinical stance, and that this allows for the construction of one natural and necessary bridge between our theories and what Rothberg calls us to see. Here, we continue to follow two threads of implication theory (each of our personal reflections high-lighted one of them) from Rothberg's social-political realm into psy-choanalysis. First is the idea of *complex implication*, which allows us as citizens and analysts to hold multiple subject positions with the feel-ings and responsibilities that come with each, where acknowledgment of multiplicity deepens the capacity to see where we are implicated. The complex implication is thus compatible with the notion of multiple self-states in relational theory but adds to it insofar as the latter tends to highlight a narrower, more specific relational context in which self-states are embedded, whereas the former locates a multiplicity of identities in particular social-structural conditions of power and hierarchy. This broader focus deepens our thinking about social and racial oppression not only outside but also inside the clinical encounter. Second is the idea of implication and, specifically, *the implicated subject*, the latter of which is a more inclusive, more accurate, and therefore more useful category located between victims and perpetrators than previous, more external positions (e.g., bystander or witness). Both threads of implication theory can help provide a useful map to the analyst for her own experience while working in areas of trauma. As many have discovered, it is inevitable in such work that analysts painfully oscillate between the perpetrator and victim position. Both complex implication and the deeply implicated analyst can help increase the space in which the analyst can think—the former by holding both positions simultaneously and the latter by holding on to a simply human, not particularly good but not horribly bad, perspective on one's self and one's participation. As important, it invites the analyst to acknowledge implication directly in moments where that is what is most crucial, both therapeutically and in terms of basic human responsiveness.

## Note

1 Stephens also includes Lacan in her analysis, a portion of the work we don't address here.

## References

Apprey, M. (2014). A pluperfect errand: A turbulent return to beginnings in the transgenerational transmission of destructive aggression. *Free Associations, 15,* 16–29.

Benjamin, J. (2004). Beyond doer and done to: An intersubjective view of thirdness. *The Psychoanalytic Quarterly, 73*(1), 5–46.

Benjamin, J. (2018). *Beyond doer and done to: Recognition theory, intersubjectivity and the third*. Routledge.

Bromberg, P. M. (2011). *The shadow of the tsunami: And the growth of the relational mind*. Routledge.

Connolly, M. (2021, April 22). What's repaired in reparations: A conversation among psychoanalytic and social activists. *Couched Podcast.*

Crenshaw, K. (1989). Demarginalizing the intersection of race and sex: A black feminist critique of antidiscrimination doctrine, feminist theory and antiracist politics. *University of Chicago Legal Forum, 1989*, Article 8.

Doñas, V. A. (2021, October 23–24). *These are not nos-otros: The paradox of integrity* [Presentation]. 2nd Symposium, International Association for Relational Psychoanalysis and Psychotherapy, online.

Du Bois, W. E. B. (1903/1994). *The souls of black folk.* Dover Publications, Inc.

Fanon, F. (1986/1967). *Black skin, White masks* (C. Lam Markmann, Trans.). Pluto Press.

Forti, S. (2014). *New demons: Rethinking power and evil today.* Stanford University Press.

Glaude, E. S. (2020). *Begin again: James Baldwin's America and its urgent lessons for our own.* Crown.

González, F. J. (2020). Trump cards and Klein Bottles: On the collective of the individual. *Psychoanalytic Dialogues, 30*(4), 383–398.

Hannah-Jones, N. (2019, August 18). The 1619 project. *New York Times Magazine.*

Hart, A. (2017). From multicultural competence to radical openness: A psychoanalytic engagement of otherness. *The American Psychoanalyst, 51*(1), 12–27.

Herman, J. L. (in press). *Truth and repair: Envisioning justice from the survivor's perspective.* Basic Books.

Kristof, N. (2021, May 6). In editorial entitled, turning child care into a new cold war. *New York Times.*

Layton, L., with Leavy-Sperounis, M. (2020). *Toward a social psychoanalysis: Culture, character, and normative unconscious processes.* Routledge.

LeBron, C. J. (2013). *The colour of our shame: Race and justice in our time.* Oxford University Press.

Mitchell, S. A. (1993). *Hope and dread in psychoanalysis.* Basic Books.

Rothberg, M. (2019). *The implicated subject: Beyond victims and perpetrators.* Stanford University Press.

Sartre, J.-P. (1964–1965). Black Orpheus. *The Massachusetts Review, 6*(1), 13–52.

Smith, B., Smith, B., & Frazier, D. (1977). *Combahee river collective statement.*

Stephens, M. (2020). Getting next to ourselves: The interpersonal dimensions of double-consciousness. *Contemporary Psychoanalysis, 56*(2–3), 201–225.

Stoute, B. (2021). Black rage: The psychic adaptation to the trauma of oppression. *Journal of the American Psychoanalytic Association, 69*(2), 265–290.

Swartz, S. (2019). *Ruthless Winnicott.* Routledge.

Tummala-Narra, P. (2016). *Psychoanalytic theory and cultural competence in psychotherapy.* American Psychological Association.

Watkins, M. (2016). *The social and political life of shame in the U.S. presidential election 2016.* Paper presented at the Massachusetts Institute for Psychoanalysis.

Yancy, G. (2012). *Look, a White! Philosophical essays on whiteness.* Temple University Press.

# Chapter 2

# Getting Next to Ourselves

## The Interpersonal Dimensions of Double-Consciousness[1]

*Michelle Ann Stephens*

This essay explores, in a speculative and reflective rather than heavily researched mode, how we might think as psychoanalysts about the interpersonal dimensions of double-consciousness. I begin by sharing briefly the convergence of ideas and disciplines that I am bringing together: the original conceptualization of double-consciousness in black studies and critical race theory; and psychoanalytic discussions of intersubjectivity. I then tell two stories, both involving my experiences of incidents of racial tension in educational settings. These experiences inspired me to perform an informal online review of writing in the mental health field on guilt and rage—the powerful pair of feelings that seemed to emerge, repeatedly and consistently, in scenes of public, racial discussion and confrontation. I then turn to discussing "white double-consciousness" and "black mirroring," extending psychoanalytic interpretations and their application to the psychic dynamics of interpersonal, interracial relating. Double-consciousness is placed in dialogue with understandings of the mirror stage, intersubjectvity, radical openness, and thirdness, theorized, respectively, by Jacques Lacan (2007), Philip Bromberg (1996, 2008), Anton Hart (2017), and Jessica Benjamin (2007). Along the way, I also draw from the work of Frantz Fanon (1986/1967). Ultimately, my goal is to think with and respond to a recent call by Lynne Layton (2019) for us to develop a psychoanalytic framework for thinking about white double-consciousness. This essay reflects my own journey, comparing and contrasting methods and theories across academic disciplines and psychoanalytic schools, to imagine what a 21st century double-consciousness could look like, if informed by an interpersonal psychoanalytic understanding of racial relationality.

DOI: 10.4324/9781003265146-2

Between 1903, when W. E. B. DuBois first wrote the following words, and 1964, when Jean-Paul Sartre wrote his, much had happened in the history of racial formation across American and European worlds. Du Bois's statement came from the third paragraph of the first chapter of his canonical work, *The Souls of Black Folk*, published in the aftermath of American slavery. *The Souls of Black Folk* represented his effort to describe the special social and psychic conditions black Americans faced at the turn of a new century. Du Bois stated:

> The Negro is a sort of seventh son, born with a veil, and gifted with second-sight in this American world,—a world which yields him no true self-consciousness, but only lets him see himself through the revelation of the other world. It is a peculiar sensation, this double-consciousness, this sense of always looking at one's self through the eyes of others. . . . One ever feels his two-ness,—an American, a Negro; two souls, two thoughts, two unreconciled strivings; two warring ideals in one dark body.
>
> (Du Bois, 1903/1994, p. 2)

Du Bois's observation regarding the "double-consciousness" of the "American . . . Negro" has been a defining feature of scholarship in African American Studies over the course of the twentieth century. His words were followed by two world wars, the colonial contours of which he also encapsulated in a second famous phrase from *The Souls of Black Folk*: "The problem of the twentieth century is the problem of the color line— the relation of the darker to the lighter races of men in Asia and Africa, in America and the islands of the sea" (p. 9). By the time Du Bois expatriated to Ghana in 1959, movements for political independence and decolonization had spread across the colonial world (the "worlds of color" Du Bois described as "shadowing" the imperial metropoles (1925/1992, p. 385)).

As early as the late 1930s, one of these movements found expression in the Francophone world in an aesthetic and cultural theory of black consciousness. As an articulation of blackness and black poetics, "negritude" engaged both the anti-colonial psychiatrist Frantz Fanon (1986/1967), and the existentialist French philosopher Jean-Paul Sartre (1964–1965). If Du Bois's statement at the turn of the century focused attention on black subjectivity—the soul of the "New Negro" and his and her double-consciousness as an intra-psychic phenomenon—by the 1960s Sartre was experiencing the "shock of being seen" (1964–1965, p. 13) *in* his white-ness. As Sartre described in his essay "Black Orpheus":

> For three thousand years, the white man has enjoyed the privilege of seeing without being seen; he was only a look—the light from his eyes drew each thing out of the shadow of its birth; the whiteness of his skin was another look, condensed light. The white man—white because he was man, white like daylight, white like truth, white like virtue—lighted up the creation like a torch and unveiled the secret white essence of beings. Today, these black men are looking at us, and our gaze comes back to our own eyes.
>
> (Jean-Paul Sartre, 1964–1965, p. 13)

Sartre heralded the interpersonal impact of negritude on white subjectivities in the context of world-wide decolonization.

When in 1903 Du Bois described this "peculiar sensation, this double-consciousness, this sense of always looking at one's self through the eyes of others" (p. 2), he was thinking specifically about African Americans. His focus was on double-consciousness as a source of internal conflict in the black American subject, who could not be in touch with a sense of self separate from the projections of, and imposed by, the (white) other. Years later, interpersonal and relational psychoanalyst Philip Bromberg would say something that, to my ears, echoed Du Bois. In describing his understanding of intersubjectivity as the ability "to see yourself as others see you while not dissociating from the experience of how you see yourself" (2008, p. 331), Bromberg also evoked the projective gaze of the other as an essential component of the psychodynamics of intersubjectivity. But for Bromberg, the moment he described—the experience of being able to see yourself both through the eyes of others and through your own—represents a highly developed and mature intersubjective capacity. Unlike Du Boisian double-consciousness, characterized by the subject's internal sense of holding, "two warring ideals in one dark body," for Bromberg true intersubjectivity amidst conflict is only possible when these warring ideals are able to co-exist, without negating each other.[2] For Bromberg, this is precisely the stage of development we may all aspire to but have difficulty reaching. Rather, we tend to live certain parts of our identities—for example our whiteness—as if they are the external projections of another that, once experienced, are fundamentally at war with our own internal, richer, non-racialized, senses of self.

In this reflection, I suggest ways of thinking together these multiple understandings of mental processes of relating to and with an other. Du Bois, Sartre, Fanon, Bromberg—all are writers and thinkers whose works were forged in different settings and disciplinary contexts. However, they also share the broader global historical field of racial and colonial formation, which, at least in my mind, situates their works in conversation with each other. Double-consciousness and intersubjectivity are thought here together in a way that both respects their different points of origin while exploring the implications of their convergences.

## Racial Incidents on Campus

While I was teaching at a small liberal arts college, a student came to my office hours in great distress after she and her friends were evicted from a classroom by members of the administrative staff. They had reserved a room until 4pm for a student club meeting, but their meeting was interrupted ten minutes early and they were told to leave the room for another event scheduled at 4:30. The students pointed out that they had reserved the room until 4 and still had 10 minutes, but things escalated and at some point in the encounter one of the staff members used the phrase, "you people," in demanding that the students leave the room. The students were African American and the two staff members were white. This incident became the source of public debate on campus, and the phrase "you people" became the lightning rod for a complex encounter involving issues of race and class in a fractious confrontation between working class white, female, administrative staff and middle to upper class, black, undergraduate students.

Soon, the incident spilled out of that classroom to engage the entire campus community. Over the next two weeks, there were meetings of black faculty with the students, meetings of faculty sympathetic to the staff union with members of the staff, a meeting of students with the President of the College, a forum held at the African American students' center between students, meetings between the President of the College and members of senior leadership, and finally, an open town forum held at one of the larger auditoriums at the college. I attended all of these meetings, and as the settings grew larger the emotions ran higher—tears, outrage, guilt, and rage—escalating more and more.

All of that took place about 15 years ago, at the very beginning of my teaching career. Flash forward a decade or so later when I was on the faculty of a large research university. Again, about a year and a half into my position, a student came to my office to share his distress over an incident that occurred in one of his graduate seminars. A fellow student had circulated a racist joke to a select group of students in the seminar. He had been included in the email because he was bi-racial, of fair complexion, and his classmate had not realized he self-identified as black. He alerted the Professor and the Director of Graduate Studies and seemed to feel the right steps were being taken to address what had happened. He was speaking with me more to share his growing feelings of distress, especially since I was a faculty member of color. I listened and gave some advice about how he might engage the white students in his seminar with whom he was still having difficulty interacting socially because of this incident.

Yet again, things escalated. Two weeks later I found myself in a meeting between black graduate students and faculty, where the students described a growing atmosphere of separation, hostility and distrust between white and black students, both in their cohort and in the class where the incident had occurred. Faculty members' efforts to encourage the students to interact with each other in a more relaxed and convivial setting, to try to talk together about what had been so upsetting about the original email and the events that followed, were experienced as insensitive by the students of color and an abdication of our responsibilities as faculty. They felt we were encouraging them to put themselves in the interpersonal line of fire, again, with their white classmates. At the same time, white graduate students were meeting with white faculty and expressing their distress about being perceived as racist by their black counterparts. And once again, as the academic year progressed, this incident became the lightning rod for two open forums, stories in the campus paper, postings on social media accounts and Facebook, and even larger national stories in such venues as the *Chronicle of Higher Education*.

I want to emphasize a few features both incidents share. First, most if not all of the players involved, from students to staff to faculty to administrators, across all the races involved, were well-meaning people trying to find their way through a thicket of individual emotions and feelings, and interpersonal confrontations and reactions, that were highly distressing, destabilizing—*traumatizing*, really—and by the end, no one came through unharmed. Second, in neither case was there some kind of moment of resolution, catharsis or reconciliation where the central players in the original incident found a way to talk to each other or address in any real way what had happened, without falling into defensiveness, guilt, shame, or outrage. I would not be exaggerating if I said that I went into psychoanalytic training partly due to these two incidents. They left me with a pressing set of questions about what *can* be done, and what *should* be done, when racial tensions are high, to enable people to talk to each other and to hear each other, despite the power of their projections onto each other and the defenses these produce. In my experience of both of these incidents, the two most powerful emotions these encounters seemed to catalyze were guilt and rage.

## Guilt and Rage

### *"White Guilt"*

Years later, in my search for answers in the aftermath of these incidents, an informal online review first led me to broader psychological thinking on racial guilt. In a post in *Psychology Today*, Susan Krauss Whitbourne (2012), Professor Emerita of Psychological and Brain Sciences at the University of Massachusetts, Amherst, commented:

> The traditional Freudian view is that guilt resides under the surface veneer of our behavior. The psychodynamic theory of Freud proposes that we build defense mechanisms to protect us from the guilt we would experience if we knew just how awful our awful desires really were. . . . From a cognitive point of view, guilt is an emotion that people experience because they're convinced they've caused harm. . . . The guilt of emotion follows directly from the thought that you are responsible for someone else's misfortune, whether or not this is the case.

Krauss Whitbourne then splits guilt into 5 types: "Guilt for something you did. . . . Guilt for something you didn't do, but want to." Another type of guilt involves the feeling that, "you didn't do enough to help someone," leading to a kind of "compassion fatigue." There is also a kind of "survivor guilt" that comes from "Guilt that you're doing better than someone else." Then there is: "Guilt for something you *think* you did." Krauss Whitbourne's adjectives in her description of this type of guilt, as "irrational" or involving "magical" beliefs or "magical thinking," gives us a clue into the area of the psyche where this type of guilt resides—in what Lacanians call the Imaginary (Žižek, 2007, pp. 40–78), the realm of fantasy, where we construct both images of ourselves and of the others we come into contact with.

This taxonomy of guilt then led me to some of the popular discourse on the notion of "white guilt" that we hear very often in the media. The current Wikipedia definition of white guilt is: "the individual or collective guilt felt by some white people for harm resulting from racist treatment of ethnic minorities and indigenous peoples by other white people, most specifically in the context of the Atlantic slave trade, European colonialism and the legacy of these eras."[3] The Wikipedia entry reminds us of the 2015 story of American civil rights activist Rachel Dolezal who "had been posing as African American." *Washington Post* journalist Krissah Thompson and psychologist Derald Wing Sue, an expert on racial identity, are quoted as describing Dolezal as "an archetype of white guilt," that is, someone who had "become so fascinated by racism and racial justice issues that she 'over-identified' with black people." This notion of 'over-identification' is an interesting one when seen in both racial and psycho-dynamic terms. It suggests an additional component to this form of racialized guilt, which matches most closely to the third type of magical thinking Krauss Whitbourne describes as, "Guilt for something you *think* you did." It suggests an emotional blurring of one's sense of the line between self and other. This blurring becomes particularly painful if the one with whom one is identifying, and from whom one seeks some form of recognition and forgiveness, is also the one whose behavior or mode of relating with you stimulates your feelings of shame, as well as guilt—that is to say, is the one "whose behavior (albeit inadvertently) is causing the pain" (Bromberg, 2003, 562).

Other psychoanalytically inflected terms have been applied to this type of blurring, such as Amber Jamilla Musser's notion of "moral masochism," that is, "an unconscious desire for punishment that manifests itself clinically as almost paralyzing feelings of guilt" (2014, p. 8). Citing first Freud and then Fanon, Musser reminds us of various psychological interpretations of the evidence of masochism in white Americans' identifications with black subjectivity in American popular culture. This masochism endeavors to "drain" black cultural products of any signs of their "aggression" by, counter-intuitively, reveling in what Frantz Fanon would invoke as, quoting from Bernard Wolfe, "an unconscious orgy of masochism—very possibly punishing [oneself] for not being the black man" (Fanon, 1986/1967, p. 175; Wolfe, 1949, p. 888). As Fanon described further his interpretation of the old Br'er Rabbit and Uncle Remus tales of southern American folk mythology: "In the United States, as we can see, the Negro makes stories in which it becomes possible for him to work off his aggression; the white man's unconscious justifies this aggression and gives it worth by turning it on himself, thus reproducing the classic schema of masochism" (p. 176). For Fanon then and Musser now, "white guilt" as it is expressed culturally manifests more complex dynamics of "unconscious masochism" within white American viewers and listeners. Also, for both authors and thinkers "white guilt" becomes the pathway to a more dynamic understanding of the potential place of aggression.

## "Black Rage"

If, for some writers and thinkers, guilt and masochism are intertwined in a complex dynamic within the form of racial affect termed, popularly, "white guilt," this complex links to the other emotion in the pair that emerges in moments of tense racial encounter, and that is rage. A psychoanalytic cognate here might be "aggression," bringing into sharper focus interpersonal dimensions that might be occluded in the ideas of rage or even outrage. While rage feels more primitive, outrage has a more vague target—outrage over an incident, or at an unacceptable idea—but aggression has embedded within it the idea of an object of one's attack.

In 1968, William H. Grier and Price M. Cobbs, two black psychiatrists and assistant professors at the University of California medical school, introduced the term "black rage" in their book of the same title. The work was inspired by the riots that followed the assassination of Martin Luther King Jr. In an interview with Richard Pyatt in 1969, Grier described "black rage" not as the product of a "unique black psychology" but rather as generated from and within the hostile "climate in which black people live" (Pyatt, 1969), aligning racialized subjective and psychic formation with the shift away from the intra-psychic to the relational contexts produced by and within the United States as a socially stratified, post-slavery, 'post-colonial,' society. The kinds of interpersonal interactions that might occur between individuals in such a hostile environment would get its own name just two years later, the term "microaggression" coined by psychiatrist and Harvard University professor Chester M. Pierce in 1970 to describe the insults and dismissals he regularly witnessed non-black Americans inflict on African Americans (DeAngelis, 2009).

Derald Wing Sue, a psychology professor at Columbia University, describes three types of microaggressions: micro-assaults, micro-insults and micro-invalidations (DeAngelis, 2009; Sue et al., 2007). "Micro-assaults are most akin to conventional racism, they are conscious. They are explicit racial or derogatory actions that are intended to hurt. For example, intentionally serving a white person before a person of color or deliberately referring to an Asian person as "Oriental" (Seghal, 2016). A micro-insult is "an unconscious communication that demeans a person from a minority group. Examples include a teacher not calling on students of color or a white person asking a person of color 'how did you get your job?,' implying that he or she is not qualified and got the job because of affirmative action or a quota program" (Seghal, 2016). Finally, "minimizing or disregarding the thoughts, feelings or experiences of a person of color is referred to as micro-invalidation. A white person asserting to minorities that 'they don't see color' or that 'we are all human beings' are examples" (Seghal, 2016).

As I read about this pair of terms coined just within two years of each other, black rage and micro-aggression, I was struck by a strange slippage, a merger that can occur between white and black subjects in terms of relating to and identifying with each other's racialized aggression. I found myself returning to Fanon's description of white guilt as "unconscious masochism": "In the United States . . . the Negro makes stories in which it becomes possible for him to work off his aggression; the white man's unconscious justifies this aggression and gives it worth by turning it on himself, thus reproducing the classic schema of masochism" (p. 176). In Fanon's reading at least, it would seem that this racialized aggression—black rage, which becomes and fuels a psychic and cultural story about being black in America, leads to an over-identification on the part of white American subjects through white guilt, which then displaces aggression. Whether or not such a phenomenon is fully explanatory or clinically helpful, what I found striking is the way this racialized aggression, like guilt, can pass back and forth between the subjects of an interracial dyad, or a multi-racial social collective. Fanon seemed to identify an overlapping unconscious space in which the black subject works out their aggression through a story, and the white subject takes in and submits to that aggression unconsciously through an identification that also, somehow, displaces it.

Almost everything explosive that ensued from each of the campus racial incidents I experienced took one of two rhetorical forms: accusations or confessions. The sad thing was that neither of these forms of address actually produced communication with the other. Outraged and distraught, speakers threw at each other the accusation "YOU are a racist"; or the confession "I am a racist." Neither enabled the start of a conversation; rather, they ended conversations. "You are a racist" seemed to say—confess, and I will feel vindicated. Your confession is all I need. "I am a racist" seemed to say—I have confessed to your accusation, I submit, and feel punished. This self-inflicted wound is all I need. The cycle was never-ending, as if that was the only point the conversation had been moving toward and, once we all arrived there, we merely turned around and began the conversation again. I was left often with the same question: after I have told you that you are a racist, after *you* have told *me* you are a racist, after I have told you *I* am a racist, and after *you* have told me I am a racist, what, then, do we have to say to each other? Is there anything left to say?

## White Double-Consciousness

In the late 1960s, Jean-Paul Sartre seemed to reach just such a moment in the encounter with his own "white guilt" as he engaged with the newly radicalized black negritude poets. The "shock of being seen" as a white subject prompted his own form of double-consciousness—seeing yourself as the other sees you (p. 13). Sartre's name for this figure or projection of blackness he was encountering, "Black Orpheus," seemed to be a very different figure than Du Bois's "New Negro," able to call forth in the white male subject a new vision of himself, a not-me. Suddenly, in the face of Africans' "wild and free looks that judge our world" (p. 14), Sartre experienced an upending of reality in which, "Being [l'Être] is black, Being is made of fire, we are accidental and far away, we have to justify our mores, our technics, our undercooked paleness and our verdigris vegetation" (p. 15). To Sartre, whiteness emerged into view as "a strange livid varnish that keeps our skin from breathing—white tights, worn out at the elbows and knees" (p. 14). He described this shifting perspective, or loss, as a submission and defeat:

> There we are, *finished*; our victories—their bellies sticking up in the air—show their guts, our secret defeat. If we want to crack open this

finitude which imprisons us, we can no longer rely on the privileges of our race, of our color, of our technics: we will not be able to become a part of the totality from which those black eyes exile us, unless we tear off our white tights in order to try simply to be men.

(p. 14)

Maybe it was the hint of white resistance, an inescapable feeling of resentment at needing to submit to a new global, decolonial, racial reality, that left Fanon feeling that something in Sartre's account fell short: "I do not know; but I say that he who looks into my eyes for anything but a perpetual question will have to lose his sight; neither recognition nor hate" (p. 29). As Fanon continued to explain his negative reaction to "Black Orpheus" in *Black Skin, White Masks*: "*Orphée Noir* is a date in the intellectualization of the *experience* of being black. . . . Black consciousness is held out as an absolute density, as filled with itself, a stage preceding any invasion" (p. 134). It is this positing of blackness as a gaze that is closed or filled up with itself that Fanon partly objects to, offering instead in the entirety of his work a different image of blackness as a perpetual questioning: "What is certain is that, at the very moment when I was trying to grasp my own being, Sartre, who remained The Other, gave me a name and thus shattered my last illusion" (p. 137).

In his objections to Sartre's assertions about blackness, however, Fanon missed the way Sartre's opening revelations about whiteness reflected the fragmented appearance of his own white subjectivity—whiteness as a now visible fragment of a previously universalized self, one that becomes visible in the face of 'black consciousness,' when one's "gaze comes back to our own eyes" (Sartre, p. 13). Despite his disagreement with Sartre's projective over-idealizations of blackness, Sartre's description of whiteness (in a relational confrontation with blackness) mirrored the very dynamic Fanon tried to theorize in his elaboration of Jacques Lacan's theory of the mirror stage in *Black Skin, White Masks*.

In his effort to address an interracial intersubjective context, Fanon used the psychoanalytic tools and thinkers he had available to him in his time—Freud, Lacan, Adler, Jung. Closer, then, to a psychoanalytic frame of reference, Fanon's engagement with Lacan's mirror-stage in *Black Skin, White Masks* also dialogues with Du Bois's older formulation of double-consciousness, as the latter originates in late nineteenth and early twentieth century radical black thought on racialized subjectivities. Fanon's work is central precisely because he stands at the intersection of these two traditions, psycho-analyzing the social and relational dimensions of black double-consciousness, while simultaneously deploying the central insights of over half a century of radical black thought to wrench a more social and relational analysis out of Freudian psychoanalytic theory. This is psychoanalytic black theorizing Fanon engaged in *before* French and American psychoanalysis turned more fully from the intra-psychic context of drive theory to the psyche's more intersubjective contexts.

As Homi Bhabha also describes in his 1986 foreword to *Black Skin, White Masks*, if, in Lacanian terms, the subject finds a name for itself in the signifiers of the Other, then: "For Fanon, like Lacan, the primary moments of such a repetition of the self lie in the desire of the look and the limits of language" (p. xvi). Bhabha's emphasis here is two-fold: both language and the look of the other become the source of the self's repetition of certain self-organizing signifiers. However, when Bhabha adds: "The 'atmosphere of certain uncertainty' that surrounds the body certifies its existence and threatens its dismemberment," he points to the threat of self-fracturing that can be experienced, psychically, as bodily dismemberment. It was Fanon's speculation that, as much as the splitting of the self in the face of the other's projective gaze is the defining characteristic of black double-consciousness, something parallel might happen for whiteness in a certain kind of encounter with blackness:

> It would indeed be interesting, on the basis of Lacan's theory of the *mirror period*, to investigate the extent to which the *imago* of his fellow built up in the young white at the usual age would undergo an imaginary aggression with the appearance of the Negro. When one has grasped the mechanism described by Lacan, one can have no further doubt that the real Other for the white man is and will continue to be the black man. And conversely. Only for the white man The Other is perceived on the level of the body image, absolutely as the not-self—that is, the unidentifiable, the unassimilable.
>
> (p. 161)

To deconstruct this dense passage a bit, first, by imago Fanon referred to Lacan's discussion of the ways in which one's sense of identity, one's self-image, was constituted by the specular image of wholeness the subject identifies in the mirror. The image of the subject's own body then becomes the basis for a form of intersubjective interaction in which the self finds likenesses and affinities with others on the basis of one's own sense of self. Fanon suggested that the experience of an other who could not be assimilated to the ego-imago, in the encounter with difference, would fracture the cohesions produced by the mirror image and later reinforced by a variety of other social signifiers, thereby leading to an aggressive affective and emotional response. This response, this aggression, is as much to the real other subject in the world as it is to the shadow of the not-me, the "unidentifiable, unassimilable" parts of the (white) self suddenly incarnated in the encounter with "the Negro."

Anton Hart (2017) has described a similar process using a more interpersonal psychoanalytic approach when he states, "The problem of racism and discrimination largely comes from a defensive process of disavowing one's unwanted parts, one's unwanted impulses and insecurities, locating them in the other person and then hating that other person in order to protect one's self" (p. 13). He continues:

> Rather than saying, 'I hate these aspects of myself, or these are really difficult, frightening aspects of my own experience,' it's easier for many people, perhaps most people, to experience these not as aspects of oneself, but aspects of the other, and then to hate the other. . . . [P]eople rid themselves of the things about themselves they can't tolerate, by projecting them onto others, or attributing them to others, and even by inducing them in others, and then hating or destroying them in those others.

Here Hart deploys a psychoanalytic theory of projection to articulate the experience of double-consciousness as a struggle with the projections of the self onto the other. In the Lacanian framework the reverse is the focus, as is also the case in Fanon's racialized re-reading of Lacan's mirror-stage. One feels assaulted in one's sense of cohesion if the image of the self reflected back to you is "different," and suddenly the projections of the other become the introjects of the self.

In an intersubjective enactment, however, imagine the "self" more chiasmically as a reflection that could be both, or either, of yourself and of the other, intertwined—whereby *both* the reality of seeing you as different (from me), *and* of seeing myself as different (to you), can be fragmenting and traumatic. With this act of imagination, I am suggesting an approach to racialized relating, and an adaptation and maturation of double-consciousness as both a concept and a description of psychic structure, to accommodate more than the Du Boisian sense of double-consciousness as primarily a site of conflict. It engages with but moves beyond Hart's description of hateful racial relating as constituted by acts of projective identification. Accepting racialized projections from the other as tied or linked to something that is actually in the self is an idea much closer to Bromberg's interpersonal theory of dissociation, multiple self-states, and enactment rather than Klein's theory of projection.[4] Rather, more in line with Bromberg's descriptions of dissociation, I am suggesting tolerating the idea that whatever toxic racial material and affect—rage, shame, guilt, self-righteousness—is induced in the self, be held as there in my subjectivity already, waiting to be awoken. For Hart, this is the insight hateful projections are meant to keep at bay, as they flow inward and outward in the back and forth of interracial conflict.

As long as what the other seems to see in us can be safely kept outside of the self, one's self-image, the imago, remains whole. What Fanon was suggesting in the 1950s, and Hart elaborates on in more contemporary psychoanalytic writing, is that the appearance of the racial other, to the degree that the other comes with a perception, and possible projection, of me that is different from my own self-perception, can actually summon forth parts of myself, not-me's, evoked in my relation to the other, that I am uncomfortable with. The key to the link between Fanon's earlier observations and Hart's contemporary ones, as psychoanalytic understandings of relating across the color line, is entertaining the idea that racial projections are not simply projections. Rather, they are elements in Bromberg's language of a more profound intersubjective enactment which, once the awareness of racial difference becomes a part of the dynamic, triggers a series of interactive not-me's in dynamic, chiasmic, tension and relationship to each other.

If, then, in the mirror stage the ego is created as a signifier of the self and its counterpart(s), Fanon was suggesting at the mid-twentieth century that what we might call white double-consciousness, is catalyzed by the appearance of "the negro" in the mirror. This is a self-alienating moment, involving the breaking up of those signifiers of like counterparts and self. This fragmentation, internal but also precipitated by a relational context, would then lead to aggression and other very difficult affects. It is just such a moment Sartre experiences and describes in his own self-alienating encounter with his whiteness at the very moment he faces the subject of "negritude."

Recently, Lynne Layton described a psychoanalytic and cultural pedagogical project: "to help White people acquire our own version of double consciousness, to try to see ourselves through the eyes of people of color" (2019, p. 107). White double-consciousness was, in some sense, what Fanon was looking for, what Sartre was experiencing, what Hart describes when thinking psychoanalytically about intersubjectivity in a racialized context. It represents a two-stage process, the first of which entails holding and tolerating the internal conflict generated by the realization of the other's racialized projections onto the self. Du Boisian (black) double-consciousness represents one aspect of that experience—the turn of the century African American subject's difficulty tolerating, and then moving beyond that sense of internal conflict: "One ever feels his two-ness—an American, a Negro; two souls, two thoughts, two unreconciled strivings" (1903/1994, p. 2). Sartre's (white) double-consciousness describes another, the defeated, guilty, shamed retreat into the self of those white European and American artists and intellectuals who were wrestling with the implications of decolonization: "Today, these black men are looking at us, and our gaze comes back to our own eyes" (1964–1965, p. 13). Could we, however, the racialized subjects of contemporary 21st century societies, move a bit further into the second stage of this process? This would require a deeper understanding and acceptance of these self-alienating projections of the other as tied to, even if not identical with, parts of ourselves—maybe sitting next to or alongside them? What might open up if we could tolerate, for a second, the idea that I *am* the white person, the black person, the Asian person, the Arabic person, the Jewish person, the Latino person, this other person thinks they are seeing? What not-me parts of the self might then appear in interaction with the projections of the other? And what more can I understand about our interaction when projective identifications and affective enactments around our racial identities are seen as engaging simultaneously, next to and alongside each other?

More productive and generative than either a black rage or a white guilt that can only stay defensively or defeatedly engaged with the other's imagined projective gaze, this second stage of double-consciousness strives to move beyond the internal conflict. It involves aspiring to a both/and position, holding two racialized positions simultaneously. And if we believe this type of subjective position is impossible to tolerate, we can look to the work of black entertainers and performers from the early years of the twentieth century, who developed precisely this sophisticated capacity as they interacted with turn of the century, predominantly white, audiences. One might even say, somewhat tongue in cheek, that in terms of the development of this psychic capacity, the ability to move beyond an internal state of conflict or defeat, and instead, sustain a reflective relationship to one's own double-consciousness, non-white analysands and analysts may be, given this history, more 'psychoanalysable'—less resistant, less defended, more curious, more self-aware—than their white counterparts, both analysands and analysts.

## Black Mirroring

In *Skin Acts: Race, Psychoanalysis and the Black Male Performer* (2014), I highlight this relational capacity, this ability to engage in a sophisticated mode of interracial intersubjectivity, as one of the special talents of certain black performers. Each of the subjects of my study, in their own unique ways, attempted to communicate with white audiences both by accepting and holding their audience's images and projections of themselves—Du Bois's and Sartre's white looks—while simultaneously using the relational field between performer and spectator to express, and reflect back, other aspects of the self.

Turn of the century blackface minstrel performers such as Bert Williams and George Walker, looked out from the stage onto audiences who were, "always interested in what they call 'darky' singing and dancing" (Walker, 1906/2004, p. 17). These white projections of darkness, what Toni Morrison (1993) diagnosed as "playing in the dark" of American's unconscious racial imaginations, were literally painted on the performer's face—as if the white look, the mask of white projection itself, was concretized and applied to the face, blackening the skin and turning epidermal skin color into a reified thing. And yet, as a highly successful entertainer Bert Williams was able to deploy multiple and differing experiences of himself in his comedic performances. As he described: "It was not until I was able to see myself as another person that my sense of humor developed. . . . I have studied [humor] all my life, unconsciously in my floundering years, and consciously as soon as I began to get next to myself" (1918/2004, p. 12). Getting "next to" himself—here Bert Williams found his way of saying what Bromberg (1996) has described as "standing in the spaces" between one's different states of self. What would it take, for the subjects of white guilt and black rage, to shift to these states of double-consciousness and mirroring, to "get next to themselves" and stand "next to" each other?

What Du Bois described as the "peculiar sensation . . . of always looking at one's self through the eyes of others, of measuring one's soul by the tape of a world that looks on in amused contempt and pity" (p. 2), is for Bromberg an example of perhaps the most common feature of everyday, interpersonal trauma. As Bromberg also describes, "it is not all that easy to accept an image of yourself as seen through the eyes of an [other], and it is especially hard when the other's image of you is based on what for you is a dissociated part of self—a 'not-me'" (2008, pp. 330–331). However, Bromberg also adds that learning how to relate intersubjectively fully depends on our capacity to accept the vision of the self seen in the eyes of the other while simultaneously holding onto one's own vision of oneself. I find it meaningful to use Bert Williams' phrase as the starting point for describing "getting next to ourselves" as a way of characterizing this form of interracial intersubjectivity. I think of the capacity to "get next to *oneself*" as finding a way to stand beside the other's projections of you in a way that keeps you also still standing beside, engaging with, while not over-idealizing or over-identifying, or engaging in a power struggle with, the other. "Getting next to *ourselves*" helps us to envision this further as a fundamentally multiple and relational process. "*Our*-selves" becomes the figure for subjects struggling to hold onto their own good-, bad- and not-me multiplicities, while in interaction with, and doubly conscious of, other's representations and projections of themselves. "Getting next to *one*self" can also provide some relief from internal conflict, as one acknowledges the play of multiple selves within one person. It then becomes possible to imagine, and hold onto, an internal truth that the rest of our selves can stand next to the one who is seen and projected by the other without the latter becoming "all" of us. These difficult psychic states, already challenging in dyadic contexts, are even more so in group settings such as the ones I experienced during the eruption of various racialized incidents on campus.

How does psychoanalysis stand in relation to questions of racialized intersubjectivity? Can we envision, psychoanalytically, the stance black performers know so well, of 'getting next to' oneself, allowing oneself to accept the other's desire to see you as an image, while retaining a substantive, ironic relationship to that projected shadow? Could we describe this as a form of racial mentalization that, when reflected back to the viewer of "the look," might represent a productive use of mirroring in a racialized, psychoanalytic context? Can we understand getting next to oneself as particularly difficult from within the white dyad, or from within a predominantly white American psychoanalytic field, in which whiteness is dissociated *in its form* as a type of racial "sameness"? In other words, before we simply assert that this is a myth—white people are not all the same—can we hold the ways in which whiteness is seen, perceived, mirrored back to us and possibly enacted by us, as monolithic and "the same," when placed in interaction with racial others (think here of the title of Beverly Daniel Tatum's classic study, *Why Are All the Black Kids Sitting Together in the Cafeteria*—and then think of the reverse—how the fact that all the white kids are also sitting together is probably not evident until the moment a black kid enters the cafeteria) (2003). This is what Jessica Benjamin also describes as "the aspect of intersubjectivity which is most elusive—the reciprocal, mutually influencing quality of interaction between subjects—two way streets" (2007, p. 1), expanded now to include a "twoness" inflected specifically by racial difference. An interpersonal understanding of double-consciousness would therefore have to have two parts: the experience of one's relationship to one's internal, disavowed not me's; and the stimulation by a real, here and now, experience-near, interaction with a racial other.

## Conclusion: Surrender in the Face of the Other

Fanon's and Sartre's encounter epitomizes a type of conversation between blackness and whiteness that has also, throughout the twentieth century, been distinctively male. As the famous African American author, Toni Morrison, described the orientation of the black male writers who set the terms for discussions of race throughout the twentieth century:

African American male writers justifiably write books about their oppression. . . . Confronting the oppressor who is white male or white woman. It's race. And the person who defines you under those circumstances is a white mind—tells you whether you're worthy or what have you. And as long as that's your preoccupation, you're defending yourself against that. Reacting to it. Reacting to the definition—saying it's not true.

(Love, 2012)

Jessica Benjamin describes this as the "push-me-pull-you, doer-done to dynamics" of "complementary relations," which tend to lead to "impasses" whereby "each person feels done to, not part of a co-created reality," with perspectives that are fundamentally "irreconcilable: as in, either I'm crazy or you are" (2007, p. 2). Key in Benjamin's account is the defensiveness that still lies not too far under the surface when even an "attribution of responsibility to self truly does not really help to extricate us from the feeling that the other person is controlling us or leaving us no options. Caught, boxed in, unable to think" (p. 2). The only way to get outside of this dynamic, Benjamin argues, is to find a "vantage point outside the two," a point we recognize as that of the psychoanalytic third. For Benjamin, the third itself is simply that which, "creates another point of reference outside the dyad" (p. 1). What matters more is how one deploys it, in an attitude that involves less submission and defeat as the necessary precondition to recognizing the other—the affect that seemed to precede and follow from Sartre's recognition of blackness—and more surrender: "In my thinking, the term surrender also implies the aspect of recognition, of being able to connect to the other's mind while accepting her separateness and difference." (p. 2). It is from this notion of "surrender" that one finds recognition, the capacity to recognize the other.

For, surrender "is not To Someone," some idealized or projected version of either the accuser or the accused (Benjamin, 2007, p. 2). Instead, surrender involves an outcome in which, "we have survived some process in which subjectivity is 'destroyed,' negated or modified by the other" (p. 2). While the accusatory/confessional dynamic of affectively charged racial encounters often rests on an underlying logic of submission, surrender requires an attitude toward the other Hart (2017) also describes as a "radical openness," in which both parties accept they may lose something of themselves during the exchange:

It encourages the participants to take the risk of losing understandings they have of themselves and of each other that constitute prejudices. . . . A psychoanalytic sensibility holds that the participants in the analytic dialogue—analyst and analysand, supervisor and supervisee, student and teacher, colleague and colleague—attempt to lose their own senses of mastery-based relating, to relinquish the feelings of cultural knowing and competence they may have held prior to entering into each new conversation with each new other.

(pp. 13–14)

Relinquishing "mastery-based relating" means also letting go of models of multicultural "competency," which Hart describes as still privileging "gaining a form of mastery . . . in speaking the language of the other, on becoming aware of the other's customs, vocabulary and syntax" (p. 13). Rather, radical openness as a stance towards racial relating rests first on an openness to confusion, fragmentation, and not-knowing. This is precisely why Fanon reacts critically to Sartre's over-idealization of negritude as an accusatory, closed look. Fanon's own self-questioning stance, as reflected in the very last line of *Black Skin, White Masks*: "O my body, make of me always a man who questions!" (p. 232) is a stance that can integrate the other's look from a position of "radical openness" while maintaining a sense of bodily integrity and wholeness in the face of the threat of psychic epidermalization, dismemberment and fracturing.

As valuable as the insights produced from discussions of white guilt and black rage may have been in an earlier cultural moment, contemporary psychoanalytic perspectives can raise Americans' awareness of the ways in which unconscious processes are inflected by social processes of racialization and epidermalization. Both clinically and theoretically, psychoanalysis needs to add to theories of racial subjectivity complex understandings of the interpersonal and intersubjective contexts of interracial relating. Black radical thought would be a useful interlocutor, having developed this capacity for self-reflection on processes of interracial intersubjectivity from the late nineteenth century. "I see the goal as being able to first accept, as a valid mental state in itself, the experience of observing and reflecting upon the existence of other selves that it hates, would like to disown, but can't" (Bromberg, 1996, p. 517). This has been the work of the black literary and cultural tradition, creating: "a twilight space in which 'the impossible' becomes possible; a space in which incompatible selves, each awake to its own 'truth,' can 'dream' the reality of the other without risk to its own integrity" (Bromberg, 1996, pp. 515–516). In their artistic and intellectual productions, black artists and authors have held onto and validated this dream. As they struggle with being the recipients of others' projections—extruded images of badness and degradation, the most racist of images—in their writing, performances, visual and musical productions, they have also inhabited those projections while maintaining a place that stands alongside them. To greater or lesser psychic harm, even in Du Bois's time men such as Bert Williams and George Walker were not merely conflicted in their double-consciousness. On stage, on film, in the recording studio, they remained open to the question, is this all of me? Am I part of this? Can I be part of this without this being all of me? Even within moments of assault, rage, and guilt, they found, also in the words of the writer Toni Morrison, "resources available to us for benign access to each other, for vaulting the mere blue air that separates us" (2017, p. 35). "Benign access to each other"—this phrase deserves a pause, a still moment of query and reflection on what it might mean, what it could look like, to find such an impossible "twilight space" across interracial color lines even within moments of intense conflict, internal and interpersonal (Bromberg, 1996, pp. 515–516).

Toni Morrison's words appear in a 2016 series of lectures she presented at Harvard, later collected into the book *The Origin of Others* (2017) with a foreword by Ta-Nehisi Coates. In this work, Morrison provides an anecdote involving mirrors that offers a powerful image to close on, a dream for us to freely associate with. Remembering a visit to the Vienna Bienalle, Morrison recounts:

> In one of the artworks on display, I was asked to enter a dark room and face a mirror. In a few seconds a figure appeared, slowly taking shape and moving toward me. A woman. When she (rather, her image) was close to me, same height, she placed her palm on the glass and I was instructed to do the same. We stood there face to face, unspeaking, looking into the eyes of the other. Slowly the figure faded. . . . Another woman appeared. We repeated the gesture. . . . This went on for some time. Each woman differed in age, body shape, color, dress. I must say it was extraordinary—this intimacy with a stranger.
>
> (p. 74)

Morrison's experience with this artwork is evocative, suggestive of a possible evolution of the "mirror stage" in the subject, another stage of development in which the subject could gain the greater psychic capacity to accommodate forms of interracial intersubjective relatedness.

The capacity the mirror art piece encourages is the ability to stay aware of yourself and the wholeness of your self-conception—present in the intentionality of Morrison's hand outstretched towards the other—while loosening the boundaries of selfhood enough to receive the image, and the mediated touch, of the other coming toward you. Morrison is able to settle into, and not feel overwhelmed by, this encounter as, "one to one," a series of unfamiliar others fade in and out, interacting with her as reflections, then substances, then shadows. They are both like her and not like her, "Each woman differed in age, body shape, color, dress," strangers with whom, just by being in and with their presence, she develops an unexpected intimacy. As Morrison describes touching the mirror, the mirrored surface of the images coming toward her, her gesture serves as a metaphor for me of the complex interplay of enactments and projective identifications—how what is/ in me interacts with what is not/ outside of me—that occur in tense racial exchanges when viewed from a psychoanalytic lens. The gesture of the touch itself, in other words, reminds me of the ways we "touch" each other psychically, beyond projective identifications in a flow of ongoing unconscious enactments, *even as* the other's projections rush toward us like the reflections in the mirror. The fact that the duets or dyads in Morrison's account are able to receive each other in a non-threatening way, quite the opposite from the more hostile field created from racial projections constituted by splitting, should be seen maybe less as a dream than as a scaffolding for the difficult psychic work such an outcome entails.

Theorists of the mirror stage, intersubjectvity, radical openness, and thirdness have provided us with the tools to think such a moment, however, and there are others we can turn to, in the interdisciplinary space between psychoanalytic theories of intersubjectivity and interpersonal relating, and black writing theorizing the dynamics of interracial relating and racialized subject formations. Throughout the twentieth century, psychoanalysis has developed with decolonization as a seemingly distant socio-political backdrop. In the twenty-first century, if psychoanalysis is to turn, as Sartre once did, to face that historical backdrop, naming racist and racialized projective identifications as such, as "racist," is not enough. A deeper understanding of the unconscious psychodynamics of interracial relating requires the recognition that I am also already reacting to how you are seeing me with projections of my own, feelings and assumptions about you that exist as leitmotifs, weaving their way through our complex intersubjective interaction. Like Morrison the writer, interacting with the images of multiple, refracted others, 21st century psychoanalysts of all races need to stand next to, get next to themselves and each other, watching and listening for the multiple selves that emerge in our complex confrontations and encounters with each other.

## Notes

1 "Getting Next to Ourselves: The Interpersonal Dimensions of Double-Consciousness," *Contemporary Psychoanalysis*, July 2020, reprinted by permission of the publisher (Taylor & Francis Ltd, www.tandfonline.com).
2 My appreciation and thanks to editor Sarah Schoen for helping me clarify key features of this comparison and line of thinking throughout.
3 https://en.wikipedia.org/wiki/White_guilt
4 For one articulation of the differentiations between these psychoanalytic concepts, see chapter 8, "Projective Identification, Enactment, and the Transference" in Goldstein & Goldberg, 2004, pp. 59–69).

## References

Benjamin, J. (2007). *Intersubjectivity, thirdness, and mutual recognition*. Institute for Contemporary Psychoanalysis.

Bhabha, H. (1986). Foreword: Remembering Fanon. In *Black skin, White masks* (F. Fanon. Trans.). Charles Lam Markmann. (1967). Pluto Press.

Bromberg, P. (1996). Standing in the spaces: The multiplicity of self and the psychoanalytic relationship. *Contemporary Psychoanalysis, 32*, 509–535.

Bromberg, P. (2003). Something wicked this way comes: Trauma, dissociation, and conflict: The space where psychoanalysis, cognitive science, and neuroscience overlap. *Psychoanalytic Psychology, 20*(3), 558–574.

Bromberg, P. (2008). Shrinking the tsunami: Affect regulation, dissociation, and the shadow of the flood. *Contemporary Psychoanalysis, 44*(3), 329–350.

DeAngelis, T. (2009). Unmasking 'racial micro aggressions.' *Monitor on Psychology. American Psychological Association, 40*(2). Retrieved February 1, 2020, from www.apa.org/monitor/2009/02/microaggression

Du Bois, W. E. B. (1903/1994). *The souls of Black folk*. Dover Publications, Inc.

Du Bois, W. E. B. (1925/1992). Worlds of color. In A. Locke (Ed.), *The new negro* (pp. 383–414). Atheneum. Originally published as "The negro mind reaches out." *Foreign Affairs 3*(3).

Fanon, F. (1986/1967). *Black skin, White masks* (C. Lam Markmann, Trans.). Pluto Press.

Goldstein, W. N., & Goldberg, S. T. (2004). *Using the transference in psychotherapy*. Rowman & Littlefield Publishers, Inc.

Grier, W. H., & Cobbs, P. M. (1968). *Black rage*. Basic Books.

Hart, A. (2017). From multicultural competence to radical openness: A psychoanalytic engagement of otherness. *The American Psychoanalyst, 51*(1), 12–13, 26–27.

Krauss Whitbourne, S. (2012). *The definitive guide to guilt*. Retrieved February 1, 2020, from www.psychologytoday.com/us/blog/fulfillment-any-age/201208/the-definitive-guide-guilt

Lacan, J. (2007). The mirror stage as formative of the *I* function as revealed in psychoanalytic experience. In B. Fink (Trans.), *Écrits: The first complete edition*. W. W. Norton.

Layton, L. (2019). Transgenerational hauntings: Toward a social psychoanalysis and an ethic of dis-illusionment. *Psychoanalytic Dialogues, 29*, 105–121.

Love, A. (2012, July 17). Toni Morrison on love, loss and modernity. *The Telegraph*. Retrieved February 1, 2020, from www.telegraph.co.uk/culture/books/authorinterviews/9395051/Toni-Morrison

Morrison, T. (1993). *Playing in the dark: Whiteness and the literary imagination*. Vintage Books.

Morrison, T. (2017). *The origin of others*. Harvard University Press.

Musser, A. J. (2014). *Sensational flesh: Race, power, and masochism*. New York University Press.

Pyatt, R. (1969, January 21). Interview with William H. Grier, author of *Black Rage*. Retrieved February 1, 2020, from www.wnyc.org/story/interview-with-william-h-grier-author-of-black-rage/

Sartre, J.-P. (1964–1965). Black Orpheus. *The Massachusetts Review, 6*(1), 13–52.

Seghal, P. (2016). *Racial microaggressions: The everyday assault*. Retrieved February 1, 2020, from www.psychiatry.org/news-room/apa-blogs/apa-blog/2016/10/racial-microaggressions-the-everyday-assault

Stephens, M. (2014). *Skin acts: Race, psychoanalysis, and the black male performer*. Duke University Press.

Sue, D. W., Capodilupo, C. M., Torino, G. C., Bucceri, J. M., Holder, A. M. B., Nadal, K. L., & Esquilin, M. (2007). Racial microaggressions in everyday life: Implications for clinical practice. *American Psychologist, 62*(4), 271–286.

Tatum, B. D. (2003). *Why are all the black kids sitting together in the cafeteria: And other conversations about race*. Basic Books.

Walker, G. W. (1906/2004). The real 'coon' on the American stage. *The Theatre Magazine*. p. 224, i–ii; CD booklet in *Bert Williams: The early years, 1901–1909*. Archeophone, 2004.

Williams, B. (1918/2004). The comic side of trouble. *The American*, 33–35, 58, 60–61; CD booklet in *Bert Williams: The early years, 1901–1909*. Archeophone, 2004.

Wolfe, B. (1949). L'oncle Rémus et son lapin. *Les Temps Modernes, 43*, 888–915.

Žižek, S. (2007). *How to read Lacan*. W. W. Norton & Company.

# Chapter 3

# Recognition in the Face of Harm

## Implicated Subjectivity and the Need for Acknowledgment

*Jessica Benjamin*

As put forward by Rothberg in his book *The Implicated Subject*, being implicated in domination or harming means being neither perpetrator nor victim, oppressor nor oppressed, but rather something harder to pinpoint. It includes a range of participation in systems of domination, of aligning one's interests with the perpetrators of those systems, resulting in the refusal of responsibility for ameliorating or opposing injustice. To be implicated is thus also to be responsible for harm, even when we are not directly guilty of doing the harmful thing. This responsibility, whether we assume it or not, is indeed often implicit. Reparation, or more generally repair of trauma, requires witnessing: knowing about and taking responsibility for terrible things.

When I first considered these ideas, I concluded that implication was a different and, in some ways, more precise and useful way of looking at the problem I had heretofore conceived as that of the bystander who does not take responsibility for witnessing and opposing injustice. This failure turns out to be as crucial in the configuration of traumatic experience as the injury itself. I had called this position the failed witness: failure to give an adequate response to the need every injured person or group has for validation of their injury. Without such recognition, the mind cannot recover coherence; agency is impaired (Benjamin, 2018). The failed witness position is a crucial component of traumatic experience and contributes significantly to its clinical reproduction and its social manifestations.

The denial and abdication may be traced to the reflexive self-protection and anxiety on the bystander's or potential witness's part: a refusal of knowledge of suffering and the accompanying alienation from one's own agency as a political subject. Denial is the result of a complex process

DOI: 10.4324/9781003265146-3

conceptualized as dissociation (Howell, 2005): the mind's defense against anguish that it cannot assimilate, alter, or soothe; an attempt to escape overwhelming pain and fear when there is no escape. Dissociation links the doer and the done-to; it afflicts victims and observers, the accuser and the accused, even while taking different forms. At the physiological level, dissociation is the reaction to being overwhelmed.

So now, how might we link our understanding of the failed witness in terms of denial and dissociation with the social fact of being implicated— even though they are not exactly the same? How do we walk the distance between therapeutic treatment with individuals or work with groups who have suffered in the past and those injuries occurring in real time that speak to our unconscious guilt, our complicity, and our failure to take full responsibility for the society in which we participate? We are not only politically responsible as citizens to repair historical damage and oppose the present harm, a position Rothberg derives from Arendt. We are also psychologically implicated, as our tacit acceptance of the psychic culture and the social benefits of harming—acquiescing in the state of denial— provides a vital, indeed indispensable, part of the orderly procedures that support systems of domination.

## Recognition versus Domination: The Third

With further exploration of recognition theory, especially in light of clinical experience, it seemed useful to elaborate on the idea of the intersubjective Third as the position "beyond doer and done-to" (Benjamin, 2004, 2018)—holding in tension binaries that have been split. Instead of mere reversal, a the Third is dialectical move out of cycles of victims becoming perpetrators. It represents corresponding internal and relational positions in which we are like subjects, not reactive but active in recognition of response to the impact of the Other. One original aim of this deconstruction of complementary relations was to go beyond the reversal in which the Other is simply revalued or even gains power while maintaining the binary opposition of domination. With this in mind, we can distinguish forms of seeking justice or redress of collective trauma that preserve the binary opposition between the doer and the done-to from those that occur in the context of a mutually recognizing Third.

A further iteration of the Third, I suggested, might be called the moral Third, which emphasizes not the reciprocal recognition of the Other, but the specific acknowledgment of relational and social violations. Meeting the need for acknowledgment, the affirmation of violations of expectancy, and the wrong things that need to be put right becomes the basis for the experience we might call the "lawful world." A representation of the lawful world evolves within the early dyadic communicative matrix, psychologically undergirding practices of justice and witnessing. Even when individual or collective loss and injury lies in the past and cannot be undone, acknowledgment can reestablish the moral Third, allow the injured ones to reconstitute their sense of dignity, and take action to repair damage through their own agency.

To be a witness, I argued, and more importantly an embodied witness, is to break through the disidentification that says the injured one is different, less human. Countering the tendency to dissociate one's own vulnerability from that of the Other becomes the basis for acknowledging injustice, injury, or wrongdoing. The psychic toleration of vulnerability is a condition of giving recognition, even as receiving—or having received it—is the condition of such tolerance. Our bodies and nervous systems require this recognition to sustain our connectedness to others as a fundamental basis of safety.

Only when we experience that Third can we begin to subjectively encompass the meaning of taking responsibility for our implication and for the fate of the Other who is dependent upon us. Which is to say, to acknowledge, repair, and restore the social bonds of connection based on mutual respect creates a very different kind of safety and sense of self than the one that submits or aligns with power. As Archbishop Desmond Tutu (1999) explained, in the South African tradition of Ubuntu, "I am because you are." Only a person who realizes that my humanity depends on yours can have dignity. This realization has profound implications for thinking about the motive for embracing or denying the need for social justice.

## What Implication in Clinical Enactments Reveals

As relational psychoanalysts, we have introduced within our own realm a process of reflection on the clinical version of being "implicated," one in which we are drawn into re-enacting trauma and seeking relational repair. In the context of studying our clinical enactments, we came to realize that psychoanalysts' initial denial or defensiveness regarding their own implication is due to entering what Bromberg (2006) called the dissociative cocoon—the envelope of counter-transference and transference. In analytic treatment we can trace ruptures and impasses to the confluence of our patients' and our own dissociated histories (Davies, 2004). Relational analysis revived and took seriously Ferenczi's (1933/1980) realization that we repeat a version of earlier traumatic injuries even though we have engaged as analysts to heal them; the analyst may become implicated by his neutral professional stance, creating distance and reactivating the patient's abandonment. But it is often the dedicated effort to avoid that repetition that drives its enactment, what I have called "our appointment in Thebes" (Benjamin, 2018). The analyst's failure to provide emotional embodied witnessing is then registered as part of the original injury and thus elided with causing it. This, in turn, intensifies the analyst's guilt.

We have found that therapeutic healing lies in surrendering to the inevitability of such occurrences as a process of rupture and repair. This process, whereby the patient can experience the restoration or affirmation of a lawful world in which wrongs are put right, may be compared to Winnicott's (1971) idea of surviving destruction. As the analyst is there to "receive the communication" and survive the knowledge of their own part in enactments, the patient receives recognition of their challenge—even when aggressive or disruptive—as an action that changes us. Changing in response to the Other's impact is an essential aspect of recognition.

I see in the tension between enacting failure and changing in response to it a possible parallel process for implicated subjects. To give acknowledgment and change in response to the Other requires a form of vulnerability, a surrender of self-protection. While these orientations (self-protection and vulnerability) are usually held in different self-states that are dissociated rather than experienced as open conflict, it is possible to survive the confrontation with vulnerability by accepting the culpability of self-protection as a problem common to us all. What is it that allows us to know both states as Me—Bromberg's (1998) "standing in the spaces"—to admit that we are implicated in harm and guilty of denying the Other's reality of suffering? As psychoanalysts, we have asked what would allow us to destabilize our self-protective barrier and tolerate the self-exposure and vulnerability of shame and guilt. Interrogating what this psychic exposure entails, we have recognized that we are vulnerable to losing our goodness (Mark, 2018)—or would it be more precise to say our claim to being recognized as good, as worthy? Rather than viewing this loss of imagined goodness in terms of placing our freedom from scrutiny and our professional power in jeopardy, we had to develop an appreciation for the kind of power and connection that come from sharing mutual vulnerability and discovering things we did not know about each other.

In other words, at some point, the position of imaginary goodness and invulnerability is revealed as false, a state of insecurity and disconnection from the other person. Socially, of course, the self-protective aim of off-loading shame onto the Other and claiming dignity for oneself legitimates control over vital resources of status, wealth, or even police protection. The more pernicious forms of invulnerability appear even more aggressive in this historical moment—masculine strength or paternal authority that bases its strength on the illusion of independence from the very relationships on which one depends for need satisfaction (e.g., women, workers) because one controls them. I will simply note that implicated subjects who comply with and find self-affirmation in that culture of power may be distinguished from those whose unease with the unlawful world may yet spur them to seek an alternative.

## Implication: Dialogue With Rothberg

Rothberg's definition of the implicated subject does not, however, restrict itself to benefitting from or supporting domination; it also conceptualizes authority and obedience as part of the implicated position.[1] With the purpose of locating the basis on which the implicated subject can become responsible, Rothberg aims to consider what militates against taking action on behalf of the human community to which one belongs. Framing the issue in terms of dissociation, the question of what impedes responsibility might be translated as "Why do we look away, and why do we accept what is?" Engaging with this question, Rothberg introduces the notion of obedience. Indeed, the problem of obedience to authority, if not to say an embrace of submission to the established order of things, seems to me central. If we posit that those implicated subjects who serve the actual originators of domination are enmeshed not only through material benefits but by identification with the powerful ones, we might say that such subjects are doubly implicated: the subject's actions *contribute* to the sum total that produces harm (Young, 2011, cited in Rothberg), but they are also *shaped* psychically as they mold to the structural demands of that totality (Layton, 2020). What is taken for granted in the unthinking comfort and submission to the social order is not only the privileges of belonging but also the allegiance—perhaps unconscious or conflicted—to its principles and process. The identification with ideals of impermeability, self-aggrandizement, and winning (not being a loser)—which in the United States means the imaginary of Whiteness as wholeness and invulnerability—inform the process of dissociating the denigration and harm to the Other.

It follows that a full confrontation with that imaginary would reveal how it shapes a dissociated, unthinking submission to the order of domination. We would consider ourselves as social subjects not only implicated in the harming and collective trauma of racial and colonial domination but also formed by our compliance with the conditions that produce it. That is, we would realize how enmeshed we are in the psychic matrix of Whiteness whose consequences we cannot help but dissociate. If participation occurs without realization of the way one inhabits and props up structures of violence, this fact returns us to the matter of dissociation, or what Bion saw as a refusal of knowledge. Insofar as our psyches are shaped by identities formed through the structures of domination, to think about or act in opposition to these structures generates anxiety. Opposition demands, at the least, some awareness of suffering (ours or others); most likely, opposition also requires critical self-reflection on how these identities have deformed us psychically. We might consider this reflection as a liberatory practice (see Gaztambide, 2019).

This is because, there where we deny, we find ourselves most likely to submit to purposes and structures we imagine ourselves free of. Here we can turn to Rothberg's quotation from Puar: "it is precisely by denying culpability or assuming that one is not implicated in violent relations toward others, that one is outside them, that violence can be perpetuated" (Puar in Rothberg p. 49). Going further, Rothberg cites Forti, who argues that passivity, obedience, and consent to authority deriving from the Christian tradition function to create "a normativity of non-judgment"—such acquiescence forming the core of ostensible democratic virtue and the transmission belt of political evil.

This insight parallels the analysis of goodness I have suggested. In quotidian life under regimes of "soft" domination, this masking of evil does indeed owe much to the lie of goodness and the masquerade of virtuous obedience to civility (Benjamin, 2017b). However, elsewhere the choices and consequences are starker. We have had to bear the knowledge, so clearly displayed in Rwanda, that a person will take a machete to a neighbor's child when the genocidaires threaten to kill his own child if he does not do so. But while such a person can be seen as implicated while being a victim, such a person is not "choosing" anything. Whereas in purportedly peaceful democratic societies like our own—where some of us may call out the contradictions posed by murder, incarceration, and deprivation of the others—the principle of "my life versus your life" operates quietly, sanitized of violence, as an acceptable and accepted choice. As the dominant principle that enforces all obedience, all regimes of domination, it may appear to us as so abstract that we are led to overlook the key element that is dissociated—namely, *fear*.

It would seem necessary to contextualize intersubjectively how, in such regimes of domination, fear operates: it enlists the Other to bear it. As in torture, the Other must always bear the pain and terror in order that one can be free of it. In psychoanalytic work with imaginary bodies, we use the concept of projective identification to grasp this forcing of pain and fear into the Other. By this, we mean nothing less than a psychic operation that makes it possible to feel as if the Other will be the one to die, to absorb pain and death, to bear the precarious life of fear. Where the perpetrator acts this out, the implicated subject merely imagines it. But is it going too far to say that the aim of identifying with Whiteness is to free oneself of fear by embracing the order that subjugates the Other while remaining innocent of such actual deeds? Fanon (1967/1986) recognized that victims use the identification with the oppressor to escape degradation, enacting a different form of submission, adopting the White mask. But violence itself also is masked; it wears the mask of the law. When many Americans, in the wake of George Floyd's murder, finally revolted in horror against the construct of White impunity to make the Other suffer, violence was unmasked within the agents of the law. And further exposed as protestors were confronted with the retaliatory violence of the political system that exposed our actual lack of agency to modify it, let alone dismantle it.

All systems of domination rely on some mask even as they depend on the perverse use of the desire for survival, which intensifies the choice between your life and mine; choosing the oxygen in the poisoned bloodstream of corruption. Some who comply are rewarded, some who are deemed unworthy are punished, and thus, this choice is perpetuated. It is the aim of perpetrators to ensure that individuals undo their own humanity as the moral Third itself is destroyed, to make sure there is no other choice than to kill (cite Gomez & Kovalskys, 2018; Benjamin, 2018). The gangland version of this choice is a staple of the Hollywood imaginary and its derivative video games. When we protect ourselves by denying the real-life version of this hell—which could be happening nearby on the streets where the police take no prisoners or under the rule of some autocratic oligarchy that our democratically elected government has initiated or supported—we are implicated. Our acceptance aids the inscription of this choice of "my life over your life" because we have been primed to choose it ourselves: to accept that force and coercion rule, to bear life in a world of doer and done-to, all the while producing our own alienation from the sense of lawfulness and agency on which our claim to democracy is based. What generates submission is fear, linked to the reality of a powerless that is masked by compliance and by the rewards for the privileged, concealed by the othering of those subjected to its punishments. Each of these forms a part of a larger lie about who is worthy of life or grief (Butler) and who may be left to perish.

## Only One Can Live

The metaphor of "my life or your life" is one way to analyze the fear that prevents acknowledgment of suffering and responsibility for harming. The phrase I have used to capture this worldview is "only one can live." This metaphor unconsciously organizes the struggle for recognition and for material survival—and in its ideological form, it is viewed concretely as fact, "reality," not an idea or belief.

Even though the modern era, the liberal worldview, is supposedly defined by rebellion against the authoritarian assumption that there is room for only one version of god, one marital partner with rights, one race with human dignity, or one group permitted to own the land—everyone is permitted to be an owner, to be a citizen, to have rights—the implicated subject also knows this to be untrue. In other words, there is a dissociative split between such ideals and the equally powerful belief that individual self-protection abrogates all other principles we respect. Living with this contradiction requires the same mechanism of splitting or dissociation we have already discussed. I am not harming anyone since social reality demands that some eat more and some eat less, and indeed, I am good because, after all, our society upholds the right of everyone to eat. I can read on the internet that the world has the capacity to feed everyone without feeling responsible for the institutions and actions that deliberately make this impossible. And while the ideals of equality will be contradicted by the necessary exploitation in which some accumulate and control an overwhelming share of the social wealth produced by others, I can continue to accept that what remains must be fought for under the condition of "my life versus your life." This might be seen in terms of the paradox of identifying with power while having no control; that is, a form of alienation of one's own agency in which the subject serves those whose power is respected in accordance with the internalized ideal of strength.

Given the reality of ruthless capitalist extraction that enforces the struggle for existence and undermines the social solidarity that might otherwise lead us to demand control over the wealth we produced, "only one can live" is not simply a belief. It falls in the category of what Marx understood as ideology: perceptions and appearances that are generated by real material conditions and not merely belief. That is, the ideology or belief that only one can live is not a mere illusion but a form of material relation; what is illusory is the notion that this is nature, not social construction, that there is no other way. As psychoanalysts, we need to recognize how the contradictions that are denied by implicated subjects are produced by material social relations that ensure the dominance of this mode of complementarity and its obfuscating form as nature.

This matter of how material conditions interpenetrate psychological relations is too vast for this essay, but we can recognize that as neoliberalism became dominant, a significant change occurred in our society. As austerity was enforced for the precariat, even the more privileged members of society were forced into compliance with "only one can live" by an unabashed defense of social Darwinism. In the United States, the term "liberal" became a signifier associated with the image of the bleeding heart—and after all, a heart that bleeds will itself die. Empathy, as well as welfare for those who could not manage without support, was scorned. Austerity for the have-nots was justified by "the economy," which was naturally identical to the interests of the strong who own it.

Obedience as goodness was now really only a virtue for the struggling class, while the elite and elect—in the puritan world, the predestined "saved"—were allowed to break the rules, cheat, and be greedy. We might say the shadow side of the puritan ideology of the "elect" or "saved" reached a kind of apotheosis: to be powerful meant to be deserving, not clamoring for gratification and security that one has not earned. The exaltation of power and the denigration of neediness produced this starkest of contrasts applied mercilessly in particular to the Other—Blacks, people of color, immigrants. Natural law would decree this opposition between the dignified and the discarded, or discardable sources of labor. Now the implicated subjects would accept as necessary the systemic lack of safety that allows only some to deserve to live and be relieved to have escaped precarity. For, after all, one must *deserve to live*. Thus, even as neoliberal culture demanded that the implicated subject serve a system whose unspoken premise was non-recognition of the Other's needs, it also disqualified and shamed their own need for safety, including the safety of depending on others (Layton, 2020; Peltz, 2005). The selection that splits the deserving from the discarded only appears to protect against shame and precarity— since only one can live, it is never too late to fall from grace.

The ideology of discarding the undeserving initially found its negation in a political opposition that upheld the right of the legitimate victim to accuse others of harming and thus establish the moral power to deserve and condemn. But the fear that the victim would capture the mantle of goodness and thus challenge the powerful's claim of legitimacy activated backlash. The moral claims of the victim inevitably had to be recast in terms of "doer and done-to": Black Lives Matter was deliberately misread as a reversal, signifying a claim to aggress against Whites, to "take" and "replace." Whites would now be the ones subject to aggression, denied their right to live. Recognition of suffering was again perverted into another terrain for competitive struggle rather than a basis for the moral Third of "more than one can live."

On this terrain of the doer and the done-to, we can observe the reversal of splitting take the form of the fantasy of being replaced, as those accused of harming fear being cast into the Other's role of not *deserving* to live. It would appear that to admit responsibility for harming, or even that harm has been done, would invite the danger of being cast out with the mark of Cain. My colleague El Sarraj, the Gazan psychiatrist with whom I organized the Acknowledgment Project, argued that the Israeli's guilt at harming in order to survive served to further intensify their already massive fear of being abandoned by the world (see Benjamin, 2016b). If one has lived at the expense of harming the Other, one has forfeited the legitimacy of one's right to live. I would suggest that to evade this consequence, it became necessary to argue that one's own people had already suffered more and had already been so justified through suffering that one now could not be accused of doing harm. In this way, a collective psychic economy is proposed in which the moral capital of suffering rules. Whoever suffers most deserves to live and may even harm to do so. This dynamic has now become a well-established, powerful form of the struggle for recognition. To the extent that the Other can be tainted as undeserving, the Other serves in the scapegoat function, justifying the righteous self who claims the right to violate others in the name of his own right to matter.

We can certainly understand how disidentification with the Other's suffering can arise as a manic defense against perceived loss of safety or as a reflexive shut down in the face of pain or fear. It is a reflexive aspect of self-protection that cannot be erased by moralizing; it occurs in most people some of the time (Benjamin, 2017). However, what clinical experience with manic and grandiose states shows is how individual rationalization of putting their survival or success above all may be understood as a reaction to the fear of being humiliated or left to suffer by their own families or community should they display shameful weakness. We might speculate that receiving no acknowledgment of pain or fear and being shamed for vulnerability, such as occurs especially for men in the authoritarian family, subtend the fear that one's own suffering will not be recognized, and so drives the politics of resentment.

Going further, we might interrogate the condition of competition for social recognition, in which justice claims risk playing into the dualism in which *one group's legitimacy or need can be acknowledged only and precisely by canceling that of another group.* Such deliberate manipulation of fear still plays a great role in how people become implicated in their own and others' domination. The dreaded Other becomes the projected container of aggression while the violent, chaotic behavior of the authoritarian leader, consciously embraced as protective, unconsciously intensifies the fear of being subjected to attack. It intensifies the belief in "kill or be killed," even if the subject imagines he will be protected by his willingness to use his guns. Recognition becomes a social product that is made valuable by scarcity; it is not enough to deserve life and dignity; someone else must be the undeserving discarded. The transgression of Cain was, after all, a response to being denied recognition in the eyes of the father—was it Cain or his father who was responsible for the notion that only one was worthy of life?

In the grip of the fantasy that only one can live, White supremacists imagine that they ensure their triumph by dismantling their own social safety net because it benefits the Other as well. This suggests the necessity of a politics that deconstructs that logic of competition between victims, a politics that counters the misuse of state violence by those who feel humiliated. How do we break the deadlock of subjects locked into this mindset of "doer and done-to," of the struggle between the dignified and discarded?

Concrete experience suggests that affirming the Third of provision for all to live is a way to appeal to the need for safety and mutual respect and thus dampen the escalation of such struggles and the attendant disregulation. However, when that move is blocked (deliberately, as a strategy to maintain power), when the Third fails to be upheld by social institutions that enforce fairness—breakdown heightens anxiety about safety, however unconscious that reaction may be.

For those accused of being on top, acknowledgment and witnessing are tainted with blame and submission. Overcoming this taint requires trust or belief in a form of the Third that makes possible the move beyond blame and toward integrating a form of accepting needs as universal. Acknowledgment strengthens the self when it is formulated in terms of "I, or we, have the ability to exercise agency and take responsibility for making the world more lawful, caring, and fair." If the recognition by the implicated subjects of their responsibility for repair is impeded by the psychic position of doer and done-to, then we might imagine that this can only be countered by intentionally promoting a Third that acknowledges histories of trauma and suffering, in a way that counters the deliberate efforts by those in power to split and divide, to appeal to the competition of "only one can live."

As a small illustration of this transcendence of competition for recognition, we may take Bryan Stevenson's story from *Just Mercy*, whose work in the Equal Justice Initiative fights the abuses of the carceral system—the death penalty, the persecution of juveniles, and the imprisonment and execution of the disabled.

There was a particularly aggressive white prison guard who deliberately humiliated him with a strip search when he came to visit the mental disabled prisoner he was defending, trying to save from the death penalty. As luck would have it, this same guard was assigned to bring the prisoner to court on a day when Stevenson and his team detailed the trauma and abuse this accused man had suffered as a child in foster care. At their next encounter in the prison, Stevenson was shocked to find out that the guard had done a 180. He declared to

Stevenson how much he respected what he did, and then revealed that while listening in court he was overwhelmed by hearing him acknowledge and describe the same kind of trauma and abuse he himself had suffered coming up in the foster care system. Suddenly his eyes were open, he realized that this had happened to others, he was not alone, someone recognized his suffering. Indeed, it seems that this recognition made his own suffering real. The guard then added, somewhat offhandedly, that driving the prisoner back to jail he'd violated the rules and stopped at Wendy's. For months he'd heard this imprisoned man at every visit pleading with Stevenson to bring him a chocolate milk shake; he now took his chance to defy the rules, express solidarity; to dignify the prisoner's need and make repair for the debasement he had caused.

We are reminded that opposing self-states—compassionate and self-preservative—exist in most people and that what is decisive is how we live the conflict between them. The guard's story parallels the experience of relational analysts in which the self-state shift to embrace one's own suffering and vulnerability can be stirred by empathy and identification with the Other. Thus, as Layton (2020) and Kabasakalian-McKay and Mark (this volume) have also argued, the implicated subject must allow all projections of shame and vulnerability to be returned to himself. The realization of vulnerability connected to suffering can arise through the desire to be rid of the falseness and oppressive deadness of denying it, simultaneously permitting a release from aggression and grievance that have no place to go. That is, the need to not be alone in one's suffering and to escape the aggressive hell of my life versus your life gives rise to the urge for transformation. From this desire for social attachment and solidarity also comes the urge to repair the world, to make it more lawful and less violent/violating.

The self that does not discard or split off weakness and vulnerability and instead poses a demand for acknowledgment of humanity can *dignify suffering*. My experience suggests that this reversal whereby the visage of dignity disrupts the conventions of power and strength can have a surprising, even electrifying effect.[2] The reclamation of suffering by the social demand for dignity and respect is a dialectical move, I would argue, in the historical evolution of self-assertion by the oppressed. Demanding recognition, victims become agents in challenging and transforming implicated subjects; implicated subjects can embrace their reparative capacity moved by insight into the difference between the competitive struggle for recognition and the moral Third. This is pertinent to the question Rothberg raises, to theorizing more closely the material social psychological process whereby implicated subjects are, as Rothberg puts it, "transfigured."

## Baldwin's Witness[3]

I think, of all writers about America in the last century, Baldwin offers the most insight into the problem of how implicated subjects might collectively and individually transform our condition. It is not surprising that, after the disillusionment our society faced with the election of Trump, Baldwin's words have been recognized and, shall we say, redeemed from earlier repudiation. One can't help but feel that the critics who judged him to have strayed too far into politics might well have regretted their own implication these last years. After all, Baldwin offered us the sharpest critique of Whiteness as an ideology and material reality of domination: White, he said, was not a description of the world but a "metaphor for power"—indeed, "simply a way of describing Chase Manhattan bank" (Baldwin/Peck, 2017).

I understand the prophetic force of Baldwin's (1963) early rhetoric in *The Fire Next Time* to lie in his belief that politics must be inspired by love, by the drive to repair and heal as opposed to hate. "It is a bomb that is a balm, and a tool for healing everyone," said his interpreter, Charles Reese. The choice Baldwin so clearly demarcated was between power and love, retaliation and reparation, surrendering to hate and putting it down. However, this does not mean that the heat of anger did not infuse his words—rather, it would seem that he sought to preserve the tension between that anger and the desire for love and reparation—and burn them in one fire. Of course, to be angry in order to protect what we love is common, but Baldwin's anger had the uncommon aim to unmask those attachments that, while invoking the name of love, are rather sustained by denying our common humanity, by hatred and demonization of the Other, by lying about the vast harm that has been done.

Speaking as witness and prophet, deliberately refiguring his assigned role as discarded, othered, Baldwin gives voice to the moral Third, addressing the wrongness of America and the destructive madness of European Christian civilization. His method demonstrates that one can be both traumatized by that civilization and yet use its ideals for witnessing with clarity the violence and hypocrisy of those who other him, giving meaning to the position of the outsider. Witness here does not merely denote observe or confirm; it means, as in religious tradition, to testify.

Shortly after Baldwin's book was published, young radical Whites like myself joined the civil rights movement looking to Black leaders to articulate the same prophetic charge. This commitment was not only political but existential: seeking a connection to something truer and more life-giving than the false, dissembling world of White normalcy—as Baldwin (Peck, 2017) said, a world in which, as never before in history, were a people "so fat and so sleek, and so safe, and so happy, and so irresponsible, and so dead." This was a historical moment where being an implicated subject seemed an identity one could step out of into a collective that rejected and exposed the horror and tragedy barely cloaked by this veil of safety. Once committed to that hope, we also suffered intense disillusionment as the civil rights movement was shattered by the murder of its leaders as America persisted in the war at home and in Vietnam.

Baldwin, in 1963, wrote to his nephew,

> it was intended that you should perish . . . [but by] a terrible law, a terrible paradox, those innocents who believed your imprisonment made them safe are losing their grasp of reality. But these men are your brothers . . . [this] means: that we with love shall force our brothers to see themselves as they are, to cease fleeing from reality, and begin to change.
>
> (24)

It should be emphasized that Baldwin remained true to this analysis even when he gave up hope that this change would occur—a disillusionment likely intensified by the obtuse self-satisfaction of the liberal intellectuals who honored him only until they understood that he *really meant it* when he said that they should change (Glaude, 2020).

What that change would mean seems to have been articulated too far ahead of his time. Baldwin's psychological clarity, perhaps strengthened by his utterly un-American outsider position as queer Black man, led him to an acceptance of human vulnerability even in his adversary. That is to say that he realized how the White master—and those who have identified with, propped up, and tried to mimic him—refused to recognize the vulnerability and the aggression for which he "invented" the container in the Black Other. The figure of debasement was signified by the thing Baldwin refused to be when he said, "I am not your Negro . . . not your projection." Declaring that this imaginary Negro is actually a White invention fulfilling a White need (Baldwin/Peck, 2017), a projection of his own self-hatred, is a double move: it demands recognition for the oppressed objects of projection and an admission by the master of what he has tried to evacuate from self (Markell, 2003; Benjamin, 2018). The double move speaks to the dialectic of recognition—the demand for acknowledgment by the powerful of their crimes, as well as their own vulnerability, violence, and self-hatred that these crimes were intended to offload. The demand he makes for acknowledgment ought to entail transformation for his benighted brothers (and sisters). As such, the demand for reparation by the victim participates in the bidirectionality of recognition that persists despite asymmetry, even as it aims to shatter dissociation about the ultimate cost of harming.

However, when acknowledgment fails and violence continues, a different kind of witness is needed. By the end of the sixties, Baldwin's faith in this bidirectionality had been severely weakened by witnessing the murderous repression that ended the civil rights movement. As Glaude (2020) has eloquently argued, then began our own time, the "after time." It seems to me right, as we face the persistence of stark contrast between the safety of Whites and the terror afflicting Blacks, that at the end of the decade, Baldwin claimed that the moment of fire had come, that he repudiated that mission in order to defend the separate and distinct right of his own people to save themselves from self-hatred and powerlessness. That he revealed his belief that the order of colonialism and imperialism must be overthrown, his sympathy with the socialist project seems to have provoked the establishment (Glaude, 2020). To conceive the struggle for equal human dignity as meaning that all of us have an equal chance to emulate and align with the powerful is one thing; challenging the actual systems of power is another. It is here that, historically, the rubber meets the road as questions of economic power collide with idealizing myths of freedom and nostrums about democracy. Baldwin's rejection of the lie of freedom as it colludes with adaptation to the inevitability of powerlessness also constituted a rejection of the demand to surrender peacefully to defeat and perpetuate the lies that conceal the trauma of such powerlessness.

Baldwin thus expresses Black rage, as interpreted by the African American psychoanalyst Beverly Stoute (2021), who shows its vital importance in enabling the holding of dignity and self-worth in the face of assault. Even as that rage exists in tandem with the historical imperative to love, not hate, that has been passed down through generations, Stoute maintains, "For African Americans there is a transgenerational teaching of defensive strategies drawn from collective unconscious stores that foster group identification, cohesion, and survival." To hold onto rage is to protect the self that rejects the betrayal and protects its truth without succumbing to destructiveness. In her reading of Baldwin, Stoute argues,

> He asks us to withstand hate, while maintaining our capacity to love, using "the word 'love' here not merely in the personal sense but as a state of being, or a state of grace—not in the infantile American sense of being made happy but in the tough and universal sense of quest and daring and growth."
>
> (Stoute, 2021; Baldwin, 1963, p. 95)

I would take this to mean that the preservation of the moral Third that holds the tension of love with hate is not to be confused with exculpation for harm; rather, it is a standpoint for condemning the betrayal. For in declaring that the humans who so abuse power, in fact, betray the very ideals they claim to love, outrage and indignation at iniquity serve to protect those ideals from perverse abuse.

Baldwin's efforts to disrupt the complacent identity that accepts mystification help me to bear the deep grief and fearful apprehension about our country's persistence in destructiveness. Baldwin demonstrated how the confrontation with suffering as a queer man in a violent homophobic society, with near death and trauma, led to his; taking up a witnessing position that sees clearly the weakness and brokenness of those who persecute him (Glaude, 2020). His voice embodies the necessary conviction that the normal is morally unacceptable, that America's truth is a lie, and recognizes the dreadful fact that America blew its chance to change. In fact, under the ruthless reign of neoliberal capitalism, it doubled down on savage exploitation and the political manipulation that protects it. Baldwin thus offers us some guidance through this current circle of hell, through the fog of dissociation and evasion of truth, a path into witnessing as a stance of active disruption and refusal of compliance.

What position can we, as White implicated subjects who disidentify with the social order, take toward the demands posed by Black rage? What does it mean to take responsibility for White rage? In the past it has not always been easy to mobilize against the perfidy of disowned White aggression that masquerades as law while recognizing a Third position in which everyone deserves safety and care. Rather, competition for who will be protected has accompanied a struggle over who will own the onus of aggression. As in relational enactments, the necessity of seeing one-self as the Other sees you (Bromberg, 2011) is part of what must be survived—witnessing the damage inflicted on the Other means seeing the self differently. This witness does not equate with becoming enmeshed in the blame-guilt version of doer and done-to, as Stephens (2020) has explained. Rather, as she contends, there can be a double-consciousness in which one struggles with the "not me" that the Other reflects, that can hold the conflicts between selves and the projections that racialized identities have imparted, moving beyond the dynamic of accusation and confession.

Holding that third position means we are tasked with disrupting the positive identifications with the system of domination even while we continue to be disrupted by others more oppressed than ourselves. This, all the while trying to avoid such outrage descending, as it did in the past, into the blaming position of doer and done-to that loses sight of the very truth of human solidarity it was meant to defend. In the context of his letter to his nephew, it does not seem a stretch to suggest that when Baldwin wrote that his dungeon shook and his chains fell off, an implicit meaning is that of release from the doer–done-to relation, from the helplessness of hate. Can we interpret that he had survived destruction through this collision with the harshest reality and depth of despair, that is, survived his own self-hatred?

To renounce hate and recognize the humanity of the perpetrator is to avoid the reversal of violence in which only one can live, but it need not renounce the rage or outrage that fuels the demand for a relationship in which both self and other can deserve to live. This remains difficult: finding a third position that serves the indignation that protects the injured without defending one's own righteousness, finding a way to embrace conflict and even collision within a larger containing Third, an intersubjective process governed by democratic principles in which more than one can live.

## Destruction and Survival

What does it mean to think about this process psychoanalytically in the Winnicottian terms of surviving destruction, keeping in view the clinical experience of destruction and survival that must be part of every experience of rupture and repair? When we go through a clinical collision or rupture, we experience that we survive destruction and succeed in repair when and if we are able to acknowledge that, having missed, dissociated, and defended our own goodness, caused pain but also admit to our own pain and sadness. I have argued that it is the very performance of such acknowledgment, the act of proffering it, that can release us from the shameful or guilty "doer–done-to" binds that equate to failure to survive. What allows the transition from guilt to survival clinically is the knowledge that the Other—the patient—needs us to survive, needs acknowledgment, and indeed, often needs it to be able to live (Winnicott, 1971).

The intricacies of surviving, in particular the process of surviving ruthless demand by those who have been oppressed, were analyzed by Swartz (2019) in the South African university context. In her book *Ruthless Winnicott*, she discusses her own survival as a White therapist for her Black patient but also as a Cape Town university administrator coping with failures that were seemingly inevitable responses to perturbation of the university system by students' ruthless demands needed to be acknowledged and heard. Swartz and her colleagues are positioned as implicated subjects, and as such, even when they are nominally committed to decolonization and opposition to anti-Black racism, their own positions of power and alignment with the existing institutional forms require them to endure collisions and challenges that stir up frightening feelings of rejection and badness, not to say their individual traumas. The unleashed aggression causes fear on both sides, grows to encompass gendered aspects, and culminates in a breakdown of order.

Swartz's book offers an exceptional analysis of this breakdown experience, which put me in mind of what I witnessed in German universities in the sixties, when students reckoned with the legacy of fascism. What seems most germane here is her elaboration of surviving the destruction when the formerly othered subjects insist upon their humanity and face the master subject with their own aggression (see also Benjamin, 2018). Citing Fanon (1967/1986), Swartz clarifies how decolonization demands being blown to smithereens, subjects blown up internally, moments in which those inhabiting privilege are forced to change but also those resisting continuing oppression bear the force internally of an explosion both sought and dreaded . . . speaking up against their colonization [means] . . . being asked to revisit and perform the trauma of which they speak.

This blowing up reverses perspective, emphasizing the historical actions and violence of the oppressed subject who is, as Fanon said, "demanding human behavior from the other." This surrender entails surviving the loss and destruction of formerly idealized objects on whom those identities were based, as well as acknowledgment of responsibility for the damage done by them. Swartz describes "a flow of acknowledgment" in which a history of traumatic exclusion meets "a witnessing of shame-saturated realization of damage done."

What Swartz's narrative reveals of what occurred at South African universities in the wake of the student movement Rhodes Must Fall is that historic moves toward justice require repeated ruptures and confrontations. A Third that overcomes the either/or mystification of "only one can live" must go through the fire of breakdown and collision. To overthrow the old order, its underlying split between the deserving and the discarded must be faced; it is in painful challenges to order that the taken-for-granted splits are enacted and become visible. The false goodness of paternalism—as we have seen in our own psychoanalytic struggles—must give way to a more painfully won reciprocity of respect for what the unprotected Other can teach us about destructiveness (Bragin, 2007).

The political feat is for such aims to survive collision, misrecognitions that painfully evoke specific traumas of non-recognition, to hold the vision of a containing Third for conflict even in its absence. This requires, as Swartz demonstrates, a temporal process: the holding of space for transformation, which means we hold the moral Third of recognizing the Other and restoring the lawful world in mind. While this process of surviving collision is well known to relational analysis, Swartz has shown that it is possible to conceive as part of decolonizing and struggling for justice in the long and turbulent march through the institutions.

In Winnicott's original description of how destruction brings about recognition, the subject is being destroyed and simultaneously receiving the communication; in this case, according to Swartz, to receive adequately means allowing one's own world to be shattered. Surviving destruction for the Other means they can see you as being changed—a bidirectional process of the impact that replaces doer and done-to (McKay, 2019). Where Swartz follows Orange and sunders this conception of mutual recognition from an ostensibly simple idea of giving recognition—"recognition-as"—I would contend that surviving destruction always also entails giving recognition—after all, survival means I have received your communication without withdrawing or pushing back. In living through a collision that challenges the old order, we change each other even as we negotiate new shared meanings. Thus, confronting our asymmetry, we still implicitly create mutual recognition.

As Gobodo-Madikizela (2003) has illuminated, the demands of the victims upon the perpetrators have the power to restore the latter's humanity and the moral community as they require the acknowledgment of harming. This is one of the more powerful ideas she derived from the experience in the Truth and Reconciliation Commission. The demand for reparation can be seen as an invitation to the Other—one that gives the implicated subjects—an opportunity for healing rather than shaming, for embracing that moral community (Nichols & Connolly, 2019; Bragin, 2019). However, that experience ought not to be used to shelter anodyne myths of repair through forgiveness that evade the highly complicated move involved in acknowledging wrongdoing, the necessity of disruptive truth-telling regarding the lies and mystifications, in particular the refusal of material reparations that would challenge ongoing economic oppression.

The essential act of reparation implicated subjects can make, the initial move toward rebuilding the lawful world, requires facing and proclaiming the Other's truth, that of a destructive history in which we must honestly identify our own divided selves. As we observe how the reaction to the murder of George Floyd could be so successfully overshadowed in the theater of public media by the lying attacks on the teaching of our appalling history of racial violence, we are reminded how easily our society flirts with and then rejects the Other's point of view when it comes to *doing something* material. This makes disruption our first task, but not our only one. A Third that holds the tension of a different double-consciousness (Stephens, 2020) would mean both tolerating being disrupted and producing disruption.

My aim here is to suggest a relational psychoanalytic perspective on the process by which we oppose the forces of domination, one that enlists the implicated to deconstruct and repudiate "only one can live" by show-ing how far our country is from embracing the right of "all can live." The transformation from implicated bystander to acknowledging witness cor-responds to the means by which trauma can be revealed and integrated. The traumatized can feel heard and known rather than alone. Truth-tell-ing is an act of integrating those who have been cast out and discarded while undoing our own acts of othering and exclusion. I have argued that acknowledgment can also engender a collective or individual psycho-logical transformation that overcomes implication as the acquiescence in denial in the name of survival that sustains systems of domination.

We are now at a point in which the battle is joined between those will-ing to give up the illusory power and safety of that survival and those who manipulate the fear of "only one can live" to keep power in the hands of those who would have the earth stop turning rather than give up their ill-gotten gains. With the future of our planet and our future human gen-erations at stake, implicated subjects who have been enmeshed may be motivated to realize that the inevitable disruption and collision with reality cannot be evaded. Ours is the responsibility to demand public admission of harming by the powerful who ostensibly keep us safe—as long as we do not challenge their own exorbitant self-protection.

It would seem important to link the repair of our broken civilization that condemns all to a struggle for survival that increasingly threatens all with extinction to acknowledging specific demands for reparation and redis-tribution of the global wealth to those who have been victimized in its production. As Baldwin said, our country refuses to know the price paid by its victims. Acknowledgment, we have said, means knowing something about the self—in our case, the social subjects who, in the struggle to live, have enacted a monstrous form of competition and rationalized its necessity. Acknowledgment requires breaking through and shattering the imaginary structure of necessary damage and sacrifice—"only one can live"—toward an authentic desire to restore social bonds of recognition. Therein lies the possibility for social connection, safety, and creative liv-ing that comes with honoring the moral Third in solidarity with others.

## Notes

1 This analysis bears resemblance to that of the earlier critical theory works on authority and domination of the Frankfurt School, a tradition that informed my work.

2 I gratefully refer here primarily to what I was able to witness through the remarkable efforts of Pumla Gobodo-Madikizela who invited a group of us to several conferences in South Africa where I had the opportunity to listen to some of the transformations that occurred in the aftermath of the Truth and Reconciliation process.

3 This section leans heavily on Glaude's (2020) interpretation of Baldwin's movement, as it felt largely true to my reading of Baldwin (1963) and what I observed about the historical period he lived through. It also benefits from Raoul Peck's radical film.

## Bibliography

Baldwin, J. (1963). *The fire next time*. Dial Press.

Baldwin, J., & Peck, R. (2017). *I am not your Negro. From texts by James Baldwin*. Penguin.

Benjamin, J. (1988). *The bonds of love: Psychoanalysis, feminism and the problem of domination*. Random House.

Benjamin, J. (2004). Beyond doer and done to: An intersubjective view of thirdness. *Pyschoanalytic Quarterly, 63*, 5–46.

Benjamin, J. (2011). Acknowledgment of collective Trauma in light of dissociation and dehumanization. *Psychoanalytic Perspectives, 8*(2), 207–214.

Benjamin, J. (2016b). Non-violence as respect for all suffering: Thoughts inspired by Eyad el Sarraj. *Psychoanalysis, Culture & Society, 21*, 5–20.

Benjamin, J. (2017b). The Wolf's dictionary; Confronting the triumph of a predatory worldview. *Contemporary Psychoanalysis, 53*(4), 470–488.

Benjamin, J. (2018). *Beyond doer and done to: Recognition theory, intersubjectivity and the third*. Routledge.

Bragin, M. (2007). Knowing terrible things. Engaging survivors of extreme violence in treatment. *Journal of Clinical Social Work, 35*, 229–236.

Bragin, M. (2019). Pour a libation for us. Restoring a sense of the moral universe to children affected by violence. *Journal of Infant, Child and Adolescent Psychoanalysis, 18*(66), 1–11.

Bromberg, P. (1998). *Standing in the spaces: Essays on clinical process, trauma and dissociation*. Analytic Press.

Bromberg, P. (2006). *Awakening the dreamer: Clinical journeys*. Analytic Press.

Bromberg, P. (2011). *The shadow of the tsunami*. Routledge.

Cohen, S. (2001). *States of Denial: Knowing about atrocities and suffering*. Polity Press.

Davies, J. M. (2004). Whose bad objects are we anyway? Repetition and our Elusive Love Affair with Evil. *Psychoanalytic Dialogues, 14*, 711–732.

Fanon, F. (1967/1986). *Black skin, White masks* (C. L. Markmann, Trans.). Pluto Press.

Ferenczi, S. (1933/1980). Confusion of tongues between adults and the child. In *Final contributions to the problems and methods of psychoanalysis* (pp. 156–167). Karnac Books.

Gaztambide. (2019). *A People's HIstory of Psychoanalysis: From Freud to Liberation Psychology.* Lexington Books 2021.

Gerson, S. (2009). When the third is dead: Memory, mourning, and witnessing in the aftermath of the holocaust. *The International Journal of Psycho-Analysis, 90*(6), 1341–1357.

Glaude, E. S. (2020). *Begin again: James Baldwin's America and its urgent lessons for our own.* Crown.

Gobodo-Madikizela, P. (2003). *A human being died that night: A South African story of forgiveness.* Houghton Mifflin.

Gomez, E., & Kovalskys, J. (2018). Reencounter with history and memory through a therapeutic process. *Psychoanalytic Dialogues, 28,* 102–114.

Gomez-Castro, E., & Kovalskys, J. (2013/2017). *Reencounter with history and memory through a therapeutic process.* IARPP, Santiago, Chile/ Psychoanalytic Dialogues.

Grand, S. (2000). *The reproduction of evil.* Analytic Press.

Howell, E. F. (2005). *The dissociative mind.* Analytic Press.

Kabasakalian-McKay, R., & Mark, D. (2022). *Introduction.* . . .

Layton, L. (2020). *Toward a social psychoanalysis: Culture, character, and normative unconscious processes.* Routledge.

Mark, D. (2018). Forms of equality in relational psychoanalysis. In L. Aron, S. Grand, & J. A. Slochower (Eds.), *De-idealizing relational theory: A critique from within.* Routledge.

Markell, P. (2003). *Bound by recognition.* Princeton University Press.

McKay, R. K. (2019). Where objects were, subjects now may be: The work of Jessica Benjamin and reimagining maternal subjectivity in transitional space. *Psychoanalytic Inquiry, 39*(2), 163–173.

Nichols, B., & Connolly, M. (2019). *Transforming ghosts into ancestors: Unsilencing the psychological case for reparations to descendants of American slavery.* Unpublished. IPFE.

Peltz, R. (2005). The manic society. *Psychoanalytic Dialogues, 15,* 347–366.

Rothberg, M. (2019). *Implicated subjects.* Stanford University Press.

Stephens, M. (2020). Getting next to ourselves: The interpersonal dimensions of double consciousness. *Contemporary Psychoanalysis, 53,* 201–225.

Stevenson, B. (2014). *Just Mercy: A story of justice and redemption.* Penguin.

Stoute, B. (2021). Black rage: The psychic adaptation to the trauma of oppression. *Journal of the American Psychoanalytic Association, 69*(2), 2659–2690.

Suchet, M. (2007). Unraveling whiteness. *Psychoanalytic Dialogues, 17,* 867–886.

Swartz, S. (2019). *Ruthless Winnicott.* Routledge.

Tutu, D. M. (1999). *No future without forgiveness.* Random House.

Winnicott, D. W. (1971). The use of an object and relating through identifications. In *Playing and reality.* New York: Penguin.

Young, I. M. (2011). *Responsibility for justice.* Oxford University Press.

## Chapter 4

# He's My Brother

*Cynthia Chalker*

In a monthly check-in, the editors of this book asked about my writing struggles. My reply was that things keep happening in the world and I keep starting over.

And then **THE** thing happened.

My brother died.
More specifically, he killed himself.
Let me say a little bit about my brother:
He was the youngest of my two siblings.
He is a good guy.
He was an accomplished professional who mentored hundreds of people throughout his career.
He has an infectious smile and gave the best hugs.
He was an attentive son, a loving husband and a doting brother.
He is six foot four inches tall with rich Black skin.
He had dreadlocks down his back.
He is a Black man in America.
He suffered from severe depression that he kept hidden from view;
and I didn't know to look much beyond what I saw or he told me because:

*He is a good guy.*
*An accomplished professional who mentored hundreds of people throughout his career.*

DOI: 10.4324/9781003265146-4

*He has an infectious smile and gave the best hugs.*
*He was an attentive son, a loving husband and a doting brother.*

He resisted treatment for his alcoholism, a disease that, again, only one or two people knew until he was forced into treatment.

In the world in which he lived and worked, he was one of a few_____
(choose all that apply):

    a)  Men.
    b)  Black men.
    c)  Men with graduate degrees.
    d)  Black men with graduate degrees.
    e)  All of the above.

A successful Black man that shouldered everyone's expectations.
And dreams and fears of what a Black man in America could be.

In the last year of his life he purchased a gun.
He said because he didn't feel safe,
living as a Black man in the United States.

Chapter 5

# Psychoanalytic Spaces, Implicated Places

*Carnella Gordon-Brown, Natasha Holmes, Beth Kita, and Lynne Layton*

## Introduction

In the course of several conversations, the four of us co-authoring this chapter, two white women and two black African American women of different generations, began by talking about why each of us had chosen to participate in this project on implicated subjects. We had originally come together because we were all involved in a project called Reflective Spaces/ Material Places and thought we would discuss how implication functioned in those spaces, one in the Bay Area and one in Boston. We soon realized, however, that we could not speak about "implicated subjects" without addressing how we each have experienced psychoanalytic spaces. Because our social locations are crucial to understanding that experience—and crucial to any hope of creating an implicated relational psychoanalysis—we begin this chapter by introducing and locating ourselves; we then describe how and why the focus of the project changed. In writing this piece, our aim has been to preserve our distinct voices as we speak to the ways each of us has experienced psychoanalytic spaces as implicated places; we end with our fantasies of a better, more honest future for psychoanalysis.

## Who We Are, Why We Are Writing, and Who We Are Writing For

### Carnella

I am a black woman and an elder in my black community. My pronouns are she/her. I am a social work clinician with almost a decade of clinical community mental health experience working with consumers who were,

DOI: 10.4324/9781003265146-5

for all intents and purposes, invisible: the disenfranchised; those consumers and their families who were all too often also the unhoused here in San Francisco; and those who were often survivors of traumatic experiences. I have so much appreciation for having had an opportunity to provide both case management and psychodynamic therapies to assist these consumers and their families in their life-affirming journeys. It was both a humbling and cherished honor to have practiced this community work in the city of my birth: San Francisco, California.

I want to acknowledge the Ramaytush Ohlone, who are the original ancestors and guardians of this land that is now known as San Francisco, California. (To support the original peoples of the San Francisco Peninsula, visit the Association of Ramaytush Ohlone's website at this link: www.ramaytush.org/about-the-aro.html.)

I am not a part of the "talented tenth." I am basic. I grew up here knowing that my city was not invested in the likes of me. I was never supposed to "make it" off of the Hunter's Point Hill projects. Nevertheless, I was relocated from the Hill. Relocation for me meant for my family to be removed from the Hill and relocated first into the Sunnydale public housing projects. Followed by another relocation into the public housing projects in Double Rock. I was never supposed to graduate from high school. I didn't graduate from high school. I was an honor roll student and an active student body officer and leader in my San Francisco junior high school (what's known as middle school today) and at graduation was one of two students who qualified for entrance into San Francisco's, if not California's, crème de la crème public high school, Lowell High. I needed day care. I was shown to the welfare office. I put on my best churchgoing outfit and proceeded to get a job. I was 15 years old. I love that part of myself. I love her spirit, bravery, and authenticity.

It is in this spirit that I am writing this piece for this publication, which is in and of itself a form of an implicated psychoanalytic space. I live in a city where my black women colleagues, working in community mental health, are providing a myriad of baseline therapeutic and maintenance services to hundreds of San Francisco's most vulnerable citizens on a day-to-day basis. These colleagues are mostly highly skilled, mostly underpaid, all overworked, and mostly invisiblized. They are mostly invisiblized through the structural utilization of the informal professional ostracization rule of hiring "only one," a.k.a. "being the only black" professional to be found per unit, per division level, and sometimes per floor in community mental health agencies. In a supervision session, Mahesh Francis, a sensitive and brilliant MFT student, likened the pain of this structural ostracization to a wounding deeply lodged inside of one's body when one is so "hugely missed" (personal communication). And one is so hugely missed so often. Amen.

### Beth

I am a cis white woman living and working in the unceded and stolen ancestral homeland of the Ramaytush Ohlone people, an area now known as San Francisco, California. I have been working as a social worker for the past 20 years. I work for an outpatient program that serves people who have returned to the community after serving long-term prison sentences, have a private psychotherapy practice, and teach in the MSW program at UC Berkeley. I grew up identified with my mom's Irish Catholic family and their experiences of poverty and trauma and their social justice values. I entered into social work with a strong desire to commit myself to be part of movements/efforts that were about ameliorating the suffering caused by inequality. As much as I was inculcated into believing in racial and economic equality, I was taught that the path there was colorblindness and assimilation—my parents taught me that everyone was equal and deserving, which appeared to be radical at the time. Social work was an easy fit—spend your life earning less, working more maybe, but make it matter for other people. My family might have espoused equality, but we locked all the doors when we drove through black neighborhoods, criticized people who gave their kids "black" names, and quietly assumed—while watching it on live TV—that there weren't any alternatives to dropping a bomb on the MOVE family.[1] I didn't know at the time—I didn't have the capacity to know in the beginning and then was helped along to continue to not know in every facet of my white life—that I could be working toward preserving a structure that I thought I was invested in undoing. As much as the structural forces that created inequality might have been recognized, the way that those same structures buoyed me was not.

### Lynne

I am a white cis Jewish woman born in 1950 to lower-middle-class, college-educated parents, who, escaping the antisemitism of their own upbringing, chose a white, nearly all-Jewish neighborhood of small businessmen as the place to bring up their children. Even as my parents deemed the neighborhood "safe," a clearly race-coded designation, I was aware of the very recent genocide of Jews and dimly aware of antisemitism in the US culture at large. In part, my commitment to social justice begins there. Money was an area of deep conflict in my downwardly mobile family. I am currently part of the 1% and live in a predominantly white suburb on unceded Massachusett land; my psyche is split between the social justice work I have always done and the way I have chosen to live.

I went to college in the '60s and encountered several social justice movements. Because sexism was what was most conscious to me as the cause of my psychic pain, I was most active in second-wave feminism and its demand for workplace equality, but also in the black, socialist, and difference feminisms of the time that countered hetero-patriarchal values with values centered on relationality, interdependence, and care. I was drawn to psychoanalysis because I early on became aware that, despite my professed desire for liberation and to be considered a full human, I had internalized hetero-patriarchal norms that led me to marry at 22, put constraints on what I had hoped to achieve, and created a lot of psychic turmoil. Because of my faith in the power of the unconscious and the power of the repetition compulsion, I always intended to pursue psychoanalytic training. But I was unable to do so until a partnership with a high-earning man made it financially possible. My analysis was transformational for me, but as the above makes clear, my white analyst never poked at the race or class contradictions I was living. And as one result of that unconscious collusion to reproduce an upper-class white subjectivity, I spent my career mostly treating middle- and upper-middle-class white patients in private practice. At the same time, I was teaching, writing, and putting on programs about racism, classism, and heterosexism. Implication resonates deeply for me as a way to think about and grapple with these contradictions.

### Natasha

I am a child of the African diaspora, a descendant of enslaved African people forcibly brought to the Caribbean and Americas. I am my ancestors' wildest dreams (Ledet, 2019). I am a 33-year-old, black, African American, able-bodied, cis-gender, queer woman. I was born and raised in Seattle, Washington (on stolen Duwamish tribal land), by a working-class family. I am the eldest of three children, a first-generation college student, and a descendant of Marcus Garveyites. In 2010, I left Seattle to attend graduate school in Portland, Oregon (on stolen Tualatin Kalapuyas tribal land). In 2014, I moved to Boston, Massachusetts, to complete my predoctorate and postdoctorate trainings. In 2015, I graduated with my doctorate in clinical psychology. In 2018, I founded my solo private practice. In 2020, my solo private practice grew into a group practice. Today, my group practice, And Still We Rise, LLC (ASWR; located on stolen Massachusett tribal land), has grown to three locations across two states. Today, I live on the South Side of Chicago, Illinois (on stolen Kickapoo tribal land). And today, I am healing—healing from the pain of racism, classism, and sexism, from the experience of being the only black person in white spaces, the only financially broke person in wealthy spaces, the only working-class person in upper-middle class spaces—today, I am healing after being *the only* for many years. The space for this healing is a recently gained privilege and one that only came after creating ASWR. I am thankful for ASWR, a space where the personal and professional parts of me can finally merge—where I can be the whole me. My goal throughout the following is to maintain this whole self, to speak from a place of strength, and to share my truth.

## The Evolution of Our Chapter

As mentioned earlier, the four of us came together because we had all been active in Reflective Spaces/Material Places (RSMP), an organization of social-justice-oriented psychodynamic clinicians who were either working in or concerned with community mental health. RSMP, founded in 2011 in the Bay Area, and RSMP-Boston, founded in 2016, were spaces intentionally created outside of each area's psychoanalytic institutes, although some analysts from those institutes were central in creating and running both groups. At first, we intended to write this chapter about how implication played out in RSMP. We chose to do this for several reasons, one of which was our suspicion that RSMP might be holding something unconscious that had been dissociated from our respective psychoanalytic institutions. Beth and Carnella set out to talk about SF RSMP and realized that they could not: over time, from when Beth was a founding member to when Carnella joined years later, it had evolved from being an alternative space to analytic institutions—a space that centered community mental health and agency life—to feeling like an extension of an analytic institution.

Beth was surprised to find out that Carnella was surprised to find out that RSMP was not actually an arm of an analytic institute. Their experiences of SF RSMP were so different that there wasn't *an* SF RSMP to talk about. The "community mental health and psychoanalysis" intersection from which RSMP emerged had evolved to become a repository for split-off parts of the analytic institution. Idealized or otherwise used defensively, RSMP was unable to address the harm happening to black people in such space—as if the space itself was a way of being un-implicated, as if identifying with community mental health and acknowledging race/class/etc. were enough.

RSMP-Boston evolved pretty much from the beginning as a space centered on looking at conscious and unconscious racism. Natasha, on the steering committee from the beginning, argued that there were no psychoanalytic spaces in Boston (or probably elsewhere) that were talking about racism in ourselves and in the field and that taking this up would be crucial to her desire to be part of RSMP. Thus, one of the ways that RSMP-Boston functioned was as a rare place where that conversation could happen. But it also may have enabled that conversation to remain siloed off from mainstream institutes. Alternately, it may have jump-started some institutes and organizations to begin antiracism action. Whatever the case, because most of the people who came to our Boston programs were white, there were racist and classist enactments in just about every one of our bi-monthly meetings, which made it a fraught space for BIPoC members. By 2020, we had begun to meet in separate BIPoC affinity and white accountability groups. RSMP was not a "safe" neighborhood for BIPoC members.

As we began talking about our experience in RSMP, it soon became clear that Natasha and Carnella are *not* implicated subjects. It was, of course, they who bore the psychic pain of the racist and classist dynamics that occur not only in psychoanalytic institutes but also in these "alternative" spaces. Their pain caused us all to look more deeply at what goes on in white-dominated psychoanalytic spaces: specifically, forms of gaslighting, demands to assimilate as the price of admission, and what Natasha calls "white shenanigans." Beth invoked Sarah Ahmed's (2010) description of the feminist killjoy as a willful subject, and it resonated:

> We begin with a table. Around this table, the family gathers, having polite conversations, where only certain things can be brought up. Someone says something you consider problematic. You are becoming

tense; it is becoming tense. How hard to tell the difference between what is you and what is it! You respond, carefully, perhaps. You say why you think what they have said is problematic. You might be speaking quietly, but you are beginning to feel "wound up," recognising with frustration that you are being wound up by someone who is winding you up. In speaking up or speaking out, you upset the situation. That you have described what was said by another as a problem means you have created a problem. You become the problem you create. . . .

To be unseated by the table of happiness might be to threaten not simply that table, but what gathers around it, what gathers on it. When you are unseated, you can even get in the way of those who are seated, those who want more than anything to keep their seats. To threaten the loss of the seat can be to kill the joy of the seated. How well we recognise the figure of the feminist killjoy!

As "willful subjects," we decided to write about psychoanalytic spaces—including relational analytic spaces—as implicated subjects that perversely disavow implicatedness and, in so doing, make too many of us start to feel "crazy" and literally sick.

## Psychoanalytic Spaces as Implicated Subjects: Our Experiences

### Carnella

If I am being honest, to be authentic, I lost faith in there. Inside that white psychoanalytic institute, I lost faith in myself. For me, the question became a serious one: "Where do I find myself?" Holding on to the "me" of myself felt Sisyphean.

The "T" is that the experience of being a candidate in that psychoanalytic space felt like the "chip" of the last chisel in the creation of one of those ancient Greek sculptures. You know how those ancient marble sculptures are hypothesized, by some archeologists and art historians, to have been initially inadvertently spray-washed white? And how these white-washed antiquities led to the modern-day established aesthetic of the lily-white marble sculpture? One of those. Spray-washed lily-white.

Visualize, if you will. Carnella, in her assimilationists' viewing of black-woman community mental health clinician: now sculptured. She tries to imagine if the assimilationist artists stumble over themselves in stepping back in admiration of their work. She, a black-woman community mental health clinician, now sculptured, looks forward blankly and wonders, "Did I just hear someone ask me to 'dance' a jig?" She wonders if she actually heard the "clink" of the chisel hit the gleaming white marble. She wonders, "What do these white analysts see when they look at me?" What does a black-woman community mental health clinician, now sculptured, look like? It is difficult to process a gaze such as that of psychoanalysis without a mirror.

Looking back, it should not be surprising at all that my greatest wounding happened inside of a circle. This was where the granddaddy of repetitions was played out, inside that circle of analytic candidates, deep inside that white space called analytic institute. That was where a supervising analyst, in a seemingly innocuous manner, described an image that he "once saw/observed" of a black woman in a cage with a lion; they were both looking at each other, and the lion is looking at the black woman like, "You don't belong here." Somewhat shocked but incredibly curious (this was, after all, an analytic institute), I of course asked about the relevance of his statement to the training day's subject matter. I received an un-answer, which implied that my question was irrelevant. This sank all possibility of my asking the follow-up question: "Was she styling an afro?"

There is a specific moment, following the supervising analyst's laying out onto us candidates his revision of Freud's "joke," when our group circle has been silenced. I have one of those quasi-paranoid moments when a black woman finds herself questioning her reality and thinks to herself, "What the . . . did that really happen?" I, too, sat there, stunned and silent, like a female nightingale; my voice was silenced—for the moment.

At that moment, though, I felt physically sick. I was so quietly, yet so violently and quickly transformed from being the first black analytic candidate into a black-woman enslaved. From the only black-woman analytic candidate to a phantasy spook minstrel; "con"-structed into blackface, an other/outsider to these un-answering white supervising analysts. Deep inside that white space called analytic institute. Unspoken: How dare you! Spoken: You do not belong here! Unspoken: Why am I here again?

Claudia Tate (1996), in her seminal article, "Freud and His 'Negro': Psychoanalysis as Ally and Enemy of African America," describes the inception of Freud's negro joke as "dat[ing] back to 1886" (p. 53). Tate discusses "Freud's compulsive repetition of the joke" (p. 55), which in

1886 had been published as "a cartoon in the Fliegende Blätter depicting a yawning lion muttering 'Twelve o'clock and no negro'" (p. 54). Tate explores Freud's "identification with the lion" and his subsequent production of a "new rendition of the joke by conflating it with the cartoon" (p. 54). I believe that there is a plausible chance that what I heard that day was indeed a revival of Freud's "negro" joke. A contemporary liberal San Francisco revision at that. Possibly interjected there as a phantasy in homage to Freud—and at my expense. Perhaps an elitist/secret society 'private' joke/initiation? I note to myself, "In this contemporary revision of Freud's 'joke,' the signifying hierarchical binaries of lion/Freud vis à vis 'negro'/patient have become an institutionalized narrative construct of lion/faculty vis à vis the 'new' negro/black-woman candidate, and both are inside of the lion's cage." I am served! The black-woman candidate is meant to be silenced—my black-woman-ness: to be colonized. I am not buying this Kool-Aid. Read Tate's prophetic article for her thorough analysis of all of the associated implicatedness.

Not totally down. Not totally out. My observations ran much along the lines of those of Stella in Frank Wilderson's (2020) book, *Afropessimism*. In chapter 3, Wilderson describes a moment when Stella has had enough of a soul-deadening friendship with her "Karen" neighbor, Josephine. I identified with Stella. I wondered if Stella was tired of a relationship that meant she had to wear blackface to be observed in Josephine's white woman's mirror. Wilderson writes about the day that Stella had enough. That was the day that Stella told Josephine, "Hattie McDaniel is dead." Righteousness, my sista!

No disrespect to Ms. McDaniel's artistic ability. Her historical and stylized depictions of the black-woman actress—playing a role depicting the white, racist cultural-phantasy of black-woman-house-slave, a.k.a. Old Black Mammy—won her an Academy Award. Ms. McDaniel was a close friend of my great-grandparents O.M.E. and Carnella. My uncles would regale us kids with oral story about family, and their narrations often told of their being in awe in her presence. My uncles were not easily impressed. Apparently, Ms. McDaniel was a remarkable and brilliant actor, and this was a known fact in those dawning years of a thriving black community in San Francisco. The Academy members obviously knew that, too, firsthand. That mammy role remained the only black-woman role to win an Oscar for 51 years. The mammy role imagery did not escape my senses during those moments inside that white space called analytic institute. Minstrelsy writ large both then and now. I thought about how soul-piercing it can be when you are the only black woman in white spaces, whether in front of a camera, or in a community mental health clinic, or in that white space called analytic institute. Being "the only" can be special, but not always. I thought about the imperatives in my life—how my journey seeks out difference. My final thought about being at that institute was "Been there, done that. Didn't work, moving right along now."

### Beth

When I started out in social work, working in a prison-based acute psychiatric treatment program, trauma theory was nascent. Being a "good clinician" meant following the scientific, empirical, and innovative ideas of the time, mostly related to criminal minds, the *DSM*, and CBT. I found relief, space, and possibility in the psychoanalytic social workers I met there who used such theoretical ideas to make meaning, dig deeper, see symptoms as communications, and see systems—not just people—as having anxiety and defenses. I worked with people in prison who were looking everywhere for spaces to grow in a traumatogenic system that thwarted them at every turn. Working psychoanalytically felt like opening up a secret portal in the floors of those cells where at least one kind of escape became possible. I found so much comfort in the "we are all more human than otherwise" adage and strove to make sense of the fact that all of the horrors there, both done by and done to the people with whom I worked, were also possibilities within me—they were us, and we were them. The bars, locks, chains, electric fences, gates, rules, regulations, disenfranchisement, registries, jumpsuits, and numbers that separated us from them revealed how dependent the whole enterprise was on disidentification. This led to all sorts of psychoanalytic explorations of mass incarceration and why its cruelty is so crucial to this country.

When I began to seek out psychoanalytic spaces, I had assumed that this shared humanity notion was a fundamental one, a motivating force for why we were all in this work: being all more human than otherwise, some of us were dying alone in prison cells because our collective had failed somehow, so, clearly, we had to get to work. Although I sat through countless presentations not understanding a word that anyone said until I was halfway through a psychodynamic doctoral program, I kept showing up because I wanted something that analysts seemed to have: this capacity to think, and to feel, and to think and to feel with such depth and precision and nuance. Everything counted; everything had meaning. It was so exciting to think that there was a way through anxiety and defenses that were calcified into public institutions that were reified in our ways of thinking and being with each other that could lead to something truly transformative.

I kept doing all the translating I could—taking talks, papers, hours about private practice and trying to figure out what was still true in a clinic setting, and also what could not be "true" if it was only possible in a private setting—and tried to glue myself to other people who were doing the same. I learned to call it *applied* psychoanalysis and felt super curious when analysts pushed back on that notion and insisted that all psychoanalysis is applied. I found spaces filled with lots of people who were using analytic ideas because they helped them to make sense of their work in community mental health settings and public systems, who were thinking about race and class and gender in nonreductive ways, and who were keeping alive analytic ideas that took into account the sociopolitical and cultural influences on developmental experiences. For years, I experienced my own practice as belonging to a realm that was getting increasingly recognized in psychoanalytic spaces—RSMP, community mental health, psychodynamic social work—and looked forward to what seemed to be the inevitable day that everyone would just kind of "get" the ways in which race, class, gender, positionality are constitutive of all of our experiences.

As it turns out, which comes as absolutely no surprise to the BIPoC/ global majority writers and readers of this chapter, that day was not actually inevitable. James Baldwin (1985) said his skin functioned as a "most disagreeable mirror" to white people. As much as psychoanalysis might have been helping me to make sense of the effects of trauma, including racialized trauma, it was suspiciously silent when it came to having anything to say about what the mirror reflected back about those of us who were implicated in perpetrating harm via the violence of whiteness. The inevitability, as a result, was to perpetuate trauma.

### Lynne

Because of life experience, feminism, and earlier training in a field in which power relations and cultural hierarchies of race, class, gender, and sexuality were central, I was one of the few white psychoanalysts, from the nineties onward, who wrote and put on programs about how racism and other intersectional isms are unconsciously reproduced in the clinic. Like Beth, I've spent a long time waiting for psychoanalysis to become fully "social," to contextualize itself and our psyches in the social worlds in which we develop. As promising as relational psychoanalysis and its early feminist commitments were for me, it still has not looked too deeply at its own implication in perpetuating domination and inequality, particularly as these live, breathe, and reproduce themselves in its institutions.

It was not until I read Alexander's *The New Jim Crow* (2010) that I truly began to "get" how the fields of psychology and psychoanalysis were implicated in disavowing systemic racism in the US. Although, since then, I have been mostly involved in racial justice activism, I'm ashamed to say that it was only even more recently that I became aware of how white my psychoanalytic institution is, how whiteness operates in it, and how I have been implicated in unconsciously replicating its racism and classism. It was, in fact, at an RSMP meeting a few years ago that I was shocked into recognizing that the separation of the psychic from the social, which I'd critiqued for decades, is as much an enactment of systemic racism as it is an enactment of the denial of class and other inequalities in the US.

Reading Carnella's painful description of what it was like for her to enter psychoanalytic space made me more deeply aware of my implication in sustaining whiteness in these spaces. In my institute, I am both an insider and an outsider. While my commitment to psychosocial psychoanalysis has consistently put me outside, or, worse, made me a valued token on the inside (valued because I do have some recognition in the field and because I taught the token one-off courses on gender and culture for many years, courses that made our institute look "progressive"), Carnella and Natasha have made it clear to me that it is in no small part my whiteness that has kept me somewhat comfortably, somewhat uncomfortably inside. I called on my own institute to bring the social world into the entire curriculum, but I was able to live with the fact that it never did.

Aside from teaching, my role in my institute has been as chair of a variety of programming committees. In that role, I organized many programs on racism, classism, gender, and politics, but again, I never really felt that most members of the institute saw cultural arrangements as the least bit relevant to their work. And yet I stayed in, unaware until quite recently that these conditions made it painful or impossible for BIPoC and working-class people of all races to participate without forcing them to assimilate to white middle-class norms. Carnella brought this home, but it was also brought home during the course of my work on my institute's antiracism task force. What we white members of the task force witnessed—*and* participated in—over the year plus of our work was a particular form of "white shenanigans," what Carter Carter (2021) calls "white shame management systems," that go immediately into effect when racism is called out—moves that are meant to protect white people from recognizing how systemic racism operates interpersonally and are meant to make those who call it out the "problem." This is perhaps the most subtle form of how implication is disavowed by white people in psychoanalytic spaces.

Sheehi (2021) and Sheehi and Sheehi (2022) define what they call "psychoanalytic innocence" as the pretense that vast political and other power differences are not in operation in psychoanalytic spaces. They are, in fact, in operation in all psychoanalytic spheres: in the intimate therapy dyad, in supervisory relations, and in training relations. I left a few psychoanalytic organizations because little interest—if not active hostility—had been shown to those few of us who were determined to bring social, political, and historical contexts into clinical work. All these organizations operated under the cover of "psychoanalytic innocence," and relational psychoanalytic institutions are no exception (see Sheehi, 2021). In 2007, for example, on the flimsiest of pretexts, IARPP purged the Committee for an Inclusive Psychoanalysis that I had chaired for three years. This was a diverse committee, made up largely of people marginalized from the profession in one way or another; part of our stated mission was to de-center power relations when they upheld norms that ruled some people/categories in and some out. After the committee was abolished, I stopped participating in IARPP work but never told the story publicly until last year. And I told it then because, after a year of listening to BIPoC clinicians talk about the horrific experiences they have had in psychology and psychoanalytic trainings and institutions, I was grief-stricken at the years of transformation that we possibly could have made in the field had we been allowed to continue our work. After that experience, I think I just sought as many psychoanalytic spaces as I could find where people shared my commitment to the understanding of conscious and unconscious processes as social—for example, Psychoanalysis for Social Responsibility (Section 9 of Division 39, SPPP, APA) and the Association for the Psychoanalysis of Culture and Society, whose journal, *Psychoanalysis, Culture & Society*, I edited for many years. I tried to make space for diverse voices to be heard, creating and participating in panels like "That's Not Psychoanalysis!" where young clinicians critiqued the field's disavowal of the effect of cultural power hierarchies. Psychoanalysis as a socially decontextualized theory has its problems, to be sure, but in my opinion, even more problematic is how that decontextualization allows it to be deployed in institutions—and how power is wielded to keep these institutions as exclusively white, middle-class clubs.

### Natasha

I was initially hesitant to contribute to this section not because I had nothing to say but because I did not want to repeat myself. Part of my experience of being in white spaces is having to repeat my experience, having to explain my experience, and having to break down my experience so that it is digestible for a white audience—I don't want to do that.

In 2020, I described psychoanalytic spaces in this way: psychoanalytic spaces are white, predominately cis-male, and elitist. As a black woman in these spaces, my psyche is vulnerable. My internalized racism, sexism, and what Vaughans (2016) describes as "cultural introjects" (para. 3) emerge. I question myself and, at times, experience feelings of inferiority. I am haunted by an experience of tokenization. I am deeply aware that should I fail, my failure is a reaffirmation of my inferiority (and my people's inferiority), and yet, should I succeed, my success is a reaffirmation of superior culture (or white supremacy). This vulnerability manifests as anxiety, anger, irritation, paranoia, and distrust of others; it is managed with some combination of manic defenses and somaticizing. To succeed in this space, aspects of myself and my identity have been sacrificed, forced to split off from the parts of self that could have the effect of triggering white discomfort (Holmes, 2020, p. 115).

To add to that, I must acknowledge that my experience of psychoanalytic spaces is complicated. I was introduced to psychoanalysis in 2010 by my mentor Sandra "Sandy" Jenkins, who is not only an amazing psychodynamically oriented psychologist but is also a black woman. At the time, I was early in my training and committed to pursuing a career in forensic psychology. Sandy was curious about my interest in forensics and encouraged me to be curious about that interest too. I experienced Sandy as different from the other psychologists: the way she thought, the questions she asked, and how she engaged my mind were different, and I was intrigued. Back then, my associations with psychoanalytic theory and the psychoanalytic community included privilege, wealth, elitism, whiteness, and intellectuals—the opposite of the community-oriented work that I was passionate about (i.e., marginalized, working-class, community-oriented, racially and culturally diverse, and action-oriented/social-justice-oriented). But somehow, Sandy balanced psychodynamic theory and working within the community (read: my community). Plus, psychoanalytic theory offered something more than the behavioral theories that I was receiving training in. Psychoanalytic theory offered the tools for me to better understand myself and my experience of the world.

Fast forward to 2014, when I am months from beginning my postdoc training at a psychoanalytic institute. I am still very new to the psychoanalytic community, yet to even attend a Division 39 conference, but I am on the East Coast now, and this is where all the *cool* analysts are. I remember a psychoanalytic supervisor I had at that time whose words I can hear as clearly today as I did then, "I don't know how you reached this point in your training; you clearly aren't ready to treat clients." This supervisor was steeped in theory, and, at the time, I thought they were one of the most intelligent, well-trained supervisors I had yet to work with. They used that same theory, however, to plant seeds of inferiority, insecurity, and doubt. They would regularly remind me that what I was doing in therapy was *not* psychodynamic. In 2017, I recall a psychoanalytic instructor who, after I presented a case, encouraged me to explore how my "exoticism" may have impacted the client's transference and the therapeutic relationship. This instructor only used "exotic" when discussing transference and countertransference with BIPoC trainees. In 2018, a different psychoanalytic instructor "jokingly" (read: passive-aggressively) queried me (the only black person in the seminar) in front of the class: "Natasha, any more questions or comments [about race or class]?" The undertone of the comment was "stop using up our class time on these questions about race and class," and the comment worked: I thought twice before asking additional questions in that seminar. I thought twice despite regularly being approached after seminars by classmates thanking me for my questions and comments (many of whom, however, were silent during the seminar).

These stories are important to share because they can accumulate into pain too heavy to carry alone. These stories are also important to share because they make space for others to share their stories. The sharing of stories, of experiences, allows the community to identify patterns, specifically patterns of harm. Carnella, Beth, Lynne, and I all described experiences of harm. And what sustains this harm is a culture of silence. When I think of the implicatedness of the psychoanalytic community, I think of how the culture of silence is collusion with white supremacy.

## Fantasizing a Psychoanalytic Space That Does Not Make Us Sick

*Beth*

With all that was invaluable about psychoanalysis (and still is), here is what psychoanalysis didn't help me with: It didn't help me wonder how my mom's family actually got out of public housing (redlining). It didn't help me to bear how I might be harming black people in my efforts to "help" (see carceral social work). It didn't challenge me on my whiteness, on our "two Americas," or why on earth the "gold standard" of therapeutic intervention is one in which someone in need has to have thousands of dollars, time, space, childcare, and so on to be able to participate. It didn't help me wonder about my parents' grandparents becoming white and the cost of that to my intrapsychic life. It didn't help me to look for the anti-blackness upon which whiteness is predicated; it certainly didn't help me to see that even feeling excited that "we were all more human than otherwise" presupposed that there was a question about that to begin with, and it absolutely didn't help me to wonder who it was whose humanity was in question: black people who have been trying to live, or me, whose whiteness is built on the "death making institutions"—as Mariame Kaba (see Taylor, 2021) calls them—of racial capitalism. In all those years of social work school, PhD school, and analytic spaces, no one asked me to account for the impact of whiteness on my white patients or to think with me about how the security of my middle-class clients was purchased and with what psychic cost to them. Instead, these were the people for whom the pesky world could stay out of our work.

A "psychoanalysis that doesn't make us sick" would be one that could help me get well, which—paradoxically—would have to help me understand how I'm ill. Without theorizing about the impact of positionality, culture, and power on human development, psychoanalysis is only ever going to be a theory for people who can live as if structural forces are not at work. It requires disavowal, which makes it unclear how any analysis could ever be successful. Without reckoning with the ways in which psychoanalysis (in the US) is based on wealth and whiteness, it can ask all sorts of questions about all sorts of things but still stay in a white space: a place where the "natural" state is one that exists outside of the impingements of systems and structures—the very ones that have been created to concentrate power and wealth in whiteness. Is psychoanalysis something that can help me with my implicatedness, or does it require my implicatedness? And if I—any of us—"use" psychoanalysis in a way that attends to race and class and whiteness and racial capitalism, is it still really psychoanalysis? If so, then what isn't? If not, then what is it?

A psychoanalysis that doesn't make us sick is one that would help us get well.

### Lynne

My fantasy of a psychoanalysis that doesn't make us sick begins by tasking relational psychoanalysis to reckon fully with its implication in intersecting systems of race, class, sex, and gender inequality. While relational psychoanalysis is off to a good start in its acknowledgment that there are always two unconsciouses present in a therapy room, in my experience this movement has not always operated relationally or in a way that suggests that it sees itself as implicated in larger systems. Thus far, in my experience, and even after the "racial reckoning" following George Floyd's murder and massive protest, I have only seen tinkering around the edges and a lot of resistance to doing much more than adding "a diversity agenda" to the supposed "gold standard" of psychoanalytic curricula. Existent forms of governance are still barely questioned. This won't do.

In recent RSMP conversations, we've proposed the fantasy that everyone in a white-dominated institute engage in "dis-orientation" meetings that offer both didactic and experiential work that speaks to and works to undo the violence of interlocking systems of oppression (Combahee River Collective, 1977—black feminism has much to teach). Like the original mandate of the IARPP Committee for an inclusive psychoanalysis, a psychoanalysis that doesn't make us sick assumes that crucial knowledge emerges from the margins and that centers of power must be continuously de-centered. Taylor and Downes (2021) have fantasized about an enormously creative curriculum, a reimagined therapy training in which white students do their work on whiteness and BIPoC students have separate spaces in which to thrive. I want a psychoanalytic training program where a BIPoC trainee—and I have heard this said—would not feel that doing more than half the assigned reading would be too toxic and exhausting. I am not sure our current institutions can accomplish something like this, but I find promise when I hear about projects for new training programs, separate from institutes, where social psychoanalytic theory and practice meet community mental health. Many years ago, the education and training committee of Psychoanalysis for Social Responsibility developed a social psychoanalytic course curriculum. We tried to "market" it, but it went nowhere. Today, members of our working group on reparations have suggested that our best hope for repair might lie in asking our white members to support, financially and otherwise, separate BIPoC-led initiatives to create new anti-oppressive analytic spaces. It makes me sad to say that this might be our best chance to transform psychoanalytic spaces.

### Natasha

As I began imagining a psychoanalytic space that I would like to see, feelings of excitement and wonderment emerged. Those feelings, however, evolved into anxiety and sadness. The sadness surfaced as I began to compare my imagined space to reality, and the anxiety was tied to whether I could do justice to this imagined space. That said, let me start by describing the feeling I wish to have when entering a psychoanalytic space. I wish that I felt that I could maintain my whole self when I entered the space. I want to feel peace, welcomed, and intellectually stimulated. I want to experience the space as a place for healing and growth. I want to know that I am among allies, folks who are invested in liberation. Now, how exactly would this space look?

There is a beautiful history of psychoanalytic spaces as relatively small study groups. Groups that would gather at people's homes, in living rooms, and at kitchen tables. Spaces that were comfortable, familiar, and inviting. In many places, this tradition has persisted. My introduction to a psychoanalytic space was someone's home in Portland, Oregon. Yet as I write these words, I am reminded of an experience from 2017 when attending a party at the home of an analyst. I decided to attend the party because I was a new trainee and eager to finally meet other members of the institute. By the time I arrived at the party, it was well underway, and I remember barely making it through the door before bumping into the flood of people in the home. As I approached the bar, an older white woman asked me to take her glass and bring her another drink. She had assumed I was the help. I was the only black person in the space. All the waiting staff were people of color. I was out of place. I felt sick to my stomach, speechless. Barely five minutes in and I was already ready to go, *but I stayed*. I like the idea of gathering in people's homes. Sharing space and sharing bread with the folks we are in community with. I do not like the idea of gathering when the reality of income inequality slaps you in the face before you hit the doormat. I imagine an inclusive, intimate, representative psychoanalytic community.

Freud was a Jewish man who lived in Austria from 1860 to 1938. Following Hitler's annexation of Austria to Germany, Freud was forced to leave his country. During World War II, three of his sisters were murdered in concentration camps. Amid all this, Freud developed psychoanalytic theory. And he did so while remaining "apolitical." I can appreciate the experience of splitting parts of oneself off to be more digestible to those around you. I can appreciate that if Freud had been more "radical" in his politics while developing the theory, the theory might have been ignored or even discarded. Unfortunately, however, the psychoanalytic community maintained this split. The psychoanalytic space I fantasize about not only accounts for the sociopolitical, but it requires analysts to do their own "work" of unpacking their sociopolitical location. Could you imagine a psychoanalytic community with a foundation in the sociopolitical? Could you imagine a psychoanalytic community committed to decolonizing? Or a community founded by people who recognized the atrocities being committed against BIPoC and then organized to do something about it? I imagine a psychoanalytic space where white comfort is deprioritized.

In a December 2020 presentation, Lara Sheehi presented an anti-oppressive psychoanalysis. She described this psychoanalysis as being explicitly anti-capitalist, anti-imperialist, anti-racist, inclusive (particularly of queer, trans, nonbinary, and gender-expansive folks), as well as resistant to ableism, purism, xenophobia, and nationalism. When imagining a psychoanalytic space that I would like to see, I imagine all the cultural values that Lara outlined that day.

At one of the writing meetings for this piece, the phrase "it's not the theory, it is the culture" emerged. The idea was that psychoanalytic theory is revolutionary; the culture of psychoanalysis, however, is problematic. The psychoanalytic community that I imagine is possible, but it would require a fundamental shift in the culture of psychoanalysis. A revolution, if you will. An intentional organizing and collaboration among folks who are committed to doing "the work" and a dismantling of systems, structures, and institutions that are committed to maintaining the status quo.

## Conclusion

Commenting on the 1954 *Brown vs. Board of Education* decision, Ann Pellegrini (2021) noted that part of that decision rested on the results of the doll test in which, by and large, black children chose the white doll as the good doll. The conclusion was that separate and unequal school systems were breeding inferiority complexes in black children. What Pellegrini incisively points out, however, is that the decision also rests on a white superiority complex that was never questioned. This captures much of what we have spoken about here: what makes us all sick in psychoanalytic spaces, relational or otherwise, is the demand to assimilate to white upper-middle-class norms that privilege decontextualization, individualism, and, in neoliberal times, vast wealth.

Although difficult to capture in written form, this chapter came out of multiple conversations that were at times painful, at times joyful relational work. In our first conversation, we wondered why some of the BIPoC RSMP organizing committee members we had approached to work on this had said no. We learned that one BIPoC former member declined because they no longer wanted to participate in white-led projects. This spurred us to think about what conditions for participation would satisfy those of us who had chosen to participate. What could we ask of ourselves and the book editors that, for us, would make us feel we were walking the walk of implication and not just talking the talk? Perhaps, even from the outset, we were fantasizing about an accountable psychoanalytic space that would not make us sick.

We decided to ask the editors to reflect on this project's implication within historical and current power relations and publishing norms. Beyond reflection, we asked them to take material steps toward the repair of these conditions and histories. With Natasha's lead, we arrived at two requests: knowing that, in general, book chapters are invisible to those who do not or cannot buy the book, we wanted the editors to commit to disseminating the BIPoC contributions to the book as widely as possible. And knowing, also, that it is only the book editors who receive royalties on books, we wanted the editors to give a portion of the royalties to BIPoC, queer, and trans organizations and/or causes to be chosen by the BIPoC contributors to the project. The editors agreed to these requests. Further, they reached out to the editors of the Routledge Relational Perspectives Book Series, who acknowledged that they, too, are implicated in inequitable systems and thus offered to contribute to the cost of making the papers accessible. Having attained the editors' commitments, we set out to write this chapter.

## Note

1  https://www.vox.com/the-highlight/2019/8/8/20747198/philadelphia-bombing-1985-move

## References

Ahmed, S. (2010). Feminist Killjoys (and other willful subjects). *Scholar and Feminist Online, 8*(3). http://sfonline.barnard.edu/polyphonic/ahmed_01.htm

Alexander, M. (2010). *The new Jim Crow*. The New Press.

Baldwin, J. (1985). *The price of the ticket: Collected nonfiction: 1948–1985*. St. Martin's Press.

Carter, C. (2021). *Whiteness and the columbine high school attack: A psychoanalytic case portrait*. Doctoral Dissertation, Smith College School for Social Work.

Combahee River Collective. (1977). *The Combahee River Collective statement*. Retrieved January 9, 2018, from http://circuitous.org/scraps/combahee.html

Holmes, N. (2020). The motherland, my ancestors, and me: My experience navigating psychoanalytic spaces. *Studies in Gender and Sexuality, 21*(2), 113–118.

Ledet, R. J. [@drrussellledet]. (2019, December 14). We are our ancestors' wildest dreams. In the background, an original slave quarter. In the foreground, original descendants of slaves. *[Tweet]. Twitter*. https://twitter.com/drrussellledet/status/1205998323355803648?lang=en

Pellegrini, A. (2021, April 24). *Beyond woke: Why the focus on unconscious bias will not address systemic racism*. Online presentation for New Orleans-Birmingham Psychoanalytic Center.

Sheehi, L. (2020, December 5). *Reimagining psychoanalytic practice: Toward an anti-oppressive praxis*. Paper presented at the Philadelphia Society for Psychoanalytic Psychology. Zoom.

Sheehi, L. (2021, September 19). *Psychoanalytic innocence: The ideological underpinnings of theory and praxis*. Plenary Talk Presented Online at Psychology & the Other Conference.

Sheehi, L., & Sheehi, S. (2022). *Psychoanalysis under occupation: Practicing resistance in Palestine*. Routledge.

Tate, C. (1996). Freud and his "Negro": Psychoanalysis as ally and enemy of African Americans. *Journal for the Psychoanalysis of Culture & Society, 1*(1), 53–62.

Taylor, F., & Downes, R. (2021). Re-imagining the space and context for a therapeutic curriculum—A sketch. In D. Charura & C. Lago (Eds.), *Black identities + white therapies* (pp. 88–97). London: PCCS Books.

Taylor, K. Y. T. (2021). The emerging movement for police and prison abolition. *The New Yorker*.

Vaughans, K. (2016). African-American boys and adolescents under the shadow of slavery's legacy. *American Psychoanalyst, 50*(3).

Wilderson, F. B. (2020). *Afropessimism*. W. W. Norton.

Chapter 6

# The Other Within

## White Shame, Native-American Genocide

*Sue Grand*

My awareness of collective racial shame began during a visit to Prague. I was standing in the Spanish synagogue in the Jewish ghetto. Awed by the Moorish beauty of this synagogue, I was chilled by its history. Case after case held Jewish artifacts, plundered by the Nazis. Sacred objects, purged of the living hands that once held them. Then shipped across Europe, to be displayed in a museum, once the Final Solution was complete. After the triumph of the Reich. For the gaze of a purified, Aryan race. I am imagining them, gazing at my extinction: blue eyed, blond, unknowing, unthinking. Reading informational plaques that rewrite my extermination. We would simply vanish into Aryan modernity.

Standing in the Spanish synagogue, I think about genocide and extinction, about who writes the history of atrocity. I am haunted, but I am innocent. Then, memory and history crack open. Suddenly, I am an adolescent, looking at another display under glass. I am looking at the Indian displays and dioramas at the Museum of Natural History in New York City. What, precisely, am I seeing? Life size, three-dimensional portraits of hunters and gatherers. An enormous stuffed Buffalo, ancient pottery, primitive tools, loin cloths, beaded leather, feather headdresses, peace pipes, artifacts of burial. For us, as children, these dioramas were alluring portals to a mythic past. They were realistic and yet magical, sealed and enclosed, but surely possessed of some hidden door—we wanted to get inside them, and time travel to the "wild west." Intriguing and primitive, these still-life Indians were figural archives of ancient knowledge, spiritual links to the natural world. They were formidable warriors, sensual and cruel, powerful, fearless, both noble *and* savage. They were the precursors to white modernity, barefoot trackers lost to New York City pavement. They were

DOI: 10.4324/9781003265146-6

the legendary ghosts of "our" prehistory. None of us actually knew a "real Indian"; they had simply vanished with time.

In the Spanish synagogue I am having dual vision. I am here, now, imagining Aryans looking at *my* extinction. And I am reading informational plaques that rewrite the Indian extermination. I am brown eyed, blond, unknowing, unthinking, oblivious. Gazing at these still-life hunter/gatherers, everything seems pastoral, and then, simply, not. Times changed; the buffalo disappeared. At one moment, I am just standing there in my Jewishness, looking at plundered silver candlesticks, prayer books, menorahs. I am certain about the locus of good and evil, and I know which side I am on. But then, my perspective and my identity shift. The Nazi intention refracts white American mythology, and I am no longer sure who or what I am, or where good and evil reside, or what racist lives inside me, or what moral axis I am living in. Imagining Aryan eyes on *my* bones, I discover myself, looking through *Aryan* eyes *at* Native-American bones. My persecuted *Jewishness* flips into a predatory American *whiteness*, and there is an all-seeing Native-American eye on that whiteness. I am suffused with shame. *On whose soil have I made my home?*

## Shame as Revelation

My innocence is lost. As Layton (2015) suggests, my collective self has multiple identity markers, and two of them are exactly what is visible and received: American and *white*. White: my Jewishness is slippery; my skin is marked by predation. My life is inscribed with multiple historical legacies in which I am both a victim of destruction *and* a collusive agent in the destruction of others. Shame awakens me to this complexity; it is a being-seen, in a first encounter with alterity (see Wilson, 1987). In this condition, the "vanished" Indian Other possesses his or her own gaze and penetrates my white blindness. I have looked through my "Aryan" eyes; I have been seen in that look, and shame refers to a failure of my own ego ideals (Wurmser, 1987; Morrison, 1987). But I am in agreement with Lynd (1958): this shame can also be a call to fulfill those ideals.

In the reckoning with genocidal history, collective racial shame can have a paradoxical effect. This shame can feel persecutory, it can reify subject-object splits and moral categories; it can readily collapse into violence, denial, and vengeance, and turn us *away* from knowing the other. But it also encodes the voice of this Other; it can be a call to conscience, an awakening to social pathologies. In its more problematic form, shame seems to divide the sacred and the profane; it certainly imagines that the clean do not shit; it denies the ordinary human-ness of our humanity. It obscures the messiness of intersubjectivity and ethics. It conjures a cold, unforgiving eye upon us. It vacates our world of empathy and self-compassion, and makes us want to hide from the Other.

But collective shame also anticipates movement: from moralism to ethics, from solipsism to I-Thou conversation, from denial to collective responsibility. All of this is inspired by an emergent Other, possessed of an all-seeing eye on our transgressions. To be seen by this eye can feel like an exposed, all-consuming badness; a sense of radical nakedness in relation to radical scrutiny. But as Lynd theorized back in 1958, shame is not simply an exposure of unwanted aspects of self. Shame disrupts our societal roles and false values—because it introduces us to another perspective that is outside of us. In the arena of race, then, collective white shame can rearrange the field of perception, and produce a crack in memory and history, when the other has been "vanished" as white America has vanished the Indian. When we are exposed to the eye of the vanished Other, when we allow ourselves to experience our own "deserved shame" (Watkins, 2016) about cultural evil, that shame allows "our moral sense to tune in to the beacon of goodness and justice" (Lebron, 2013, p. 7). This can inspire us toward the depressive concern and restorative justice that moved so many veterans to protect the recent protests at Standing Rock.

## Creative Shame and the Restoration of History

Psychoanalysts have tended to emphasize the sheer destructiveness of shame—as a toxic form of splitting and projection, a cruel and dangerous affect. Thus, *shame* would seem to *reduce* our capacity to make amends for our own destructiveness. But does it? In this article I am suggesting a more nuanced understanding of shame as *affect, intersubjective process, and cultural commentary*. I am complicating shame's toxicity by highlighting shame's *creative moment*: that breach in our white blindness that permits us to see the Other, *who we could not see before*. As many analysts (e.g., Kohut, 1977; Leighton, 2004; Orange, 2010; Wurmser, 1987) have noted, shame can inflame the disintegrating self, incite aggression, and destroy the human links that we are seeking to restore. I am certainly *not* an advocate of this kind of toxic, destructive shame. In fact, I endorse another kind of shame that I do see as constructive. As Watkins (2016), Lebron (2013), and Braithwaite (1989) suggest, there is an ethical call embedded in our retrieval of our own "deserved shame." When we cringe before the all-seeing eye, it can be a first order of engagement with the marginalized Other. We start to imagine another mind to converse with. As Lewis puts it, "The 'me' emerges in distinction from the 'other' . . . it is the eye of the other in the me who beholds my transgression" (Lewis, 1995, p. 92). If we can acknowledge shame and mitigate its inflammation, the Other outside can become increasingly visible. And this visibility enables us to query cultural evil and our collusion with that evil. This shift is potentiated as the *I* (eye) of the oppressed perceives, externalizes, and separates from its oppressor (Gaztambide, 2017). Now, as Benjamin (1988) describes it, there is, "a new possibility of colliding with the outside and becoming alive in the presence of an equal other" (p. 221).

To defeat this dialogic possibility, psychopathic regimes often construct seamless insularity for the dominant, so that this visibility is occluded. In her work on "white fragility," DiAngelo (2006) describes these formidable white arrangements: radical forms of exploitation and segregation that foreclose all encounter with our racialized Other. In such radical segregation, there is no hope of finding our way toward reparative guilt. Reparative guilt is predicated on our proximity to the wounded Other, and it is predicated on our wounded Other seeing *us*. Reparative guilt is threatening, and destabilizing, for racist regimes; it is precisely why oppression is hidden from view. When this concealment reaches its apex, the master narrative is almost seamless. This is precisely what whiteness achieved with the "vanishing" of the American Indian. In this mythic vanishing, there was no agentic destruction. Shame cannot rupture our insularity or expose our agency. Ambivalence cannot be evoked; reparative guilt is preempted before it can arrive.

The American genocide has been an exemplar of this malignant cultural condition; it has produced a seamless, nonreflective, collective white narcissism. Whenever we are in this cultural condition, we need to be startled by an outside that is outside of us. Repair cannot begin with depressive concern and reparative guilt. It must begin with the rupturing gaze of wounded otherness. If we are not psychopathic, and if we have a way to tolerate the induced shame, history will begin to penetrate us. It can feel toxic to experience what Watkins (2016) refers to as our "deserved shame." But if we hold each other well enough in the first shock of this mortification, that zone can become facilitative of racial justice.

The question, for me, then is *not* how we *avoid* experiencing *creative shame*—a form of shame that actually increases our awareness of the Other and has constructive effects on our relational and cultural contexts. It is how we contain, empower, and decode this together, within a shared sense of tragic complexity, and an understanding of our flawed human goodness. This allows us to resist participation in psychopathic structures. Without this containment, we can get locked down into persecutory systems of *malignant shame*. There, we will try to put our shame back into the Other, reproducing their sense of "undeserved shame" (Watkins, 2016) in escalating systems of cruelty. To affirm creative shame while we mutually contain shame's potential for savagery is our collective challenge. To face this challenge, we need to understand this: creative shame is not a stable state or an individual capacity. It is an intersubjective *moment* in a fast-moving intersubjective *process—a process that readily becomes toxic*. We need to greet creative shame in a spirit of compassion, so that we don't slide into malignant shame. This empathic reception is not false forgiveness; it does *not* obscure our transgressions *or* the emergent subjectivity of the Other. Rather, it restores our humanity, so that we can begin the movement towards restorative justice.

For me, this collective responsibility began in the Spanish synagogue. Once, I was riveted by the dioramas at the Museum of Natural History. I wanted those still-life Indians to come alive. Suddenly, in Prague they came alive with a vengeance. They have continued to rupture my white blindness, and they have called on me to know history. Now the

Holocaust will be forever linked to the Native-American genocide, which Hitler praised for its inspiration (Coates, 2014; Sterba, 1996; Stannard, 1992). As Sterba notes (1996), our atrocities certainly rivaled Hitler's, and our "manifest destiny" became his "Lebensraum."

## Strategies of Racial Disappearance

Ever since my experience in Prague, I have been thinking about racial guilt and racial shame and genocidal vanishing. I am thinking about the differential structures of racial subjugation; the differential myths that sustain these structures, and the ways they evoke/suppress our deserved shame and guilt. In the United States, black slavery and indigenous extermination were twinned; they were parallel, interdependent regimes for constructing white wealth. But they also had distinctive arrangements of visibility and/or vanishing; I believe that these arrangements have bearing on our capacity for collective shame or guilt.

The enslavement of Africans, the extermination of the Indians: these systems were both clearly genocidal. At the first European contact, it is estimated that the Native population in what would become the territorial United States was 5 million. By 1890, there were 248,000 (Bruyneel, 2007). The number of African slaves who died during the middle passage is estimated in the *millions* (see Sterba, 1996), without accounting for their deaths *in* slavery. In the colonial era, both peoples were enslaved by Europeans for trade and free labor.[1] Both were starved, tortured, and rapidly worked to death.[2] Beginning in the 1600s, settlers in Rhode Island engaged in the trans-Atlantic slave trade, exchanging Native captives for African slaves. As Gallay (2009) put it, "both Indians and Africans were depicted as savage heathens" (p. 3).

But by the 18th century, our home-grown genocides bifurcated into divergent pathways. These pathways overlapped, converged, and exacerbated each other[3]; but they differentially constructed racial presence and racial absence. With regards to this differential project, George Washington put it rather succinctly: "The gradual extension of our Settlements will as certainly cause the Savage as the Wolf to retire; both being beasts of prey tho they differ in shape" (as quoted in Saunt, 2005, p. 17).

## The Differential Math of Genocide

Africans arrived on this continent stripped of everything except their labor. Indigenous peoples would be exploited for labor, but also for skills, resources, and land. For settler imperialism, both redness and blackness became subservient to whiteness; both Africans and Indigenous peoples had to absorb malignant projections and justify white dominance. But, over time, white dominance required the visibility and controlled proximity/distance of "whites" and "blacks." On the East Coast, in the 18th century, the plantation sugar economy expanded. This economy relied on vast infusions of slaves. The Native population was already decimated by slavery, extermination, starvation, and disease, but African slaves were constantly being replenished. By the 18th and 19th centuries, skin color was raced, and slavery was raced as *black*. African slave labor didn't entirely replace

Native slave labor in the territorial United States, but by that era, another genocidal project became more salient, involving the Native population: that is, the land and dominance to be gained from their extermination and/or removal.[4] Thus, African American slavery was grounded in proximal castes of whiteness and blackness. Native-American extermination became a divine mission of westward expansion and Indian absence. To build the U.S. economy, "redskins" had to "vanish" from the landscape of whiteness. And such is the perversity of racism: once slavery was raced as black, the historical truth of Native-American slavery *vanished* from white guilt and white consciousness, as did the Native Americans themselves.

Of course, throughout our history, to be black is also to be disappeared and/or murdered. Jim Crow, convict labor, lynching, mass incarceration, police shootings—these atrocities are acts of disappearance. But before and after the Indian Removal Act, U.S. wealth has been grounded in the regulated *presence of* whiteness and blackness, and in Native-American "vanishing." Whiteness has always extruded blackness but whiteness has not written blackness into an extinct, distant past. Indeed, whiteness has claimed superiority through its opposition with blackness. But after the 18th century, land seizure required the disappearance of "redskins."

"Redskins" were further sequestered from whiteness by master narratives about American origination. These narratives tell us that Europeans "discovered" America; that U.S. civilization began with European settlement. They tell us that *we* created modernity, that this modernity was an essential good,[5] and that Indians were unable to adapt and assimilate, thereby writing *them-selves* out of existence. As O'Brien (2010) notes, local histories of 19th-century New England were regularly identifying the "last Indian."[6] This narrative of disappearance was mythologized in James Fennimore Cooper's "American masterpiece," *The Last of the Mohicans*. A disappearance through a failure of adaptation, this myth is contradicted by historians. The indigenous population was extraordinarily adaptive to its colonizers (see O'Brien, 2010; Dunbar-Ortiz, 2014; Gallay, 2009; Miles, 2005; Saunt, 2005). Nonetheless, those who survived extermination, cultural annihilation, and disease were forced to march, starving, and nearly naked in the snow, to the barren "Indian territory" west of the Mississippi. Most of them died on this "trail of tears."

White settlers were infinitely inventive in their practices of extermination and erasure. Those Indians who somehow remained in physical proximity to whiteness were often reinscribed as not-really-Indian. Here, there is a stunning, predatory differential between the twin genocides. In African-American slavery, the one-drop rule was used to define blackness. As white masters raped slave women, questions arose about the condition of the children. Did they follow the condition of the slave mother, or that of the master father? If they followed the father into whiteness, these children would gain their freedom. With the one-drop rule, slave states determined that just one drop of blackness disqualified these children from claiming whiteness, thus protecting the slave economy from the financial losses of manumission. Through rape, the one-drop rule of African slavery actually *increased* the number of black slaves, while sustaining the (relative) visibility of blackness to whiteness. But the Native-American predicament operated in reverse: A drop of whiteness was used to eradicate "redness," although redness could never acquire the full privilege of whiteness. In the official narrative, only the "full bloods" were "real Indians," who always maintained traditional practices. In most land treaties (all of which were broken), only these "full-blooded Indians" held land rights. But, of course, over centuries of slavery, rape, accommodation, and assimilation, Native Americans had engaged with white settlers and black slaves and black freemen. There were intercultural penetrations, cultural transformations, intercultural kinship networks, mingled DNA, the destruction of indigenous land, culture and economies, and therefore, fewer "full bloods" living traditional lives. Because only "full bloods" had land rights, most Indians could be expelled from their land.

Here we can see the differential math of white wealth and racial subjugation: Black slaves are multiplied by their one-drop rule whereas the Indian population is subtracted through its inverse. When Native Americans did assimilate and adapt, their "semi-whiteness" disqualified them as "real Indians." Reading history, one has the impression of an unseen psychopathic hand arranging all this madness. These strategies constructed and sustained the myth of the "vanishing Indian" as Native peoples were regulated out of their own identity and existence. This myth recast genocide as evolution: Redskins just seemed to fade away into white *homo erectus* (see Saunt, 2005; Senier, 2014; Gallay, 2009; Newell, 2009; Snyder, 2010; Miles, 2005).

It is no accident, then, that centuries later, U.S. psychoanalysis has been silent about this atrocity and its traumatic legacies. In the 21st century, mythic narratives continue to erase atrocity, writing the Indian out of existence. Certainly, with the exceptions of Apprey (2003), Gump (2000,

2010), Alan Bass (2003), and Grand (2014), psychoanalysts have barely attended to African-American slavery. But we have attended not at all to the Native-American genocide. This absence in psychoanalysis parallels the void in our national narrative. Where Native-American trauma should be inscribed, there is only an *absence without commentary*. This mirrors the problem of *who* writes on psychoanalysis, and what culture and region of the United States they are writing from within. White psychoanalysts of the urban North East live in some proximity with anti-black racism; many white analysts are addressing that racism (Altman, 2000; Grand, 2014; Suchet, 2007). But—and this is a terrible admission—for analysts in the urban Northeast, Indians can seem archaic and so absent that they can't even elicit this white racial address. This psychoanalytic silence perpetuates our national myth.

To break up this myth, we need these moments of creative shame. White presence, Indian absence: this was not about evolution. It was about centuries of warfare, rape, starvation, and enslavement; disease; broken treaties; laws that forbid Indians from hunting, trapping, and fishing on their own land; land theft; narrowing racial laws; the purposeful slaughter of the buffalo and provision of smallpox-infected blankets; and the maddening switchbacks through which whites defined the "blood quantums" of "real Indians." And this absence is not about innocent white settlers under attack by savage warriors. This is a history of asymmetrical violence, of white predators, and Native-American victims. As Dunbar-Ortiz (2014) points out, the colonialists *always* addressed indigenous tribes with practices of total extermination, using atrocities against them that were previously unknown to indigenous warfare. Scalping was invented *by* white settlers (Dunbar-Ortiz, 2014); Indian scalps were sold for profit, and celebrated as conquest.[7] In all of this malignancy we obscured Indigenous protest: "Why should you take by force that from us which you can have by love? Why should you destroy us, who have provided you with food? What can you get by war? . . . You see us unarmed, and willing to supply your wants, if you will come in a friendly manner, and not with swords and guns, as to invade an enemy" (Wahunsonacock, Powhatan, 1609, quoted in Wilson, 1998).[8]

Refusing gratitude and denying their own dependency on native resources and generosity, whiteness clamored about "manifest destiny." White greed moved west with ethnic cleansing, erasing indigenous culture, befouling and stealing the land, removing survivors to remote and unwanted land. And insofar as whiteness did have proximity to its victims, whiteness kept extruding its "deserved shame" (Watkins, 2016) into the imago of the "drunk Injun."

## Slaves and Masters: Transmissions of Shame and Malignance

Throughout all of this predation, white dominance ensured that the natural alliances that could have defeated it were not allowed to form. In our early history, Africans and Indians were enslaved, starved, tortured, and persecuted *together*. Their alliance would have been formidable. But American wealth has always been grounded in a divisive hierarchical system of "vanished Others," of those who have been raced, classed, and gendered into subjugation, exploitation, antagonism, and mistrust. All arranged in layers of relative privilege, colonized by scarcity, written and divided by the master narrative, so that unity and resistance are weakened. It's all here, in this terrible history.

In the colonial era, the French, Spanish, and British were in contest for dominance, all of them enlisting Native warriors, commanding them with threats and promises, seducing them with European goods and weapons, enlisting them as partners in commerce and as slavers, exploiting their prior intertribal conflicts, so that intertribal alliances were in continuous flux.[9] In every region, each tribe was its own nation with distinct language, culture, economies, land, and religion. There were no *Indians* until European presence made "them" into *redskins*. From the beginning, Europeans persecuted these nations as one, even as they exploited their preexisting rivalries and alliances. The effect was bewildering, and solidarity was belated. Indian confederacies could not be formed until the indigenous population was being decimated, and diverse nations recognized themselves as the annihilated Other, raced by Europeans as *redskins*:

"Brothers—my people wish for peace; the red men all wish for peace; but where the white people are, there is no peace for them . . . The white men . . . do not think red men sufficiently good to live . . . Brothers—if you do not unite with us, they will first destroy us, and then you will fall an easy prey to them. They have destroyed many nations of red men because they were not united, because they were not friends to each other. Brothers—we must be united, we must smoke the same pipe; we must fight each other's battles" (Tecumsah, quoted in Nabokov, 1999, pp. 97–98).[10]

Colonization arouses our mutual terror and our hatred; it violates, starves, and degrades us; it pits us against one another in gradations of privilege, objectification, survival, and abjection. Who is a subject? Who is disposable? Predatory conquest is brilliant and incisive. It perceives and foments our rivalries, our competitions, our cravings for wealth, status, and inclusion. In these conditions, we can all become agents of the machine that is destroying us. We can commit what I have called, the "bestial gesture of survival" (Grand, 2000), dehumanizing those who are suffering the same fate.

Divide and conquer: U.S. wealth is a historic register of this obscenity. If Indian resistance was much less violent than whiteness imagines, it is not always innocent. Native peoples were both slavers and the enslaved. There were slaving tribes who captured other tribes, entering into commercial arrangements with the very colonists who would subsequently enslave these Indian slavers. While Africans were being kidnapped by Africans in Africa for shipment to American colonies, Indians were being captured by Indians for shipment to the Caribbean colonies, Canada, the Great Lakes region, and from the South to the North in the territorial United States (Gallay, 2002; Newell, 2009; Rushforth, 2012; Snyder, 2010).[11]

On our shores, Indians were enslaved *with* Africans, and they formed familial bonds. Insofar as African slaves and Native peoples sustained their alliances, they effectively threatened the genocidal regime. The Tuscarora provided sanctuary for escaped black slaves, and formed an underground railroad as early as the 1600s; the earliest slave revolt was jointly mobilized by Native and African slaves in New York City in 1708 (Miles, 2009). The Seminoles of Florida welcomed fleeing black slaves, formed kinship systems, became fierce warriors of resistance, and were renown as the "undefeated tribe" (see Brooks, 2002; Henson, 1849; Hill, 2009; Krauthamer, 2013; Miles, 2011; Saunt, 2005). But according to Saunt (2005) and Miles (2005), alliances between black slaves and native peoples were sparse. And when these alliances occurred, white dominance could read its future defeat. Black slaves and native tribes would be purposefully divided by racial hierarchies, the racing of slavery, and by the false promise of Indian survival if they assimilated to white "civilization." The resulting divisions between redness and blackness were exacerbated by laws that criminalized sanctuary of fleeing African slaves (Krauthamer, 2013; Miles, 2005).

The pressures of indigenous survival undermined alliances between these two persecuted peoples. Nonetheless, Miles, Snyder, Saunt, and Gallay all conclude that native peoples did share culpability in the African-American genocide. Until about the mid-19th century, Africans were enslaved *with* Native peoples. Throughout the Southeast, Northeast, and Indian Territory, Indians had been stripped of the resources that defined and sustained them; but they were also lit up by the greed that lit up their colonizers. These tribes owned, and traded in, black slaves. According to these historians, Indians had a significant role in the African slave trade, even as they formed bonds of kinship and mingled DNA (Saunt, 2005; Snyder, 2010; Miles, 2005).

And by the late 17th century, colonists had established their separate and contradictory "one drop rules" for Africans and Indians. They had "bizarre blood-quantum requirements claiming that Native identity 'dissolves' with intermarriage . . . [colonists] began recasting indigenous people as 'colored,' 'mulatto,' 'French'—anything but 'Indian'" (Senier, 2014, p. 2). Blackness was, as always, at the lowest rung of the caste system, and, given the one-drop rule of *African* slavery, blackness could *never* attain *either* redness *or* whiteness. For a Native person to be labeled "colored" or "mulatto" or kin with blackness could further dilute Native-American identity and land claims and would distance them forever from any entry into "white civilization." And to have one-drop of blackness was to be at risk for being sold into black chattel slavery. Native-American survival would increasingly require the affiliation with whiteness and the corresponding disavowal of blackness.

In these ways, the white incursion broke apart the natural alliances that would have defeated it, and mutual antagonisms were inflamed. Black Indians often found themselves doubly abased and vanished, by both whiteness and redness, existing at the marginalized nexus of this complicated history. Blackness *could* be absorbed into Indian kinship systems, but only if this blackness was denied and vanished. But Southeast Native tribes would also acculturate, and accrue wealth and status by establishing plantations, enslaving blacks, and repudiating black kin.[12] Some Native planters enslaved *their own black kin* (Krauthamer, 2013; Miles, 2005; Saunt, 2005).[13] Free families of African descent continued to live in Indian nations (Snyder, 2010). But, as Krauthamer notes, some Southeast tribes[14] fiercely opposed abolition, supported the confederacy in the Civil War (also Saunt, 2005), and resisted emancipation in Indian Territory even after the War was lost. Fleeing slavery, blacks often encountered reenslavement as they sought sanctuary in Indian Territory. The resulting alienation and animus has haunted generations;[15] it splintered familial bonds *and* political alliances.[16] Recently, there have been an effort to repair this legacy and to recognize the black Indian.

## Flawed Human Goodness: Redeeming Our Shame

Any genocide that lasts centuries is not going to be a pure story. But in this history, there *are* some *very* clear lines between good and evil; between perpetrators and their innocent victims. However, in these conditions, we don't know what we ourselves would do. The complexity of this history can further bewilder our "deserved" and "undeserved" shame; it can make us more resistant to knowing history. Most of us cannot escape from bias and greed, from collusion, from the exigencies of terror and hunger and survival, or from the prejudicial myths written by master narratives.[17]

To resist racist regimes, we need to find a way to restore the human bonds that genocide seeks to destroy. But to speak to the Other, the all-seeing eye of shame must be softened by another kind of vision. This is a compassionate sight that sees our flawed human goodness, and allows us to witness our own ignorance and welcome the stranger even though we are not yet purged of our prejudice. This is a form of the "radical hope" that Lear (2006) found in the dream of Plenty Coups. This radical hope has been passed through the ages; it is in this story told by Josiah Henson in his encounter with the Native-American stranger,[18] as he fled African-American slavery:

> We were instantly on the alert as we could hardly expect them to be friends. The advance of a few paces showed me they were Indians, with packs on their shoulders; and they were so near that if they were hostile, it would be useless to escape . . . they looked at me in a frightened sort of way for a moment and setting up a peculiar howl, turned round, and ran as fast as they could. . . . [W]hat they were afraid of I could not imagine, unless they supposed I was the devil whom they had perhaps heard of as black. . . . [M]y wife was alarmed too, and thought they were merely running back to collect more of a party, and then to come and murder us, and she wanted to turn back. . . . [A]s we

advanced, we could discover Indians peeping at us from behind the trees and dodging out of our sight. . . . [T]he chief . . . soon discovered that we were human beings

. . . and now curiosity seemed to prevail. Each one wanted to touch the children who were shy as partridges . . . a little while sufficed to make them understand what we were, and whither we were going and what we needed; and as little, to set them about supplying our wants, feeding us bountifully, and giving us a comfortable wigwam for our night's rest. The next day, we resumed our march . . . they sent some of their young men to point out the place where we were to turn off and parted from us with as much kindness as possible. . . .

(Henson, 1849, pp. 53–54)

## Notes

1 O'Brien (2010) notes, for example, that the Pokanoket in Cape Cod were enslaved in 1614.
2 Gallay estimates that before 1715, approximately 30,000–50,000 Native people were taken as slaves by the British.
3 Most notably in the arena of African American slavery. In the 18th century Native Americans had a considerable role in African-American slavery. See Krauthamer (2013).
4 Jackson passed the Indian Removal Act in 1830.
5 This mythology is ongoing. David Brooks (2015) writes in "The American Idea": "America was settled, founded and built by people who believed they were doing something exceptional. . . . American was defined by its future, by the people who weren't yet here and by the greatness that hadn't yet been achieved . . . once the vast continent was settled the United States would be one of the dominant powers of the globe."
6 Thus "Ishi," as the last known member of the Native American Yahi people, would be celebrated and studied as the last "wild Indian" (Kroeber, 1961); Even now, there seem to be ongoing disputes about this firsting and lasting. In 1996, the 8,500-year-old skull of "Kennewick man" was discovered in Washington, and claimed as Caucasian. Native Americans said that these were the bones of their ancestors, and tried to reclaim Kennewick Man for burial. Lawsuits contested repatriation. Recently, Danish scientists settled this dispute over identity and history: they conclusively determined that Kennewick Man is most closely linked to Native Americans. Nonetheless, repatriation is still in doubt.
7 The term, 'redskin' originated as a descriptor of the wounded craniums of these scalped bodies (see Dunbar-Ortiz, 2014).
8 Also, for example, in their effort to dominate South Carolina, the British attacked French-allied Choctaws, and also attacked the Apalachee to strike at the Spanish. The Chickasaws switch alliance from the French to the British,

and take native slaves for the British (Gallay, 2002). In the King Philip's War (1675–1676), New England colonists went to war with their allies—Mohegan and Pequot—against Wampanoags, Narragansetts, Nipmucs, and others. For Native Americans, there were 5,000 casualties (Gallay, 2009).

9 By the mid-18th century, the capture and sale of Native slaves decreased east of the Mississippi as tribes formed confederacies and refused large-scale slaving (Gallay, 2009).

10 Native slavery was officially outlawed in the mid-18th century, but it continued.

11 These tribes included the Choctaws, Chickasaw, Cherokee, and Creeks. Miles (2009) traces Native American plantation slave practices through the Cherokee family of Shoe Boots and the Cherokee Van family (Miles, 2005). Krauthamer (2013) highlights these practices of the Choctaw and Chickasaw in Indian Territory.

12 According to black slave narratives, conditions varied—often Indian masters were described as more humane. See Minges, 2004.

13 The Choctaws did not develop slave codes until after removal. But later, their laws would forbid marriage with African Americans, and prohibited black slaves from learning to read or from owning firearms, in disturbing mimicry of white masters (Snyder, 2010).

14 The Choctaw, Chickasaw, Cherokee, Creek, and even the Seminoles (Krauthamer, 2013).

15 With the Dawes Act of 1887, federal land allotments are determined by "blood quantums," with "full blood" Indians receiving the largest allotments, and former black slaves the smallest (Krauthamer, 2013).

16 The transgenerational legacy of this complexity persists: in the recent controversy about removing the Confederate flag flying above the South Carolina capital, a white conservative wanted to erect a monument to a Cherokee chief who became a confederate general (Pitts, 2015). To this day, there are tensions between Native tribes and "black Indians" (Saunt, 2005; Miles, 2005); By contrast, Northern Creeks actually anticipated the 13th Amendment, abolishing slavery, granting freed slaves equal tribal status in September 1863 (Saunt, 2005).

17 As Snyder (2010) put it, "rather than a one-way monologue crafted by the white elites, the language of race was a dialogue shared by whites and Indians and shaped by the violent intimacy of the Southern border wars. New articulations of race blended with—and complicated—older notions of Native identity. Challenging colonialism, Indians drew on their experiences with 'Virginians' to craft a racial ideology underpinned by nativism" (p. 172).

18 Northern Ohio, tribe unknown.

## References

Altman, N. (2000). Black and white thinking: A psychoanalyst reconsiders race. *Psychoanalytic Dialogues, 10*, 589–605. doi:10.1080/10481881009348569

Apprey, M. (2003). Repairing history: Reworking transgenerational trauma. In D. Moss (Ed.), *Hating in the first person plural* (pp. 3–29). Other Press.

Bass, A. (2003). Historical and unconscious trauma: Racism and psychoanalysis. In D. Moss (Ed.), *Hating in the first person plural* (pp. 29–45). Other Press.

Benjamin, J. (1988). *The bonds of love*. Pantheon Press.

Braithwaite, J. (1989). *Crime, shame, and reintegration*. Cambridge University Press.

Brooks, D. (2015, September 25). The American idea and today's GOP. *The New York Times*. https://mobile.nytimes.com/2015/09/25/ opinion/david-brooks-the-american-idea-and-todaysgop.html?referer=https:// www.google.com/

Brooks, J. F. (2002). *Captives and cousins: Slavery, kinship and community in the Southwest borderlands*. University of North Carolina Press.

Bruyneel, K. (2007). *The third space of sovereignty: The postcolonial politics of U.S. Indigenous relations*. University of Minnesota Press.

Coates, T. N. (2014, January 16). Hitler on the Mississippi banks: Thoughts on Timothy Snyder's *Bloodlands*. *The Atlantic*. www.theatlantic.com/international/ archive/2014/01/hitler-on-the-mississippi-banks/283127/

DiAngelo, R. (2006). My race didn't trump my class: Using op- pression to face privilege. *Multicultural Perspectives, 8*(1), 51–56. doi:10.1207/ s15327892mcp0801_9

Dunbar-Ortiz, R. (2014). *An indigenous people's history of the United States*. Beacon Press.

Gallay, A. (2002). *The Indian slave trade: The rise of the English empire in the American South, 1670–1717*. Yale University Press.

Gallay, A. (2009). Introduction. In A. Gallay (Ed.), *Indian slavery in colonial America* (pp. 1–33). University of Nebraska Press.

Gaztambide, D. J. (2017). A "psychoanalysis for liberation": Reading Friere as an act of love. *Psychoanalysis, Culture & Society, 22*(2), 193–212. doi:10.1057/ s41282-016-0033-9

Grand, S. (2000). *The reproduction of evil: A clinical and cultural perspective*. Analytic Press.

Grand, S. (2014). Skin memories: On race, love and loss. *Psychoanalysis, Culture & Society, 19*, 232–249. doi:10.1057/pcs.2014.24.

Gump, J. (2000). A white therapist, an African American Patient: Shame in the therapeutic dyad: Commentary of paper by Neil Altman. *Psychoanalytic Dialogues, 10*, 619–632. doi:10.1080/10481881009348571

Gump, J. (2010). Reality matters: The shadow of trauma on African American subjectivity. *Psychoanalytic Perspectives, 27*(1), 42–54.

Henson, J. (1849). *The life of Josiah Henson: Formerly a slave, now an inhabitant of Canada, as narrated by himself*. Arthur D. Phelps.

Hill, Sr. R. W. (2009). Rotihnahon:tSi and Rotinonhson:nI: Historical relationships between African Americans and the confederacy of the six nations. In G. Tayac (Ed.), *Indivisible* (pp. 99–109). Smithsonian, National Museum of the Native American.

Kohut, H. (1977). *The restoration of the self*. International Universities Press.

Krauthamer, B. (2013). *Black slaves, Indian masters: Slavery, emancipation, and citizenship in the native American South*. University of North Carolina Press.

Kroeber, T. (1961). *Ishi in two worlds: A biography of the last wild Indian in North America.* University of California Press.

Layton, L. (2015). Beyond sameness and difference: Normative unconscious process and our mutual implication in each other's suffering. In D. Goodman & M. Freeman (Eds.), *Psychology and the other* (pp. 168–188). Oxford University Press.

Lear, J. (2006). *Radical hope: Ethics in the face of cultural devastation.* Harvard University Press.

Lebron, C. J. (2013). *The color of our shame: Race and justice in our time.* Oxford University Press.

Leighton, J. (2004). The analyst's sham(e): Collapsing into a one-person system. In W. J. Coburn (Ed.), *Transformations in self psychology: Progress in self psychology* (Vol. 20, pp. 169–188). Analytic Press.

Lewis, M. (1995). *Shame: The exposed self.* Free Press.

Lynd, H. M. (1958). *On shame and the search for identity.* Routledge and Kegan Paul.

Miles, T. (2005). *Ties that bind: The story of an Afro-Cherokee family in slavery and freedom.* University of California Press.

Miles, T. (2009). Taking leave, making lives: Creative quests for freedom in early black and native America. In G. Tayac (Ed.), *Indivisible* (pp. 139–151). Smithsonian, National Museum of Native American.

Miles, T. (2011, Summer). Of waterways and runaways: Reflections on the great lakes in underground railroad history. *Michigan Quarterly Review.* www.michiganquarterlyreview.com/2011/10/of-waterways-and-runaways-reflectionson-the-great-lakes-in-underground-railroad-history/

Minges, P. (2004). *Black Indian slave narratives.* John F. Blair.

Morrison, A. (1987). The eye turned inward: Shame and the self. In D. L. Nathanson (Ed.), *The many faces of shame* (pp. 271–291). Guilford Press.

Newell, E. M. (2009). Indian slavery in colonial New England. In A. Gallay (Ed.), *Indian slavery in colonial America* (pp. 33–67). University of Nebraska Press.

O'Brien, J. M. (2010). *Firsting and lasting: Writing Indians out of existence in New England.* University of Minnesota Press.

Orange, D. (2010). *Thinking for clinicians: Philosophical resources for contemporary psychoanalysis and the humanistic psychotherapies.* Routledge.

Rushforth, B. (2012). *Bonds of alliance: Indigenous and Atlantic slaveries in New France.* University of North Carolina Press.

Saunt, C. (2005). *Black, white, and Indian: Race and the unmaking of an American family.* Oxford University Press.

Senier, S. (2014). Introduction. In S. Senier (Ed.), *Dawnland voices* (pp. 1–21). University of Nebraska Press.

Snyder, C. (2010). *Slavery in Indian country: The changing face of captivity in early America.* Harvard University Press.

Stannard, D. E. (1992). *American Holocaust: The conquest of the new world.* Oxford University Press.

Sterba, J. P. (1996). Understanding evil: American slavery, the holocaust, and the conquest of the American Indians. *Ethics, 106*(2), 424–448. doi:10.1086/233624

Suchet, M. (2007). Unraveling whiteness. *Psychoanalytic Dialogues, 17*(6), 867–887. doi:10.1080/10481880701703730

Tecumsah. (1999). Tecumsah. In P. Nabokov (Ed.), *Native American testimony: A chronicle of Indian-white relations from prophecy to the present, 1492–2000* (pp. 95–98). Penguin Books.

Watkins, M. (2016). *The social and political life of shame in the U.S. presidential election 2016*. Paper presented at the Massachusetts Institute for Psychoanalysis.

Wilson, E. (1987). Shame and the other: Reflections on the theme of shame in French psychoanalysis. In D. L. Nathanson (Ed.), *The many faces of shame* (pp. 162–194). Guilford Press.

Wilson, J. (1998). *The Earth shall weep: A history of Native America* (p. 55). Grove Press.

Wurmser, L. (1987). Shame: The veiled companion of narcissism. In D. L. Nathanson (Ed.), *The many faces of shame* (pp. 64–93). Guilford Press.

## Chapter 7

# Don't Blame the Mirror for Your Ugly Face

## *A Russian Idiom*

## *Ofra Bloch*

"*Because you are not white*." There was nothing unusual about her response. This is what I often hear from Black patients when I ask them why they have chosen to engage in treatment with me. After such an exchange, I usually feel rather pleased that my new patient can easily recognize that I'm one of the "good guys" and not a descendant of her slave-owning oppressors.

Not this time. This time I had a different reaction. I imagined myself going down the street and encountering an African American who didn't recognize my accent or my first name as foreign. In my imagination, what this person might see was a white face like any other white face, imprinted with the map of chattel slavery. My patients' assumptions about my race have served as a hiding place in which I can avoid feelings of guilt and responsibility for the damage racism has done in this country. On the other hand, it has also contributed to my feeling that I am a perpetual outsider. I'm not a refugee, and I haven't been expelled from my home, yet even though I've lived in New York City for over 40 years, I still feel un-homed here and everywhere else, for that matter. However, awakening to my white skin and owning its meaning has made me realize the gains of avoidance inherent in my continued feeling of not belonging. I wonder about my own contribution to being in that permanent state and whether it's time I exercise a choice in the matter.

Back in the treatment room, the discussion with my African American patient turned into explorations of why she did not choose to work with an African American therapist. I could easily identify with her need not to be seen by a Black therapist, as it is very important for me not to be seen by

DOI: 10.4324/9781003265146-7

an Israeli therapist, who, based on the sense of familiarity and intimacy that exists among Israelis, might use projections and pigeonhole me. Owning my whiteness has affected my clinical practice in a different way—I have become more able to recognize my patients' own hiding places from the truths about racism and oppression of the past and in the present, whether in the US, Israel, or elsewhere, and try to help process it together.

In this chapter, I will try to bring to light the journey I have taken to own my whiteness and to understand that by virtue of that whiteness, I am an implicated subject who has benefitted from the wrongs done to Blacks and other people of color in this country. In order to arrive at this point, I had to face my own part, while I still lived in Israel, in being a perpetrator, and in the years since, my own implication—as a Jew, an Israeli citizen, a US citizen, and a human being—in crimes committed by Israel against the Palestinian people.

This specific encounter with my patient happened in 2018, when I was in the final stages of editing my documentary film *Afterward*, and my response had everything to do with my reflections before, during and after the production process. Six years earlier, after making two documentaries about second-generation survivors who processed the Holocaust trauma through their art, I realized that I had never given any thought to the impact of the Holocaust on the descendants of German perpetrators. I wanted to talk to Germans face-to-face and perhaps rid myself of the hate and fear I was raised to feel toward them, even if these subjects belonged to a generation who had done nothing other than having forebears who tried to kill my people. I set out to make a documentary about how Germans of today experience the presence of the past in their daily lives. I had no idea that I was about to embark on a journey that would turn into my own personal analysis and eventually lead me to talk face-to-face with Palestinians, the other group of "others" whom I was raised to fear and hate. There was no way I could have imagined that the camera would later turn on me. I didn't originally plan to be a subject in the film, and the Palestinians were not originally part of my film, but my unconscious took over in mysterious ways and led me along bumpy back alleyways to where I was viewed as a victim by the Germans and as a victimizer by the Palestinians. In hindsight, I realized that I needed first to encounter the Germans and evacuate the space in my mind, which was filled with an ongoing terror and dread of them, so I could move away from gazing constantly backward at the traumas of the past and instead allow my focus to shift to the present traumatic reality of the Palestinians.

*Afterward* began screening in festivals and theaters, and the documentary received criticism by some as "not pro-Palestinian enough" and by others as "anti-Israeli." There were even those who refused to watch it on principle, based on such expectations. In some way, I thought that I must have done something right if people representing completely opposite political orientations were all angry with me. After all, I didn't make a film about "sides." And while making the film, I realized that looking at ourselves through the lens of the victim-victimizer binary creates an airless collapsible space. More truthfully, evil resides in all of us, with the potential for us to become, under certain conditions, both victim *and* victimizer. Michael Rothberg offers the concept of the "implicated subject" to aid in creating a figure, beyond those concepts, of a subject who, either consciously or unconsciously, remains distant from knowledge through denial and avoidance and benefits from the privileges inherent in systems of injustice and inequality, thus reproducing the conditions necessary for the continued oppression (Rothberg, 2019).

*Afterward* ended up being about my own struggle to navigate the complexity of the transgenerational victim-victimizer matrix without a script, literally and figuratively. The seven years I worked on the documentary enabled me to enter a state of reflective self-awareness, of being both subject and object, participant and observer, guilty and/or implicated. It allowed me to embrace, sometimes begrudgingly, my own complicity and responsibility and comprehend on a deeper level my implication as well. I hope that recognizing it will lead me to become a political subject who can break out of the realm of implication and join others in active forms of resistance to structures of violence and exploitation (Rothberg, 2019).

The making of *Afterward* has accelerated my awakening to who I am in the world. This journey was not about a change in my political views concerning the Israeli-Palestinian conflict, which have been firmly leftist since 1968. It was about getting underneath ideology, through the maze of historical narratives, beyond membership in an exclusive tribe, and actually meeting the gaze in people's eyes that could eliminate my distance from the events that informed my being. I did not choose the privilege of ignorance; in a way, it was imposed on me. I grew up in a home that prevented my exposure to political ideology. I was not permitted to join a political youth movement because my parents feared that I would be brainwashed. They read their newspaper in English, which I was unable to read as a child and because there was no Israeli TV broadcasting until 1966, my exposure to the news was limited to the state-regulated radio. However, when I look back, my political roots began way back in childhood when I went through a variety of experiences, some of them as a child-witness and later as an adult, unaware of the impact of my own involvement, or lack of involvement, on others.

I was recently asked how I identify myself. I'm not fond of categories, yet I answered, "I'm an implicated Israeli ex-pat and a captive Jew." A captive Jew because as long as there is anti-Semitism in the world, it is others who impose on me a Jewish identity, and I yearn for the day when I can choose to be Jewish (or not) out of my own free will and not based on the gaze of others.

In order to explain being an implicated Israeli ex-pat, I have to go back to my own beginning as a "perpetrator in the making." My story is not unique, and in a sense, that is what makes it interesting: everyone can find himself or herself participating under certain conditions in evildoing. I want to examine closely the set design of the theater of my childhood, which includes the many myths and untruths that supplied the narrative. I also need to elucidate how I've since become an implicated Jew in the diaspora. I choose to add the term "implicated" to my identity not because it is a permanent state of being like the other parts of my identity, but because I want it to serve as a constant reminder of my political and moral accountability in the world.

It's 1956. I live in Jerusalem. What do I know?

I know that there is a war.

Did I hear about it from my mother when I helped her glue long strips of paper on the windows to prevent the glass from shattering if we were bombed? Did I deduce it when my mother explained to me that we needed to save on electricity as she warmed water for my bath on the primus stove? Or perhaps it was my father who told me about it when he returned home and explained that during the war he went through training as a medic. All the while, the children in my second-grade class all knew the victory song even before the battle had begun. The song compared the end of the war in Sinai to the moment when God revealed himself to Moses through a burning bush. I remember humming the song with excitement.

Years later I learn that on October 29, 1956, the first day of the Sinai War, the Kfar Qasim massacre took place when Israeli Border Police killed 49 Palestinian civilians returning to their village from work; a curfew had been imposed earlier in the day, unbeknownst to them.

I am six years old, and I discover that there is no God. I catch my father drinking the glass of wine we left for Elijah the prophet after the Passover Seder. I look at my father, and he says nothing. Neither do I.

I'm eight years old. It is a special day filled with celebrations. I'm observing the 1958 Independence Day Parade through the window of my father's office. A lot of soldiers in different uniforms are marching in rows below, and I see tanks for the first time in my life. I know that we are not allowed to have planes in the sky. Jordan has a Jerusalem of its own across the walls, and if the planes cross the border in the sky, there can be war.

I know that my pioneer grandparents immigrated to Palestine in the early 20th century, when it was still part of the Ottoman Empire. Some of them escaped pogroms in Lithuania and Ukraine, arriving in Palestine, hoping to build a safe homeland for the Jews. Still, others ran away from poverty in Poland to sweatshops in New York City and landed in Canada but chose to pursue the Jewish renaissance in Palestine in 1925. I was told that they arrived in a land empty of inhabitants and set out to make the desert bloom.

I'm still in elementary school, and I'm learning that Zionism was a liberation movement in response to anti-Semitism. I hear that there is "the Jewish problem" in the world and that Zionism is seeking to build a safe home for the Jews in their ancestral land. Another branch of Zionism emphasizes the idea of Jewish revival after periods of intellectual decline and strong assimilation, something that can only happen in the biblical land promised to the Jews by the Almighty.

I'm told that most of the Palestinians who lived within the State of Israel in 1948 ended up running away out of fear. Fear was certainly a factor in the mass flight after the Deir Yassin massacre in April 1948, which was the first of numerous incidents in which Jewish fighters killed Palestinian civilians. It is only when I reach adulthood that I am able to comprehend that when new life for Jews began on that land, about 750,000 Palestinians were uprooted and not allowed to return. The extent of the transfer plans that were made before the State of Israel was officially established has only recently been revealed with the opening of certain state archives.

I'm fifteen years old, and I walk by the border that cuts through Jerusalem, separating it into two. I can see Israeli and Jordanian soldiers patrolling and children playing in the streets. I spot the boarded-up windows in the apartment building where my parents' friend Masha lives. She is fearful of stray bullets. I reach the Notre Dame monastery, which is located on the border facing no man's land, and climb to the roof, from where I can see Palestinians going about their daily lives, exactly like we Israelis do on our side of town. They look so far away and out of reach.

I notice graffiti on the wall across the street, "Revoke the Martial Law," and I don't know what it means. "What is martial law?" I ask and do not receive an answer. Later on, I discover that the Palestinians who are citizens of Israel lived under martial law from 1948 to 1966, which imposed on them travel restrictions and therefore impacted their access to work, commerce, health care, education, and personal relationships. I had met only a few Palestinians during those years. My father had a few Palestinian friends who worked in the local YMCA, where he played tennis. In addition, we used to frequent the restaurant in the neighboring Palestinian village of Abu Gosh when we wanted to escape eating matzos during Passover. At that time, they were not referred to as Palestinians but rather as Arabs, reflecting the denial common at that time and expressed by the Israeli prime minister Golda Meir, in an interview, that there was no such thing as Palestinians. It was only in the late 1970s that one could hear a reference to Palestinians as those who resided in the occupied territories as distinguished from Arabs who resided within the State of Israel. It was during those years that I had a chance to meet more Palestinians and to discover the horrific conditions of the infrastructure in many of their villages, which had sewage running in the streets. Later on, when I mention this in conversations with other Israelis in New York, I'm met with disbelief.

Even today, in 2021, the right to claim previously owned properties is allowed only to Jews under the Absentee Property Act. Palestinians don't hold the same right to claim their old properties, which are often inhabited by Jews. It is quite an irony that when Poland recently passed a law that puts limitations on the return of properties confiscated during the Nazi occupation and then by the communist ruling party, the State of Israel, ignoring its own hypocrisy, criticized Poland harshly.

The State-Nation Law gives the right of self-determination only to Israeli Jews and establishes the goal of Jewish settlement as a national value, resulting in Palestinian citizens having a status inferior to Jewish citizens by law. There has been an effective freeze on family reunification for Palestinians who were abroad when the 1967 occupation began. The Palestinians who live in Israel face mass residency revocations or restrictions, large-scale land confiscations, and categorical denials of building permits.

From early on, I am told that we, the Jewish people, are the "chosen people" and therefore a beacon of light to the world. I believe wholeheartedly that I am living in a society based on just and equal rights. After all, they tell me this wherever I go.

It takes me longer to realize that the still prevailing myth of the "chosen people" has served to create for Israeli Jews a frame of superiority toward the Palestinians. The tears of a grieving Palestinian mother are not viewed as equal to the tears of an Jewish Israeli mother. It is a concept that breeds indifference to the plight of others and causes a profound lack of empathy.

It was hard for me to realize that an unconscious part of me continued to believe in the myth of the chosen people. My own reaction upon hearing about Mohammad Abu Khdir, a Palestinian teenager who was burned alive by Jews, in apparent retaliation for the murder of four Jewish boys, was of total horror but also shock. I was unable to imagine that Jews, who carry vivid memories of being burned by fire throughout history, were capable of such atrocities.

When I look back, I can point to one distinct moment in my childhood when my father said something that broke the spell and planted a seed of doubt about the reality that surrounded me.

It is the early 1950s, and I often listen to radio announcements about border infiltrations by Palestinian fedayeen and about Israeli retaliations against them. I hear Israel claimed that these fedayeen attacks are reasons to join in the 1956 Sinai Campaign. Later, in my 30s, I discover that the early Palestinian infiltrations were motivated by economic considerations as they tried to return to their homes and land. Israel adopted a dogged position to prevent their return and in retaliation attacked civilians. After a notorious Israeli attack in October 1953 on the Jordanian village of Qibya, which killed 70 Palestinians, Israel shifted its policy toward striking military targets instead of civilians in response to border incidents.

My father had no way of knowing any of that when he shared with me that he wondered whether the government of Israel was initiating those border incidents in order to distract Israelis from various economic crises. I vividly remember him looking straight into my eight-year-old eyes and saying, "Don't ever believe everything you read in the newspapers!" I'm sure he didn't realize that he had just caused the first crack in my mirror, planting that seed of disbelief in what is being presented to me by others.

It's June 5, 1967, my last day of high school. Israel launches preemptive airstrikes against Egyptian airfields, and we debate with our history teacher whether Jordan will attack us in retaliation. As we talk, a siren goes off, and the first bombs land on Jerusalem. When there is a pause in the bombing, my father arrives at school and picks me and a few of my friends up in his car and takes us home. I spend the day and the following night in a shelter underneath my home. One Jordanian bomb lands in my building's courtyard. I'm scared but say nothing. Nobody does, as if what is going on is totally normal.

During the tense and anxious period before the 1967 war, after Egypt's president removes the UN Peace Force from the Sinai and closes the Straits of Tiran to the passage of Israeli ships, we are glued with mounting anxiety to our TVs, watching the Egyptian army marching. Radio Cairo promises for quite some time that all the Jews will be thrown into the sea. Everybody expresses fear that a second Holocaust is imminent. I am worried because I don't know how to swim. Six days later, Israel conquers East Jerusalem, the Old City, and all of the West Bank from Jordan, along with the Golan Heights from Syria and the Sinai Peninsula and Gaza from Egypt. The joy at our victory and the euphoria that follows knows no bounds.

Shortly thereafter, I join the Israeli army. I do my service during the War of Attrition—between 1968 and 1970—and am assigned to the artillery unit of the Southern Command, which is involved in duels with the Egyptian army. I am given a high-security clerical job that involves typing the coordinates of the Egyptian artillery targets, which are provided by daily aerial photographs. This was is happening away from the spotlight and seems to continue without an end in sight. There was nothing out of the ordinary about my path. It was a clear continuation of a common transition from kindergarten to elementary school to high school and then from high school to mandatory army service. I managed to be rebellious throughout this course, expressing that spirit by breaking rules and regulations. At no point do I ask questions about the purpose and meaning of my army service. I am convinced that I am here to defend the right of Israel to exist and provide protection from the next Holocaust that is planned by the Arab countries surrounding Israel. Yet, I'm unable to envision that the shells shot from our cannons are likely to hurt human beings, who happened to be soldiers like me. My imagination goes only as far as destroying their cannons that shoot at our soldiers. I have the mind of an 18-year-old, lacking the intellectual or emotional depth needed to truly appreciate and process the multilayered reality that surrounds me. It is a structured and regimented environment and yet, paradoxically, I feel such a sense of freedom, not unlike American young adults who leave home for college, only that in my case, there is a substantial loss of life on a daily basis for both sides.

I form strong friendships in my army unit that have lasted to the present. One day, I have coffee with my close friend Leah. I take small sips and turn to her and state, as if it were obvious, "I can't wait for Israel to return the Occupied Territories to Jordan." I barely manage to finish the sentence when she shoots back, "We will never return the Liberated Territories." We both gaze at each other in silent astonishment as we realize that a new element has invaded our friendship. Fifty-three years later, we still don't know how to go about sorting out our opposing political views.

The 1973 War, also known as the Yom Kippur War, feels like a continuation of the Six-Day War, but with a different flavor. Israel is caught by surprise on the holiest day of the Jewish year, and the fear we feel during that war isn't a response to enemy propaganda but rather to the realities reported by our own leaders. The very same Moshe Dayan who once said that it's better to have Sharm el-Sheikh (the tip of the Sinai Peninsula) without peace than to have peace without Sharm el-Sheikh, looks gray and exhausted as he gravely announces that Israel might be facing the destruction of the Third Temple.

Wars are a unique and special time in Israel in terms of the atmosphere. There is a "during" phase and there is an "after" phase. I go back in time and look around. There are hardly any men in sight. There is a weird cheerfulness among the women and children, as if we are celebrating the occasion. We cook lots of food, although nobody seems to have an appetite and there is an abundance of joy, which is associated with feelings of unity and confidence that this war is going to be as short as the previous one and that we'll emerge victorious as well. Bad news about failures on the battlefields and about distressed besieged soldiers and the increasing number of dead and wounded Israeli soldiers begins to filter in. I'm not sure what I'm feeling and whether it has a name. Everybody is volunteering to help keep our little universe going. I volunteer in the Little Gallery, an art gallery/café, and along with some friends keep the place open until the owner returns home. It becomes a hub for soldiers returning from the war and for foreign correspondents. After the war, I'm afraid to call on friends and find out they lost a family member. The list of 2,656 names of dead soldiers is published. It doesn't include the names of the 7,000+ wounded. For a country with a population of approximately three million, these numbers are a lot. I shed tears and mourn the loss of so many lives, many of them belonging to my generation and some of whom I knew personally.

It is still hard to describe my emotional experience during that war and the years that followed. Time was passing too slowly and too fast at the same time, and there is a numbness that I can't pierce through. Sometimes I get a glimpse of my very deep fear of extinction that I have experienced especially in the first two weeks of the war, yet at other times, I can't be sure I was even there.

A few decades after the end of the 1973 War, I learn along with everybody else that the war, which was regarded as a no-choice war, was actually a war of choice, the choice of Israel's prime minister Golda Meir and her advisers. All efforts to reach a peace agreement failed, including President Sadat's initiative in 1971, because Golda Meir was unwilling to negotiate with the Egyptians, fearing that a peace agreement with them might lead to the return of the territories that Israel occupied in 1967.

I view this as the last big lie in a long series of lies that I have been exposed to since childhood, which have eventually been unearthed but often too late. I can easily imagine my father looking into my eyes in silence and hear his unspoken words: "I told you so." But of course, there is nothing victorious about his being right. It is a visceral feeling that has been building up throughout the years: that there is no one truth that I can hold onto or rely on.

The atmosphere of the following years is one of constant anxiety. Terrorist attacks kept happening as if without a pause: bombs explode in busses, markets, and cafés, killing civilians, including women and children, and hostages are taken as a bargaining chip for the release of political prisoners. I can remember the details of so many of these incidents, like the abduction and murder of the Israeli athletes at the 1972 Olympic Games in Munich. It is hard to forget the tension surrounding the 1976 hijacking of an Air France plane on a flight from Israel to Paris with 248 passengers aboard. Once it landed in Entebbe, Uganda, the non-Israeli passengers are released, and 94 Israelis, along with the 12-member crew, are kept as hostages. The Entebbe Operation, led by Israel, rescued 102 of them. It is hard to forget the horror in the town of Nahariya in 1979, when a father was kidnapped from his home along with his four-year-old daughter. The father is murdered and his daughter's skull smashed with a rock from the beach. Her mother, who was hiding in the bedroom crawlspace, accidentally suffocates her two-year-old daughter in an attempt to keep her quiet so they wouldn't be discovered.

I remember these events vividly, yet my internal emotional reaction is dissociated. It is as if it is locked away and the key is missing. What I do remember is a dark humor conversation with my roommate following one particular act of terrorism. It is 1974. At a school building in the town of Ma'alot, in the north of Israel, 105 schoolchildren and ten adults are held hostage for two days by members of the Popular Front for the Liberation of Palestine (PFLP), who are demanding the release of Palestinian prisoners. Israel will not negotiate with terrorists and an Israeli commando unit storms the school building. The hostage-takers react with gunshots and grenades, killing 25 hostages, including 22 children.

My roommate and I joke and consider practicing jumping out of the window of our first-floor apartment in preparation for the possibility that terrorists might try to take over our apartment. We even make a pact that in case one of us is held hostage, the other one will do everything possible to convince the Israeli government to negotiate in our particular case with the terrorists.

I leave Israel in 1980 and am spared more experiences of war, scud missiles, suicide bombings, stabbing and killings, the murder of children and babies, rockets aimed at civilians, and balloon bombs that burn entire fields. However, my distance in miles from Israel hasn't diminished my emotional engagement with every piece of news from there. After decades of life in New York, that particular anxiety about possible bombs isn't out of my system and I still freeze and get out of breath at the sight of an unattended package. The experience of living a double life continues to this day.

By the time of the first Lebanon War in 1982, I am no longer living in Israel. Instead, I watch in shock images of the Sabra and Shatila Massacre on American TV. The Lebanese Christian right-wing militia storm these refugee camps, and in the course of two days and within plain sight of the Israeli forces surrounding them, they massacre their Palestinian inhabitants (estimated between 500 and 3,500). Watching this event along with my Holocaust survivor husband takes us back to the everlasting horror of the Holocaust, and we realize in an unequivocal way that descendants of victims of that trauma are enacting through role reversal in the present the role of the participant-observer. We speak through tears of devastation, but words fail to describe the heavy responsibility we felt as witnesses, and our shame as bystanders.

In April 2016, I conducted an interview with the Palestinian psychiatrist and psychotherapist Dr. Samah Jabr for my documentary *Afterward*. I am trying to face those I was raised to hate and fear in order to better understand the identity-making narratives of the Holocaust and the Nakba. During the interview, Dr. Jabr shares an observation: "Whenever the Palestinians want to discuss their acute predicament, their acute problems in life, their difficulties with the Occupation, the history of the Holocaust is being brought up to silence them, to make them understand that there is nothing comparable to the Holocaust. The history of the Holocaust is silencing the world."

I point out that Israeli society has continued to suffer from PTSD symptoms related to the Holocaust and that Israeli leadership in recent years has made cynical use of the Holocaust. They have not only cheapened the memories of the Holocaust but have also manipulated the situation by amplifying the threats by Iran and Hamas to destroy Israel, thus creating a permanent state of hypervigilance and paranoia. Later, I regretted that I didn't tell her that although those threats seem very real, Israel is also a very strong military power and is capable of defending itself.

I am very aware of my inclination to do exactly what Dr. Jabr complains about, but not for the purpose of silencing her or privileging Jewish pain, or in order to justify the Nakba and the Occupation, but because I'm convinced that it is the constant fear of annihilation that operates like non-extinguished kindling in the fireplace, ready to be ignited, that prevents many Israeli Jews from seeing and hearing the Palestinian other. I fight my urge to share with Dr. Jabr how it felt growing up in the shadow of the Holocaust, experiencing it as an ongoing event that showed no sign of lessening its grip. I want to share with her that I was introduced to the Holocaust when I was five years old through jokes told by my great uncle Binyamin about the years he spent in concentration camps. In his stories he used to cut the hair of Germans officers and make fun of them. I remember laughing along with him as he joyfully imitated them being tricked by him in various ways. My mother shared with me shortly afterward that Binyamin had lost his wife and two children in that camp. Perhaps that was my first encounter with affect not being congruent with a traumatic experience. Before his death, Binyamin would complain of having a taste of ashes in his mouth.

How can I explain to anyone the Holocaust ABC game we used to play as children, which was based on the first letter of the various concentration camps? How can I describe listening daily to the radio program *Search Bureau for Missing Relatives*, along with everybody who didn't lose hope of discovering relatives who somehow survived? I want to tell her about the horrific testimonies I heard during the Eichmann Trial when I was 11, about how I started to read everything I could about the Holocaust and never stopped, about the recurring nightmares. I want to describe the Holocaust humor that has developed in recent years and the effect of the Holocaust on language association and hidden meanings, like in the example of words like "train" or "twins." I want to say all this, but I don't.

I don't want to seek empathy from the oppressed for her oppressor or expect her to spend time and energy trying to understand the emotional undercurrents of the Israeli psyche. I don't feel entitled to make her listen to me, at least not until I hear and understand the essence of the Palestinian pain. My thinking is influenced by Jessica Benjamin's ideas about the need for two-way directionality of acknowledgment and recognition between subjects and about the creation of the "third", as a mental space in which inter-subjective relatedness can be created through the surrender and acceptance of the differences and separateness of the other (Benjamin, 2013). My wish to share my experiences is not an attempt to compete for the title of biggest victim, deny the cynical use of the memory of the Holocaust to justify unchecked oppression and silence criticism, or provide an excuse for what is done to the Palestinians. That wish is based on my conviction that comprehending the mind of the Israeli Jew can shed light on the reason that many Israelis buy into the mantra that "there is no partner for peace." It is because they live in a sort of survival mode where no amount of military power is going to lower their level of existential fear.

Another aspect of the intergenerational transference of Holocaust trauma is the transference of shame. During the Holocaust, Jewish resistance fighters urged Jews to rise up and not "be led like sheep to the slaughter." It's not for nothing that when the Holocaust Memorial Day was established in Israel, it was officially named the Holocaust and Heroism Memorial Day. The message was clear: the only way to guarantee "never again" was by the sword. Until the Eichmann trial, the Holocaust was not discussed openly. The Zionist leaders wanted to raise in the newly established State of Israel a new kind of Jew, one who wouldn't succumb to his enemies and never cease fighting. Weakness was frowned upon.

After the Holocaust, there were allegations that the Germans had manufactured soap from the human fat of dead Jews. Years later, Israel absorbed many European immigrant children who came from communist countries. They were rather pale and not nearly as muscular as we, Israeli-born children, who were deeply tanned and imagined ourselves to be very powerful because of our skin tone. Their light shade seemed like evidence of weakness, perhaps a residue of the passivity of their parents, who didn't resist their perpetrators. We called them "soap" because that was what their parents allowed themselves to become.

Transgenerational shame has played a major role in the development of a culture dedicated to fighting and glorifying sacrifice, creating blindness to the suffering inflicted on the Palestinians. The post-Holocaust generations continue to hold tight to the identity of victim, all the while claiming moral superiority because of it. I wonder whether that shame might also prevent them from admitting that in order to have a land to which they are always allowed entry, they have created an open-door policy only for Jews, while excluding the Palestinians who have a rich history on that very same land.

Some Jews tend to bring up anti-Semitism not only when the Palestinian predicament is discussed but also when the suffering of any group is being mentioned, including that of African Americans in the US. There seems to be a desperate need for exclusivity, accompanied by a fear that any other traumatic group narrative might diminish or belittle the magnitude of the Holocaust.

The governments of Israel take the lessons of the Holocaust to mean that their main goal is survival. They believe that if they want to remain alive, their only option is to develop the strongest army possible and never cease to fight. I remember meeting groups of Jewish Israeli teenagers on a visit to the labor and death camps in Poland. A year before they will be drafted into the army, they walk the paths of Auschwitz-Birkenau wrapped in the Israeli flag, singing, "The people of Israel are alive." The connection is obvious, and the message that is delivered is that soon it is going to be their turn to fight for Israel's survival and live forever by the sword. The sanctity and glorification of death, the ultimate sacrifice for one's country and its people, is part of their culture and is expressed between the lines.

What chance do they have to use a different lens to view and understand the reality that surrounds them in order to explore other options short of war? It is probably naïve of me to continue to believe that it is still possible for Israel to change the music of the military march and allow for different lessons to be gleaned from the Holocaust.

And what were my options? Going to demonstrations and having political arguments in cafes did not require much courage. My protest against the Occupation was limited to a self-imposed ban on traveling to the West Bank, East Jerusalem, and the Old City. But looking back, I wonder if my unconscious was attempting to avoid learning about the Palestinians' reality, opting instead to remain ignorant under the guise of pure protest. Was I hiding behind my unconscious choice of selective blindness in order to avoid gazing into the reality that was staring me in the face?

Avoiding knowledge can be useful to the participant bystanders. It makes me think of a particular day in Warsaw in April 1943. Czeslaw Milosz, the Polish poet, was on his way to visit his friend, the writer Jerzy Andrzejewski, when he passed by the burning ghetto. There was a Ferris wheel just outside the ghetto walls, and Milosz saw the smiling faces of those riding it as it circled up and down, exposing them to the burning ghetto. When he arrived at his friend's home, he wrote the poem "Campo dei Fiori," in which he describes how he was reminded of that lively market square in Rome, filled with stalls of fruits and vegetables and flowers, where the Inquisition burned to death Giordano Bruno because he refused to recant his heretical ideas. Milosz compared the people of Rome to the people of Warsaw, who continued to laugh and make love and avoided taking in the horror. Those riders on the Ferris wheel ignored the loneliness of the dying, allowing the horror to fade into oblivion even before the ghetto's flames died down.

Is it really possible to live in Israel and not know? There is a component of choice in denying the reality of the Palestinians, but reality can't be avoided forever. When I made the decision to film in the Occupied Territories and crossed the Qalandia checkpoint, I was forced to face the consequences of my own mental act of avoidance, my unconscious effort of using denial. It didn't matter that I was already convinced, immediately after the end of the 1967 War, that the time was perfect already then for peace negotiations. As my hopes and beliefs diminished, I too joined the Occupation forces by making an unconscious effort not to see what I knew was done in my name.

I hear the pained questions repeated by many Jews around the world: Why Israel? Why is it singled out from other nations that do as much harm? Why is there so much focus on the Israeli-Palestinian conflict? These reactions dishearten me. Yes, it is likely true that some critique is laced with conscious or subconscious anti-Semitism. But this is an ethically fraught rebuttal. Implicit in their questions, it seems to me, is that the existence of anti-Semitism excuses other immoral behavior.

The tendency to avoid responsibility takes another form in the strains of self-righteous thought within Israel, a country that likes to wave its ethical flag high above all others. A country that even refers to its armed forces as "the most moral army in the world." Underneath this remains the ancient story of a self-described chosen people, a story seemingly proven true through modern achievements while simultaneously cloaked in a narrative of victimhood. This belief in one's inherent moral superiority, combined with the feeling of having an eternal license to act in whatever way is deemed necessary given prior dangers, creates a recipe for blindness as they drift increasingly into morally inexcusable actions.

July 2021—I drink my morning coffee while reading the Israeli newspaper *Ha'aretz*.

Israel Prison Service refuses to let Khalida Jarrar, who is serving a two-year sentence for being a member of the Popular Front for the Liberation of Palestine, attend the funeral of her daughter Suha, a 31-year-old human rights activist, who died of a cardiac arrest, even though she was supposed to be released from jail in four months.

The IDF blows up the family home of a Palestinian accused of, but not yet convicted of, murdering an Israeli after the High Court rejected a petition against the house's demolition. The idea behind this collective punishment (which is illegal according to international law) is that it serves as a deterrent. When I see the photos of innocent children witnessing their homes being demolished, I wonder whether this action will end up encouraging these children, when they reach adulthood, to pick up arms and choose violent resistance.

I try to imagine the people who gave those orders. It isn't only that their thought process is distorted, but that they must have a stone for a heart.

Other images in the newspapers catch my eye during this month: Haifa, the third largest city in Israel, has been invaded by wild pigs that control the city's streets. The irony of the wild pig, an animal with a particular negative connection of impurity for both Jews and Muslims, doesn't escape me. It feels as if I am personally witnessing the 2021 Israeli allegory of George Orwell's *Animal Farm*. After all, at the very beginning, I was told that Israel was a dream come true–a country based on liberty, justice, and equality for all its citizens–only to find out later that the Palestinians living within the State of Israel were second-class citizens and the Palestinians living in the Occupied Territories live in an apartheid state. The sight of the pigs roaming the streets makes me think of how seemingly noble ideals, which everyone ostensibly believes, dissipate when human beings reveal their pig-selves.

And then, on July 19, 2021, Ben & Jerry announce that they are ending sales of their ice cream to Israeli settlements in the West Bank. The two Jewish co-founders of the company made a principled distinction between sovereign Israel and the Israeli settlements in the Occupied West Bank because the settlements are inconsistent with their values. The decision shakes the Israeli public and its leaders and is referred to as "economic terrorism by self-hating Jews," hinting that this act is tinted with anti-Semitic hues. I could sense a different kind of panic than the usual reaction in Israel to violent acts of resistance. It is much harder to fight against nonviolent activity, the sort used by the Boycott, Divestment, and Sanctions (BDS) movement that is gaining popularity around the globe.

In contrast, I understand this as evidence of two American Jews comprehending their own implication in the Israeli Occupation and considering what that should compel them to do, what ability they have to effect change, even through the vehicle of something as seemingly trivial as ice cream.

Claiming my whiteness has allowed me to confront that I am a beneficiary of the prevailing racism in this country. When I visited the US for the first time in 1974, I did not imagine that I would end up immigrating and becoming a citizen. I learned about this country through Damon Runyon's stories and from my father's reminiscences about his university days in Philadelphia, the Great Depression, and the New Deal. When he sang, "Say, buddy, can you spare a dime?" I thought I could smell America. On the flight over, I read James Baldwin's *Another Country*, and my view of America became more nuanced and complex. During my four-month cross-country trip, I met Americans from all walks of life. I remember feeling proud when I heard about the major role of Jewish activists in the civil rights movement and feeling ashamed when I came back to New York in 1980, and heard about the racist behavior of some Jewish landlords in New York City. Thinking in such binary terms speaks to my own limitations, but when I read about the action taken by Ben & Jerry, I regress and feel for a second the taste of that old pride.

My own realization that I'm implicated in the murder of Abir Aramin in Palestine and George Floyd in the US doesn't end there and is also experienced through my being part of a universe that is unable to act together for the common interests of everyone. Nationalistic goals stand in the way of universalism; otherwise, how can Israel explain its initial decision to send its surplus COVID-19 vaccines to countries that could potentially transfer their embassies to Jerusalem instead of distributing them to the Palestinians who live under their occupation in the West Bank or under Israel's imposed siege in Gaza? By the same token, the promise of globalization has not stopped the denial of the epidemiological connection we all have with each other and does not interfere with the choice of rich countries not to provide vaccines to poorer countries, allowing the continued spread of the virus and the potential development of more dangerous variants of COVID-19.

The search for meaning in my journey of self-reflection is paved with landmarks of gazes. Gazing twice into my father's eyes in my childhood, I discover there is no God and that I'm directed to question everything. This is only the beginning of my growing curiosity. During the filming of *Afterward*, I'm privileged to encounter gazes of German and Palestinian subjects that reached me on a very deep level. I experience intimate acts of personal recognition and am seen in a new way; I feel the non-personal hate of the oppressed, and although I understand why and accept it, it scares me; I discover that my Jewish identity is still a reflection in someone else's eyes and not my own choice; I witness the love-hate relationship of the descendants of perpetrators with their parents and I don't want to trade places with them; I see the memory of landscapes in people's eyes along with the human void left behind that new history cannot hide or bury.

During this journey, I face ambiguity and feel ambivalent on so many occasions but try not to fight it. Walking through the same street of the Old City of Jerusalem, a week after an Israeli Jew is stabbed to death, I feel anger about the presence of armed soldiers everywhere, along with the wish for their protective presence. The wall of the Aida refugee camp is filled with stenciled portraits of Palestinians who took up arms to resist the Israeli Occupation. Jewish Israelis call them terrorists, and Palestinians refer to them as freedom fighters. Looking closely at their faces, I attempt to understand the despair that brought them to choose violent resistance. At the same time, I want to look them in the eye and say, "You killed my people." My conflicted state is also part of the story.

Yet there is one gaze that is hard for me to meet, the gaze of Bassam Aramin, the Palestinian peace activist whose ten-year-old daughter, Abir, was murdered by an Israeli soldier. We filmed this part of the interview in the playground in the West Bank built in Abir's memory by Combatant for Peace. I ask Bassam to tell me what happened to his daughter and when he begins to talk, it suddenly hits me like a ton of bricks. It's easy to think of "them" as those who killed Abir in the same way that it's convenient to blame the Jewish settlers as responsible for everything to do with the Occupation. Only suddenly, I am feeling acutely the "we" and the "I" and can no longer look straight into his eyes.

It is very hard to live one's life haunted by responsibility, shame, and guilt, but I don't want that sense of being implicated to ever leave me. I want it to challenge me and prevent me from drifting into passivity.

In the last scene of my documentary *Afterward*, I can be seen visiting my family home, which now serves as a mental health clinic and bears no resemblance to the environment I grew up in. But when I pass by my old bedroom's window, I discover that the almond tree across the street that used to blossom every year just in time for my birthday is gone, replaced by a concrete surface. As if from nowhere, I feel flooded with a profound, yet-to-be-named acute pain. It is only when I am back home in the editing room, viewing footage of the camera scanning my teary face, that I understand I was mourning the sweet and comfortable times of my childhood. Even though that period was laced with layers upon layers of lies, deception, and half-truths, it allowed me to buy into the myth and truly believe that I belonged with the right and the just.

What I see in the mirror is a white Jewish woman who has dual citizenship. I'm not seeking forgiveness for being an implicated subject; for a start, I hope to own it.

## Acknowledgments

I thank David Bloch, Adam Bloch, Omri Bloch, Ruth Fallenbaum, Sue Grand, Sarah Hill, Audrey Jacobson, and Sharon Zane for their insightful comments and encouragement.

## References

Benjamin, J. (2013, March). Intersubjectivity, thirdness, and mutual recognition . . . *icpla.edu*. Retrieved January 23, 2022, from https://icpla.edu/wp-content/uploads/2013/03/Benjamin-J.-2007-ICP-Presentation-Thirdness-present-send.pdf

Rothberg, M. (2019). *The implicated subject: Beyond victims and perpetrators.* Stanford University Press.

# Chapter 8

# The Complexity of Implication for Racial Minority Immigrants

*Pratyusha Tummala-Narra*

"I don't want to be canceled. So I just stay quiet. There's too much at stake." In our first psychotherapy session together, Jared, a 20-year-old Filipino American cis man, shares his experience of racism in college. He tells me that he has felt depressed and isolated amid the COVID-19 pandemic and that he has not been able to form stable friendships since beginning college. Soon after the pandemic spread in the United States, he became disillusioned with his racial position. While he had been cautioned about racism by his parents, he had always been told by people outside of his Filipino community that Asians are model minorities with privilege. Jared's family emigrated to the U.S. from the Philippines when he was four years old to escape poverty and political instability. As an only child, he wants to ensure that his parents, who are domestic workers, can finally attain financial stability. He stated, "I need my college degree and my whole family is depending on it." As our therapeutic work progressed over the course of a year, Jared shared his fears about white supremacy spreading across the nation and his fears of being associated with white racists when, in fact, he was the target of racism. The insurrection on January 6, 2021, led by supporters of Donald Trump terrified him, as he imagined a mob of angry white people assaulting him and his family, reminiscent of when he was assaulted by a white peer in high school. The recent video footage of older Asian people being harassed, beaten, and spat on by white and Black perpetrators while bystanders did nothing to help lingers in his mind. Jared has feared white and Black people on his college campus who have expressed racist attitudes against Asians and takes the strategy of "lying low," in other words remaining mostly invisible. Lying low entails not making mistakes in public, such as expressing

DOI: 10.4324/9781003265146-8

viewpoints that contradict his peers in his liberal, predominantly white college campus. It also means not speaking out against injustice suffered by other students of color on campus. In one session, he stated, "I try to say something or do something to help, but then you get judged every time. So I just keep to myself."

For Jared, being Filipino American reflects a complex matrix of experiences of marginalization, invisibility, and privilege, steeped in racial dynamics that have been created and perpetuated long before his family's migration to the U.S. On the one hand, he recognizes that he wants to support others (e.g., Black students) facing racism, but he feels that his voice does not matter. Being Asian American/AAPI poses challenges to his efforts, as some of his white and Black peers tell him that he is "white identified" and "not a real minority," words that cause deep pain for Jared. Rothberg (2019, p. 200) describes "complex implication" as follows:

> Implication comes in diverse forms: it describes beneficiaries and descendants, accomplices and perpetrators, and it can even attach to people who have had shattering experiences of trauma or victimization and are thus situated within "complex implication." He further proposes that we are all implicated in social injustice and must transfigure implication. Specifically, through transfiguring, one "opens the self to others—and to one's own otherness, prosthetic agency, and unacknowledged capacity to wound.
>
> (Rothberg, 2019, p. 201)

For Jared, there is a scarcity of spaces where he feels as though it is safe enough to open himself up to others, even as he empathizes from a distance.

In this chapter, I explore the complexity of implication for racial minority immigrants and its manifestations in psychoanalytic psychotherapy and education. I begin with the disavowal of race and non-Black/white racial dynamics in psychoanalysis, including within training institutions, and then discuss the complexity of privilege and marginalization for racial minority immigrants and their children. Additionally, I explore how we might move toward recognizing the challenges of being implicated subjects in psychoanalytic education and practice. I emphasize how racial trauma, in the context of family, community, and broader U.S. society, shapes how an individual comes to experience the self and the other as the perpetrator, the victim, the bystander, and the implicated subject at different moments. Clinical vignettes illustrate how these various self-states interplay in psychotherapy, particularly within the contemporary context as we contend with local and global crises, such as the COVID-19 pandemic, discrimination and violence, and mass displacement.

## Disavowal of Race

González and Peltz (2021, p. 410) recently noted a renewed interest in community psychoanalysis, stating that

> institutional psychoanalysis is having a moment of awareness: a coming of consciousness of buried parts of its more radical history, a recognition of the pernicious limitation of calcified perspectives, and a renewed attention to the voices of a marginalized analytic community of practitioners outside of its walls.

Indeed, since the 2016 presidential election of Donald Trump and, subsequently, the murder of George Floyd, engagement with issues of race and racism among psychoanalytic practitioners has been burgeoning. Scholars have emphasized the absence of diversity within psychoanalysis and the history of racism within psychoanalysis (Holmes, 2016; Powell, 2019) and have called for an interrogation of white supremacy within the psychoanalytic theory (Powell, 2019; Steele, 2021; Tummala-Narra, 2022). Steele (2021) describes the defensive reactions by many analysts in interrogating white supremacy within the American Psychoanalytic Association, where on panels on racism, white people rush to defend themselves rather than looking within, a reaction that is antithetical to the psychoanalytic process. Powell (2019) further describes the way in which analysts are silent bystanders when they remain silent not for the purpose of reflection but to rationalize and avoid deepening reflection and dialogue about race.

Several white psychoanalytic scholars have explicitly recognized the problem of disavowing race in the white analytic community (Anen, 2020; Benjamin, 2021; Grand, 2018; Harris, 2019). For example, Harris (2019, pp. 309–310) points to the "investment of white people in many projects of denial and historical amnesia" and the challenges of white people's "guiltiness," which is characterized by narcissism and anxiety, impeding mourning and reparation. She underscores the importance of white people immersing in intellectual and emotional labor required to unpack racism and how it is enacted among white people. Interestingly, she names the outrage felt by people of color who write about racism when their work is not being heard by white people. In other words, many white people remain bystanders to racism. Benjamin (2021) reminds us that connecting with the suffering of others is essential to repair in the face of collective trauma and recognizes herself as an implicated white American who occupies a privileged position. She describes the struggle to admit that one is implicated as a significant challenge to real efforts to connect with others' suffering. In particular, alternating between altruistic intentions and behaviors and defensive responses ripe with guilt and shame can render a sense of helplessness. Benjamin (2021) proposes that liberals must grapple with and overcome splitting that protects a personal sense of goodness and confront one's own implication and complicity in social injustice. Relatedly, Grand (2018) suggests that collective racial shame, while experienced as persecutory, can also awaken one's conscience and awareness of social pathology. In her perspective, racial shame can mobilize individuals and communities toward racial justice.

While scholarship on race by white and BIPOC psychoanalytic authors is critical to the journey of exploring and transfiguring implication, literature that closely examines complex implication within the experience of racial minorities remains scarce. Ironically, although the effects of racial trauma on people of color have been increasingly elaborated in our literature, there remains a notable gap between white practitioners' and BIPOC practitioners' experiences. BIPOC practitioners' experiences of being marginalized in their own training, practice, and supervision of others remain less visible in training institutions and professional organizations. We are often viewed as holding expertise in areas such race and immigration rather than practitioners with multiple clinical interests that may intersect with multicultural and social justice issues. Most often, in conversations about race, there is a focus on people of color who are victimized and white people as oppressors who need to examine their privilege. Inadvertently, we reproduce binary thinking about privilege and marginalization in the spirit of recognizing and repairing entrenched systemic racial injustice. It is important to note, however, that there are missing pieces in grappling with the complexity of race and racial trauma faced by people of color, which have consequences for our conceptualization of the implicated subject (Rothberg, 2019). Binary approaches to racism perpetuate the dehumanization of non-white and white people in ways that obstruct a real engagement with implication and, as Rothberg proposes, complex implication.

### Institutional Disavowal of Racism

In my experience of working in academic and clinical settings, the disavowal of racial dynamics and racism by an institution significantly contributes to racial enactments within training programs. This is the case even within liberally oriented programs that are idealized as safe spaces for dialogues on social justice. Yet there is often a disconnect between idealizing fantasies of institutions and faculty and the reality of race continuing to be a source of discomfort. For example, while an early career psychologist at a city-based hospital that prioritized long-term trauma-informed care for patients coping with severe distress and limited economic resources, I observed how the pressure to see more patients less frequently diminished the help provided to patients, not to mention the morale of staff and trainees. The hospital's mission of meeting the needs of underserved communities was further diminished by the growing emphasis on broader discipline-based policies emphasizing time-limited empirically supported treatments (e.g., American Psychological Association Clinical Practice Guideline for the treatment of PTSD in Adults, 2017). Such professional guidelines contribute to a demoralized context in which individual faculty and trainees carry the burden of providing care at the cost of their own economic security and mental health.

The lack of access to in-depth care for marginalized people has only become more entrenched during the COVID-19 pandemic. Mehta and Fauci (2021) recently described the challenges of providing care to traumatized adolescents in an inpatient treatment setting. They state, "For the youth who come to us with deep attachment traumas, the COVID-19 pandemic has been an earthquake, introducing yet another way in which their lives are in perpetual risk, and yet another way in which they feel unworthy of and unable to reach care, love and support" (Mehta & Fauci, 2021). They point to the problem of the closure and/or reduced capacity of residential and community-based treatment programs, which has left many adolescents waiting in and essentially feeling "stuck" in inpatient units. Mehta and Fauci (2021) note, "For patients with severe attachment traumas, this disruption left them feeling not only trapped, but also alone.

Given their histories, it felt personal and was proof of their greatest fear: no one really wanted them." The mental health professions' implication in the neglect of children and adolescents, particularly those who are socially marginalized, based on race, sexual orientation, immigration status, religion, gender identity, social class, and (dis)ability, is profound.

In a different training context, as a professor in a doctoral program in counseling psychology, I am among the faculty responsible for helping students learn how to conceptualize psychotherapy theory and practice. Our students experience immense pressure to see more patients, increase their productivity, and they work with patients coping with severe trauma and mental illness early in their training, rather than having the progressive, sequential, and developmentally appropriate training that should be offered in the training process. Our students ask what can they can do to help someone facing complex trauma and address sociocultural complexities in four to six sessions and how to help their patients manage relational disruptions when their patients have been repeatedly transferred from one therapist to the next. One can imagine that manualized treatments offer solace in the face of the anxiety faced by faculty and students under these circumstances. As a professor, I'm torn between offering my students what they wish for (a straightforward solution) and knowing that most mental health issues are far more complex for people than what we currently meet in mental health care. I have typically approached this dilemma by asking my students to consider that there is empirical evidence for treatments guided by various theoretical orientations and then ask them to consider the economic realities guiding access to treatment. Still, the work they are being asked to do runs counter to our program's social justice mission.

A program's self-perception is one that can inadvertently take its social justice mission for granted, particularly when faculty have been invested in multicultural psychology and social justice in their research and practice. Our students, though, have rightfully asked us to face our neglect of certain areas related to diversity and social justice, such as sexual orientation, gender identity, and intersectionality. Our international students and our Asian American students have shared more recently the microaggressions they face on and off campus. Increasingly, my graduate students ask for more complexity in our thinking about racial minority groups, and both racial minority and white students have shared their frustration with not being able to speak freely in class about their experiences. They most often share these experiences with me in private because they don't want to be perceived as offending someone else, and they don't want to be targeted/canceled by someone else. I want to underscore that these dynamics are not unique to any particular institution, but rather they are emblematic of broader societal tensions concerning marginalization and privilege.

In each of these training contexts, the institution's self-perception as only the good object impedes the possibility of self-reflection, particularly as it relates to implication. When we can see ourselves as doing only good, we are unable to see the racial pain in which we are implicated. Consequently, there is a lack of attention to the experience of people and communities less visible within the institution (e.g., Jared). Conversely, when an institution is perceived to be only a bad object (e.g., perpetrator), we are less able to see the complexity of the experience of white and non-white people and rather apt to externalize our own responsibility for social injustice. Therefore, we must move beyond binary thinking about racism, recognizing that we are all socialized with racial, ethnic, and religious stereotypes, and we all engage in ways that connect us to each other and harm each other. Moving beyond binary thinking about racism requires that we end academic and theoretical debates about whether race matters in psychotherapy and focus more on how it matters to the patient and the therapist and to institutional culture. Understanding how race matters requires respect for the complexity of human experiences, including marginalization and privilege, a task that is well suited for psychoanalytic conceptualization.

## Complexity of Marginalization and Privilege for Racial Minority Immigrants

Psychic experience is inherently intersectional as human beings are influenced by multiple social contexts (e.g., family, school, neighborhood, workplace, social media) in which interactions with significant people leave an indelible mark on identity (Belkin & White, 2020). Racial minority immigrants typically face traumatic and non-traumatic separations from loved ones and familiar cultural environments that shape their experiences in a new country throughout their lifespan, often involving a loss of sense of continuity (Boulanger, 2015). The process of immigration encompasses anxiety and mourning as one leaves familiar spaces and navigates acculturative stress, such as linguistic and cultural barriers and racism (Akhtar, 2011). Further, as noted by White (2015), acculturation can produce compartmentalization and dissociated self-states. It is a common experience for many immigrants and their children to unconsciously shift from one context to another without a sense that one has the opportunity to bridge the distinct experiences from each context. For example, a person whose heritage language is Spanish faces the challenge of both linguistically and culturally translating an emotional experience in a non-Spanish-speaking context (e.g., school, workplace).

Psychic shifting across contexts also involves racial dynamics. Most immigrants are unaware of the deep entrenchment of racial trauma in the United States. They may have heard about the legacy of slavery and genocide in the U.S., but typically have little knowledge about how historical traumas may impact their everyday life. The American myth of meritocracy assumes a color-blind approach that offers optimism for immigrants seeking better economic and educational opportunities and safer living conditions (Bhatia, 2020). Immigrant parents are most often unaware of the detrimental impact of racism on their children's and their own mental health and in securing the opportunities they had hoped for through migration. In fact, the expectation that their children will fare better than them in the U.S. with regard to educational opportunities and securing a sense of belonging is often diminished in the face of racism (Tummala-Narra, 2016). There is ample research indicating that racism-related stress has an even more significant impact on the second generation (US-born children of racial minority immigrants) and that the second generation suffers from worse educational and mental health outcomes as compared with the first generation (those who arrive to the U.S. as adults) (García Coll & Marks, 2012; Tummala-Narra, 2020). These findings suggest that growing up in the US as a racial minority person poses risks to one's health and one's sense of belonging in the broader mainstream context.

It is important to note that the psychic toll of racial trauma faced by racial minority immigrants is often minimized within and outside of one's ethnic and religious communities. Specifically, racism is sometimes viewed as a necessary cost incurred in immigration, a sacrifice one must tolerate in order to achieve a better sense of security for oneself and for one's family. Paradoxically, efforts to achieve the American Dream can result in disillusionment regarding one's sense of belonging and security when immigrants and their children are perceived to be perpetual foreigners regardless of the length of time lived in the U.S., immigration/documentation status, and/or national identity (Eng & Han, 2000; Tummala-Narra,

2020). Conflicts concerning belonging are not only rooted in contexts outside of one's home or ethnic or religious community but also within one's family or community. For instance, sexual orientation may be a stigmatized issue in a family or a church, and LGBTQ+ people may be alienated across these multiple contexts (Belkin, 2018).

The marginalization that occurs within immigrant communities in part reflects social frameworks that have been internalized in a heritage country or culture. I have previously written about the internalization of colorism and caste in South Asian immigrants' conceptions of social and economic status (Tummala-Narra, 2020). These pre-migration frameworks interact with racial hierarchies in the U.S. to create new understandings of racial dynamics. For example, an immigrant who believes that they hold a special status because they belong to a high caste or social class in the country of origin may feel superior to another immigrant who is associated with a lower caste or social class, even when both have similar incomes or racial positions in the U.S. Recently, while meeting with a community of refugees from Bhutan in Massachusetts regarding mental health and substance abuse concerns, I was struck by how some members refused to engage with fellow refugees from a lower-caste background. The frameworks for social position, in this case, while distinct from race, have profound implications for the support offered to community members with lower social status. At the same time, refugees who hold either higher or lower social status within their ethnic community suffer alienation and invisibility within broader U.S. society. Rothberg's notion of complex implication is relevant here as there is a "coexistence of different relations to past and present injustices" (Rothberg, 2020, p. 8).

For some racial minority immigrants, being implicated in slavery and genocide within the U.S. context poses significant dilemmas, as they may benefit from being associated with whiteness, depending on their race, gender, and social class, and at the same time be marginalized by stereotyping, racism, and other forms of discrimination. Rothberg (2020, p. 19) notes that acknowledging our implication is necessary to "remain on the side of justice." Yet for people who contend with ongoing racism, xenophobia, and religious discrimination, the recognition of one's implication can feel implausible. Specifically, immigrants whose countries of origin have histories of colonization seek liberation from social, religious, and economic oppression in their heritage countries, much of which is a direct consequence of Euro-American colonization. Therefore, it is especially challenging for these immigrants to recognize themselves as implicated subjects.

The impact of colonization on the internalized frameworks concerning race, gender, and social class is evident in David and colleagues' conceptualization of the colonial mentality (David et al., 2017). These scholars (David et al., 2017), in describing the influence of Spanish colonization on feminine values among Filipino Americans, note the objectification of women based on white ideals. Importantly, they also underscore a paradoxical emphasis on women becoming leaders, pointing out that the Philippines has already elected two female presidents. The contrasting objectification and idealization of women are striking, reflecting unconscious and conscious efforts to liberate oneself from colonized histories, albeit within a new country (e.g., the U.S.) with deeply entrenched racist ideologies.

As an Indian American immigrant, I witness the tensions that many Indian Americans feel with regard to being implicated in racial injustice in the U.S. Some Hindu Indian Americans support the Indian prime minister Narendra Modi, despite his oppressive policies aimed to persecute Muslims, and Donald Trump, even while they feel victimized by racism within the U.S. In this case, the fantasy of having power through majority Hindu status in India is juxtaposed against the dissociation of stereotyping and discrimination they and their children face in the U.S. Adding to this complexity are layers of discrimination within Indian American communities that center on gender, caste, skin color, and sexual orientation.

The psychic experience of tensions between privilege and marginalization carries a sense of alienation for many immigrants. For example, discrimination based on race, caste, skin color, and other aspects of identity is felt to be deeply shameful for many Indian Americans, particularly the second generation, who navigate multiple sociocultural contexts in which they experience both privilege and marginalization. Many of my Indian American patients grapple with feeling shame about their family's anti-Black and anti-dark-skin-color attitudes and their rage about racism that they and their family members have endured since migrating to the U.S. One patient, Aditi, stated, "You can't just write off your parents or your aunty or uncle because they say these stupid things about dark skin and fair skin. They have been through a lot, you know, like people calling them sand n——. So what do I do? I just don't talk about it with anyone." Aditi proceeded to tell me about how no one at her workplace recognizes the discrimination faced by Indians, assuming that she is okay with jokes/ microaggressions about Indians being terrorists, dangerous, or exotic: "When no one really understands what it's like to be Indian, then you are not sure what your place is. It's just a problem between white people and Black people. I'm on the outside."

The dilemmas raised when a person faces multiple instances of marginalization across different contexts have been explored by scholars such as Kris Yi, who coined the term "cultural dissociation." Yi (2014) described cultural dissociation as an experience of distancing from one's heritage culture and community and instead immersing in primarily white mainstream society in the face of enduring trauma within one's family and/ or community. While the distance from the location of trauma can offer a sense of safety and comfort, it can also promote dissociated self-states such that heritage and mainstream experiences cannot be bridged (Bromberg, 2012; Yi, 2014). As such, cultural dissociation poses a complex, if not impossible, dilemma in coping with traumatic stress within one's family and community. Recently, Yi (2021) reported the experience of her Asian American patients who expressed their grief upon hearing of the Atlanta spa shootings, when six Asian American women, a white woman, and a white man were murdered by a white man who claimed to have a sexual addiction and attempted to eliminate sexual temptations by killing people at the spa. Specifically, Yi noted how, for Asian American women, the shootings triggered memories of earlier experiences of racism and sexual victimization and objectification, typically perpetrated by white men. Yi (2021, in review) pointed out that the internalization of the model minority stereotype makes it challenging to recognize the "illusion of inclusion" in a "culture saturated with sexualized stereotypes of Asian women." It is important to note that Asian American men are conversely desexualized by both Asian and non-Asian people (Yi, 2021, in review). In the face of compounding traumas, such as sexual trauma and racism, it is especially difficult to parcel out one's implication in gendered racism.

Yi's account of Asian Americans' experiences of internalizing the model minority stereotype while simultaneously being targeted by racism and sexual objectification or devaluation raises questions about belonging in broader American society. Eng and Han's (2000) description of racial melancholia captures the impossible bind of dreaming of belonging in the U.S. and facing the reality of racism and stereotyping as perpetual foreigners. The mourning of racial trauma rests heavily on the collective recognition of racism among both Asian Americans and non-Asian Americans. In other words, mourning is only possible when all people can speak truthfully about their own anti-Asian prejudice. Therefore, the movement toward recognizing one's implication is a collective effort rather than only an individual's or a single community's effort. When Asian Americans' racism-related distress is minimized or ignored, their sense of belonging is diminished. It is then challenging to see one's own implication in injustice against other racial minorities when you are not seen as a real American.

Another illustration of the complexity of privilege and marginalization is evident in the experience of Black immigrants and their children in the U.S. Interpersonal and structural racism can have a profound impact on the identity and mental health of Black immigrants (Meyer et al., 2021). The marginalization of cultural and religious beliefs and a lack of understanding of pre-migration and post-migration stress by others, including mental health practitioners, contribute to isolation from broader U.S. society, including from African Americans whose ancestors were forced into migration through slavery. For many Black immigrants, the conflation of race and culture in the U.S. is problematic, where there is minimal or no recognition of the immigrant experience and its distinct sociocultural vicissitudes. In fact, the experience of culture being erased while adopting racial labels is a source of distress and a source of conflict among family members.

My patient, Tamara, a second-generation Haitian American cis woman in her 30s, described her feelings of alienation from her family and Haitian community as she moved to a different region of the U.S. to attend college and later accept a professional position in which she earned a significantly higher income than her family members. Tamara, the first in her family to attend college, became increasingly aware of people's perceptions of her as a Black woman, which contrasted with her self-perception as a Haitian American. Her cultural heritage, her connection with her church, and her family's migration history remained invisible to most people. She shared in one of our sessions, "Not many people see who I am or where my family comes from. They see a Black woman. Even other Black people, they don't really accept me at times. If they are Jamaican, they look down on me, you know, make assumptions about how poor we are." Tamara further expressed her apprehension in sharing these feelings with me, her Indian American therapist: "It's a little strange telling you this. I don't want you to think that Black people have all these problems with each other." As I listened to Tamara in this session, I resonated with the anxiety about revealing to non-Indians aspects of my experience within my Indian American community that are problematic or dysfunctional. These fears are based on real stereotyping and racism directed against racial minorities. As such, impression management, where we defensively present only features of our ethnic or religious communities in positive terms, becomes a mechanism through which we attempt to ward off racism and stereotyping (Kanukollu & Mahalingam, 2011). Nevertheless, being able to share these hidden aspects of the self is critical to psychoanalytic work. I responded to Tamara by stating, "I resonate with the feeling that you don't want to share something that sounds negative to someone who isn't Black or Haitian, and at the same time, I appreciate you sharing your feelings more fully with me. I feel like I understand more about you."

As our conversation proceeded, Tamara shared with me her frustration with the racism she experienced in her workplace, where she was called "hostile" and "unempathic" by her white supervisor in a performance review. Tamara stated that whenever she expressed an opinion that differed from that of her supervisor, she was perceived as hostile. She has been heartbroken about the murder of George Floyd and police brutality against Black people and posed the question several times in our sessions, "Why did it take a video of a Black man being murdered by the police to get how bad it is?" I responded each time by sharing my sadness about the denial of racialized violence, and in one session, I stated, "Isn't it odd that you are the one being seen as hostile at work?" Tamara expressed, "Yes, it's backward." The complexity of holding the various forms of discrimination is overwhelming at times, as Tamara feels that there are few spaces where she can openly talk about what she loves and what she fears in each of her contexts (e.g., family, Haitian community, broader U.S. society). Our discussions about racism connect very directly to her safety on a daily basis, where she unconsciously and consciously assesses where she will be physically and psychologically protected. Over the course of two years of our work, Tamara has begun to question whether she should say something when one of her Haitian American friends makes negative comments about Chinese people. This particular friend blames Chinese people, including those in the U.S., for the COVID-19 pandemic. Tamara felt conflicted about sharing her disappointment in her friend's comments, as her friend has been victimized by sexual trauma and racial violence. In psychotherapy, we continue to consider whether she feels ready to speak honestly with her friend.

## Moving Toward the Recognition of Complex Implication in Psychoanalysis

Powell (2019, p. 1042) notes,

> Racism does most of its damage psychologically . . . It is up to us, as therapists and analysts, to provide an atmosphere, a container, where communication is welcomed, with an eye to mutual understanding. An important part of addressing race entails accepting a certain humility, even a clumsiness, about addressing these issues straightforwardly with our patients.

Developing a therapeutic space in which this type of communication is the norm rather than the exception is critical for patients and therapists of all sociocultural backgrounds. For patients and therapists of color, such therapeutic space is even more vital when coping with racial loneliness, which Suslovic (2020, p. 488) defined as encompassing complex affects "associated with being the only or first person of color in otherwise all-white settings." The experience of racial loneliness involves feelings of ambivalence, grief, rage, and/or lack of belonging (Suslovic, 2020). Drawing a parallel with Eng and Han's concept of racial melancholia, Suslovic (2020) emphasizes that racial loneliness is not a diagnosis but rather a description of social conditions shaped by white supremacy and accompanying normative unconscious processes (Layton, 2020).

One of the most significant consequences of the grief that characterizes racial loneliness is the loss of community. For many people of color, such loss is experienced repeatedly across different contexts where they are either marginalized or dismissed. Recently, Judith Herman (in press) has elaborated on the importance of a moral community in securing justice for survivors of complex trauma. She argues that the "relationships of dominance and subordination are incompatible with justice, which must be based on principles of trust and fairness that are found only in relationships of mutuality" (Herman, in press). For people of color whose experiences remain invisible within their racial/ethnic/religious communities and outside of these communities, the lack of moral community is palpable.

The concept of moral community is especially important in recognizing oneself as an implicated subject, particularly in the current sociopolitical climate, which is highly polarized politically, racially, and socioeconomically. Creating a moral community entails recognizing that people of color and white people have distinct experiences of race and that, regardless of their unique experiences with race, perpetuates stereotyping, bias, and discrimination at individual and/or systemic levels.

In considering the institutional and individual implication of racial injustice, it is critical that psychoanalysis engage with the notion of a moral community. We must revisit our institutional cultures that largely neglect the experiences of racial minorities and other marginalized communities (Bhatia, 2020; González & Peltz, 2021; Merson, 2021). This includes reflection and modification of our theoretical perspectives and clinical formulation and technique (Tummala-Narra, 2016). Developing a moral sensibility in which the integration of racial justice in theory and practice and honest dialogue about racism is essential for transfiguring implication (Rothberg, 2019; Tummala-Narra, 2022). It is not enough to recruit candidates of color in psychoanalytic institutes, for example. Rather, examining and shifting the culture of the institute is essential for creating an inclusive and moral community. Recently, I have proposed some considerations for decolonizing psychoanalytic theory and practice, which are relevant to the process of transfiguring implication. These include the therapist's willingness and ability to humanize cultural narratives, where a patient is seen in their entirety, "a whole person with all of the intertwined complexity of intrapsychic, interpersonal, and sociocultural aspects of life"; confront one's own painful affect associated with privilege and marginalization and approach therapeutic work with humility; engage with the depressive position, recognizing both the limits of the analytic relationship and the hope of repair; and integrate new cultural narratives in training (Tummala-Narra, 2022). Each of these approaches to decolonizing theory and practice requires a moral community within psychoanalysis in order to be optimally effective in achieving racial equity and justice.

Therapists' ability to grapple with our sense of vulnerability and power and with histories of marginalization and privilege is critical to recognizing our implication in racial injustice and to a more racially inclusive psychoanalysis. McKay (2019, p. 81) describes recognition as distinct from empathy, occurring when "the person on the receiving end makes the transition from feeling understood to feeling known." Her description of recognition is especially compelling as it calls upon the therapist to move beyond empathizing with a patient. Recognition further entails engagement with one's vulnerability. A number of scholars have emphasized the therapist's ability to bear the vulnerability of the patient and their own vulnerability in addressing dissociation of feeling bad or a sense of badness in the context of race and racism (Benjamin, 2021; Kuchuck, 2018; Layton, 2020; Orange, 2020). For example, Kuchuck (2018) describes how silent disclosures, where the therapist contemplates whether to make a disclosure to the patient, allow for the therapist to access dissociated content, including affects, cognitions, and the intersubjective dynamics between the therapist and patient. Other scholars have focused on the analysis of counter-transference and the powerful role of witnessing the patient's suffering as mechanisms for breaking through dissociative defenses related to race and culture (Benjamin, 2021; Boulanger, 2012). Additionally, many white analysts and practitioners have begun the emotional labor required to recognize their implication in racism and move toward dismantling racist ideologies in theory and practice (Harris, 2019).

Still, much of the psychoanalytic literature has focused on Black-white racial dynamics without consideration of the unique experiences of other individuals and communities, and specifically how immigration shapes one's experience of implication in broader racial dynamics within the U.S. In facing the history of white supremacy and colonization, Benjamin (2021, p. 402) notes the importance of "both acknowledging harm and providing a vision of repair as its alternative." In psychoanalysis, we have yet to face histories of colonization and ongoing discrimination faced by immigrants and their children. In fact, the history of white, European immigration remains largely dissociated in psychoanalytic theory, education, and practice. Just as it is critical to expand our understanding of Black-white racial dynamics within psychoanalysis, we must further recognize and explore the complexity of and transfiguring implication in therapeutic work with patients whose racial position and immigration experience lies both within and outside of Black-white racial dynamics. Importantly, the guilt and shame that are described by white people with regard to racial privilege may be qualitatively different than that experienced by people of color since we (people of color) carry colonized histories and continue to encounter racism as we examine our own stereotypes and racist attitudes toward other racial minorities (Tummala-Narra, 2020). Further, as people's identities and social locations are inherently intersectional, guilt and shame are produced and uniquely experienced within a complex matrix of privilege and discrimination (Belkin & White, 2020; González & Peltz, 2021).

In my practice, I have increasingly grappled with the challenging task of navigating privilege and marginalization with my patients. Specifically, how do I recognize patients' and my own conscious and unconscious stereotyping and racism while working through our own racial trauma and pain? Returning to my opening vignette of Jared, I have found it to be useful to share some of my emotional responses to his dilemma of helping and protecting other students of color on his campus and protecting himself from further marginalization. For instance, I told him, "It's not easy to figure out the right thing to do when you have been hurt so many times." Jared asked me directly about my own experiences of racism, and although I had not shared specific incidents of racism, I shared with him that I, too, felt at times that racism directed at me, my family, and my South Asian friends has been minimized. Recognizing this shared experience has been important for ameliorating some of Jared's racial loneliness. At the same time, I have been examining how my economic privilege stands in contrast to Jared's economic struggles and the enormous pressure he feels to care for his family's financial needs. My parents both attended college, and although they faced and continue to face racial and ethnic discrimination, they were able to pay for my college education. I have a doctoral degree which has enabled me to secure financial stability. The high stakes of completing college are evident for both me and Jared. Yet I have not felt the same pressures of supporting my parents financially.

As a professor, I am well aware of the challenges students such as Jared face with few people on campus recognizing the unique experiences of first-generation immigrant-origin students. I also realize that I contribute to the alienation of these students through my participation in the graduate admissions processes and curriculum development, even as I advocate for first-generation, immigrant-origin students. In my therapeutic work with Jared, I have begun to name our differences in racial and socioeconomic positions. I shared with him that I have not had the same struggles as him, and yet I experience racism and work with students who are facing racism and financial pressures. Jared responded to me, letting me know that he felt affirmed by me. He also shared some of his negative attitudes about "rich white people and people who are just given things in their life," which I understand as reflecting his sadness and anger about having to work so hard and his frustration with me, his therapist, who has been "just given things." Explicitly recognizing the injustice of having to work so hard and prove himself in ways that are beyond what is expected of his peers, all while bearing racism, has been a meaningful part of witnessing (Benjamin, 2021; Boulanger, 2012). This engagement moved us toward further exploring his hesitation to support other students of color. Jared started to question his own implication in racism directed against Black students on his college campus and has been contemplating whom he can trust to share his views more openly on his campus.

## Conclusion

Rothberg's (2019) proposal of opening the self to others and to one's own otherness is especially relevant to psychoanalytic psychotherapy, which holds at its core the freedom to experience and express the most unacceptable and conflicting aspects of our psychic lives. Race and racism are fundamental traumas in U.S. society that pose unresolved conflicts to individuals and communities. Recognizing and engaging this reality is urgently needed in psychoanalysis. For racial minority patients and therapists, such recognition is vital for being seen as a whole self in the therapeutic relationship, a sense of belonging in psychoanalytic training programs and communities, and the ability to engage with complex implication.

## References

Akhtar, S. (2011). *Immigration and acculturation: Mourning, adaptation, and the next generation.* Jason Aronson.

Anen, S. J. (2020). Narcissistic states of privilege. *Psychoanalytic Psychology, 37*(3), 249–256.

Belkin, M. (2018). Who is queer around here? Overcoming rigid thinking and relating in patient and analyst. *Contemporary Psychoanalysis, 54*(3), 484–510.

Belkin, M., & White, C. (2020). *Intersectionality and relational psychoanalysis: New perspectives on race, gender, and sexuality.* Routledge.

Benjamin, J. (2021). Acknowledgment, harming, and political trauma: Reflections after the plague year. *Psychoanalytic Perspectives, 18,* 401–412.

Bhatia, S. (2020). Decolonizing psychology: Power, citizenship and identity. *Psychoanalysis, Self, and Context, 15*(3), 257–266.

Boulanger, G. (2012). Psychoanalytic witnessing: Professional obligation or moral imperative? *Psychoanalytic Psychology, 29*(3), 318–324.

Boulanger, G. (2015). Seeing double, being double: Longing, belonging, recognition, and evasion in psychodynamic work with immigrants. *The American Journal of Psychoanalysis*, *75*, 287–303.

Bromberg, P. M. (2012). Credo. *Psychoanalytic Dialogues*, *22*, 273–278.

David, E. J. R., Sharma, D. K. B., & Petalio, J. (2017). Losing Kapwa: Colonial legacies and the Filipino American family. *Asian American Journal of Psychology*, *8*(1), 43–55.

Eng, D. L., & Han, S. (2000). A dialogue on racial melancholia. *Psychoanalytic Dialogues*, *10*(4), 667–700.

García Coll, C., & Marks, A. K. (2012). *The immigrant paradox in children and adolescents: Is becoming American a developmental risk?* American Psychological Association.

González, F. J., & Peltz, R. (2021). Community psychoanalysis: Collaborative practice as intervention. *Psychoanalytic Dialogues*, *31*(4), 409–427.

Grand, S. (2018). The other within: White shame, Native-American genocide. *Contemporary Psychoanalysis*, *54*(1), 84–102.

Harris, A. (2019). The perverse pact: Racism and White privilege. *American Imago*, *76*(3), 309–333.

Herman, J. L. (in press). *Truth and repair: Envisioning justice from the survivor's perspective*. Basic Books.

Holmes, D. E. (2016). Culturally imposed trauma: The sleeping dog has awakened. Will psychoanalysis take heed? *Psychoanalytic Dialogues*, *26*(6), 641–654.

Kanukollu, S. N., & Mahalingam, R. (2011). The idealized cultural identities model on help-seeking and child sexual abuse: A conceptual model for contextualizing perceptions and experiences of South Asian Americans. *Journal of Child Sexual Abuse*, *20*(2), 218–243. doi:10.1080/10538712.2011.556571

Kuchuck, S. (2018). The analyst's subjectivity: On the impact of inadvertent, deliberate, and silent disclosure. *Psychoanalytic Perspectives*, *15*, 265–274.

Layton, L. (2020). *Toward a social psychoanalysis: Culture, character, and normative unconscious processes*. Relational Perspectives Book Series. Routledge.

McKay, R. K. (2019). Bread and Roses: Empathy and recognition. *Psychoanalytic Dialogues*, *29*, 75–91.

Mehta, S. B., & Fauci, J. (2021). "Why are you even here?" Relational reverberations of COVID on a pediatric inpatient unit. *The Clinical Psychologist*, *74*(4), 18–22.

Merson, M. (2021). The Whiteness taboo: Interrogating Whiteness in psychoanalysis. *Psychoanalytic Dialogues*, *31*(1), 13–27.

Meyer, M. L. et al. (2021). Racial stress and racialized violence among Black immigrants in the United States. In P. Tummala-Narra (Ed.), *Trauma and racial minority immigrants: Turmoil, uncertainty, and resistance* (pp. 147–163). American Psychological Association.

Orange, D. M. (2020). *Psychoanalysis, history and radical ethics: Learning to hear*. Routledge.

Powell, D. R. (2019). Race, African Americans, and psychoanalysis: Collective silence in the therapeutic conversation. *Journal of the American Psychoanalytic Association, 66*(6), 1021–1049.

Rothberg, M. (2019). *The implicated subject: Beyond victims and perpetrators.* Stanford University Press.

Steele, J. (2021). Fear of blackness: Understanding white supremacy as an inverted relationship to oppression. *Psychoanalysis, Culture & Society, 26*(3), 388–404.

Suslovic, B. (2020). Mitigating racial loneliness as transformative psychoanalytic work. *Psychoanalysis, Culture & Society, 25*(3), 480–489.

Tummala-Narra, P. (2016). *Psychoanalytic theory and cultural competence in psychotherapy.* American Psychological Association.

Tummala-Narra, P. (2020). The fear of immigrants. *Psychoanalytic Psychology, 37*(1), 50–61.

Tummala-Narra, P. (2022). Can we decolonize psychoanalytic theory and practice? *Psychoanalytic Dialogues, 32*(3), 217–234.

White, C. J. (2015). Strangers in paradise: Trevor, Marley, and me: Reggae music and the foreigner other. *Psychoanalytic Dialogues, 25*, 176–193.

Yi, K. (2014). From no name to birth of integrated identity: Trauma-based cultural dissociation in immigrant women and creative integration. *Psychoanalytic Dialogues, 24*(1), 37–45.

Yi, K. (2021, October). *Asian American experience: Illusion of inclusion and dissociation of otherness.* Presentation at the Massachusetts Institute for Psychoanalysis.

Chapter 9

# The Relational Citizen as Implicated Subject

## Emergent Unconscious Processes in the Psychoanalytic Community Collaboratory

*Billie A. Pivnick and Jane A. Hassinger*

## Introduction

Historian and Holocaust scholar Michael Rothberg argues that US citizens are all implicated in the crimes of history, particularly chattel slavery, and thus share in the web of costs, benefits, and accountability. As a remedy, he urges psychological exploration of the tensions baked into our multiple group identifications, cultivation of an ethos of mutual aid, and community engagement. Although this can occur in individual therapy, it is best achieved in group settings in which the psychic and social meet in ways that can be observed from multiple perspectives. In this chapter, we will discuss the mutually constitutive interactions between Rothberg's (2019) concept of *implicated subjectivity* and a new construct we (Hassinger & Pivnick, 2022) have called *relational citizenship*.

*Relational citizenship*, the interplay of intrapsychic, interpersonal, and group-based aspects of identity, is an intersubjectively constructed self-state in which the individual and the sociopolitical are dynamically linked, and the demands of belonging to one or (more) collectivity are managed. Animated by ghosts of society's cultural/political controversies and an ethic of interdependency and implication, *relational citizenship* is an expression, intrapsychically and interpersonally, of capacities for intersubjective perspective-taking and mature group relations.

These ideas evolved over five years with the Psychoanalytic Community Collaboratory—a web-based seminar and project incubator for practitioners who work on significant community problems. Within this inherently relational experience, freighted with historical trauma, participants create a temporary community in which the value of all voices and recognition of

DOI: 10.4324/9781003265146-9

mutual implication in the struggles and successes of all are foregrounded. Clinical illustrations of these experiences in two iterations of the Community Collaboratory will be presented and discussed.

## The Present of Memory

We are living in a time in which we are more aware than ever of difficult histories and our implication in others' suffering. In such times it is imperative that we pay attention to how we can form ethical communities—groups in which the one is in the many and the many is in the one—so that we can journey together with and bear witness to the pain of others, even others who have hurt us (Ulanov, 2007; Margalit, 2004; Pivnick, 2017). Since the communal trauma of 9/11, a notable shift has occurred even in our consultation rooms toward thinking about how history, beyond the family crucible, has shaped individual and group experience (cf. Pivnick, 2013, 2015, 2017, 2021). Our patients reveal concerns about their safety in their community and the wider world, about their political opinions, affiliations, and actions of themselves and others; about the narratives that underlie our cultural identifications; and about how the government structures and contains (or fails to) our private lives. Increasingly, people are searching ancestry registries to fill in gaps in their immigrant histories. Many are looking to establish links to the US history of chattel slavery—as descendants of former slaves, of former slave owners, and of both (Vaughans, 2017; Connolly et al., 2022). As individual psychotherapists, we have needed a theoretical foundation for helping us understand the impact of (and imbrication with) "the ghosts of history" (Apprey, 2004) and their manifestations in psychopathology and social marginalization. Such a theory should connect our object relations models to conscious and unconscious experiences of ourselves in relation to historical forces and social power.

Based on his work with Holocaust narratives, and in a formulation not unlike Freud's (1920) *nachtraglichkeit*, the idea that memories are re-transcribed through a process of enacting the past in the present and re-imagining the present into the past, Rothberg (2009, p. 3) believes that memory is "the past made present." To the degree that our identities are constituted by historically shared group experiences, our social lives are constituted, in large measure, by past injuries. When divergent groups and their histories encounter one another, they often compete over who is most victimized, making for battles for recognition in the public realm and dividing the spoils among winners and losers (Volkan, 2013). Rothberg contends that only by viewing memory as *multidirectional* can it be renegotiated and reconfigured in a generative way. Citing Confino and Fritsche (2002), Rothberg (2009, p. 4) asserts that this multidimensional framework treats memory as a "representation of the past embedded in social action" and can only be changed via group experiences that account for the non-uniqueness of the experience of injury while simultaneously creating new ways for groups to relate to one another. Group identity, of course, is contained within individuals, too, within the "social unconscious"—the constraining elements of culture, communication, and social arrangements that are not perceived, acknowledged, or seen as problematic yet have a profound influence on our attitudes and behaviors (Hopper, 2003; Rozmarin, 2017; Hassinger & Pivnick, 2022). For this reason, Rothberg favors facing these divergent unconscious experiences in iterative (repeating) group experiences that can restore the possibility of reciprocal communication. Theoretical support for and individual competencies with group processes are therefore crucial for navigating difficult histories as they play out in community life.

## The Psychic and the Social in Contemporary Psychoanalysis

Contemporary scholars have addressed and attempted to mend the rupture between American ego psychological theories of the evolution of the individual mind and the social surround (Sullivan, 1953/1968; Cushman, 2015; Frosh, 2001; Layton, 2019). We argue that the British group analytic theorists' perspective provides an integrative model that accounts for the interactions between individual psychologies and the sociohistorical and views individual, dyad, and group experience in dynamic relation, reflecting the "social matrix," manifestations of which appear in unconscious communications across categorical boundaries (time, geography, culture, etc.) in ways that can be observed and given meaning (Foulkes, 1964/1984; Dalal, 1998, 2017; Tubert-Oklander & Hernandez-Tubert, 2021). In this tradition, political experience (e.g., being members of groups and citizens in society) is part of what makes us human. These dynamics are best revealed and understood in groups.

In community work, issues of identity, belonging, and membership feature prominently. The group is constructed of individuals, but these members come from social and cultural groups replete with people and relationships that have been internalized through memories symbolizing both experience and loss (Eng & Han, 2000). While these images are internal, they represent external historical realities and past and recent internal responses. Thus, the past and the present, the visceral and the sociohistorical, all play a part in how we view our identities and those of others.

Particularly in times of trauma and dislocation, any of these identities can be stirred up and provoke reactions by others similarly activated. Managing incipient conflicts requires maturity and perspective-taking in citizens. This kind of citizen is discussed by Fromm (1958) and reflected in what he calls the "revolutionary character," one whose identification is with humanity at large and can therefore rise above his own narrower social location. Group theorist Hopper (2000) adds to this depiction of the model "citizen" the idea of courage and willingness to risk his own needs for the sake of social change. Both see people as always deeply involved in groups and with concerns shaped by culture external to the intrapsychic world as traditionally defined.

American psychoanalysis has had a bias against consideration of environmental factors, in part as a result of the intense pressure to "scientize"/medicalize psychoanalysis and as a self-protective response to the anti-Semitism faced by many of the European psychoanalysts as they fled the Nazi terror and attempted to settle in the United States (Cushman, 2015; Dalal, 2017; Rozmarin, 2017; Tubert-Oklander & Hernandez-Tubert, 2021). To some degree, the bias against incorporating the sociocultural in our theories of development was modified by interpersonalists and relational psychoanalysts. But we believe that the work of South American group psychoanalysts Tubert-Oklander and Hernandez-Tubert (2004, 2021), building on Foulkes (1964/1984, 1990/2018) and Pichon-Riviere (Scharff, 2018), further provides a new and superior paradigm for integrating the psychic and the social.

In the framework outlined by Tubert-Oklander & Hernandez-Tubert, the unconscious consists of a *group matrix*—dyad, group, family, and institution. The matrix bridges what appears to be a gap between the individual and the group. Integrating Foulkes' (1964) formulation of a hypothesized web of communication and interrelationship that provides a shared context for understanding the meanings ascribed to events and Hopper's

(1982, 1985, 2003) assertion that social context determines meaning, Oklander-Tubert and Hernandez-Tubert assert that it is "minds in interaction" that constitutes mental processes rather than "individuals interacting." When individuals form a group, they begin a new dynamic network of communications that combines individuals' *personal matrices*, or what Pichon-Riviere calls the network of their *internal groups*, with those of others. Oklander-Tubert's and Hernandez-Tubert's conception of the mind as a "process" rather than a "thing" leads them to agree with Foulkes' (1964/1984) and Bateson's (1972) concept of the creation of a "group mind" based on the flow of information within the group as a social system. They agree with Pichon-Riviere (as cited in Losso et al., 2017) that dynamic forces of a group function in a *dialectical spiral* in which external bonds with others become internal, then the internal becomes external again, and so forth, until a boundary is constituted that is both unique to that individual and shared with others. In this way, as any individual is changed, so is the world.

Conversely, when communication and relationships are affected by social and historical forces, the changes also influence the organization of the individual psyche (Banfield, 1967; Levine, 2017). Social influences, including the nonhuman environment, act on individuals in a container-contained relation (Bion, 1961). The community-as-a-whole functions in a manner similar to that of the mother (container) *vis-a-vis* her infant (contained) in both providing recognition and acting in ways that solve their problems; members reciprocally act to create a way of life that helps all thrive. When communities are attacked from within or without and fail to protect their own members, dehumanizing loss and trauma can occur, provoking defensive attacks on linking (Bion, 2013) accompanied by fragmentation of semantically held memories.

## How Historical Trauma Affects Group Process

The first step in repairing our ability to think and communicate after communal historical trauma involves processes characterized by dialogic thought (Beebe et al., 2013; Boulanger, 2011; Davoine & Gaudilliere, 2005; Pivnick, 2011, 2013; Pivnick & Hennes, 2014). As with children, whose "play in the presence of another" fuses dissociated emotions and creates tolerance for interpersonal separation, it is a dialogue that brings to life split-off traumas so they can be contextualized within a full range of experiences in shattered communities and individual psyches.[1] Often this dialogue arises in group experiences that create transitional space, what we have termed a *collective third*—a form of adult group cooperative play (Hassinger & Pivnick, 2022)—that helps to counteract a community's persistent sense of helplessness and victimization, or what Volkan (2013) calls a large group's "chosen trauma." Without recognition and mourning, such chronic injury is often counteracted with splitting and projection, leading to intergroup conflict that can lead to violence and even war. Without formal memorializing, spontaneous recreations (enactments) often arise unconsciously and create disruptions that can benefit from communal or therapeutic intervention.

## Recognizing the Implicated Citizen Self

We know that the development of self-as-citizen is as integral to mental health as working well and loving well (Samuels, 2004, 2016). Interestingly, Shapiro (2020) has proposed that "psychological citizenship," a sense of being a responsible contributor to the well-being of one's community, is an essential feature of mature adulthood and a psychological outcome of experiences in groups. Taking account of this observation makes it possible to understand object relations as including a much broader web of familial, social, and cultural connections. This is a bidirectional process in which individuals' affectively charged identities, as well as the contours and characteristics of their group memberships, are also shaped by the community context and its politics. In the case of US structural racism—the "warp" in the tapestry of US history—these dynamics reproduce almost unbridgeable social and economic inequalities.

Mature citizenship pivots on acceptance of our responsibility toward our communities and our implication in the suffering of others (Davoine & Gaudilliere, 2005; Frie, 2017; Layton, 2019; Rothberg, 2019). Rothberg's (2019) implicated subject shares in responsibility for the crimes of history and can accept a share of costs, benefits, and responsibilities for repair and reparation. Rothberg's formulation enlarges our field of vision beyond traditional categories of perpetrators and victims, heightening the need for awareness by others who claim either ignorance of the true nature of the crimes or view themselves to be innocent bystanders.

Shared denial of implicatedness is a telltale sign of widespread social amnesia and normalized dissociation, which provides cover for the proliferation of inequitable and discriminatory social practices and policies, reduced expectations for citizen engagement, and an increasing indifference to the vulnerabilities and needs of citizens (Jacoby, 1975/2017; Layton, 2019). When citizenship is stripped of the values of accountability and mutual aid, the individual is left feeling uncared for and uncaring.

Implicated subjects in denial tend to identify with those who are more privileged. Thus, Rothberg's broadened definition of implicatedness helps to restore the historical facts of our country's beginnings in ways that can lead to collective psychological recovery of dissociated or decontextualized elements of personal histories and social circumstances. These inevitably humbling recollections can provide opportunities for problem-solving without pathologizing and othering (cf. Pivnick, 2021; Pivnick & Hassinger, 2021). By emphasizing community responsibility and mutual aid, rather than blame and guilt, we are better able to accept our multiple identifications and their costs, benefits, and associated responsibilities, both in the past and present.

These often-conflicting identifications can be understood in part as reflections of a society's cultural/political controversies and, in the psychic register, dynamic self-states intersubjectively evinced in particular group situations in community life (Hassinger & Pivnick, 2022). Shapiro and Carr (1991) describe profound contributions to one's ability to claim one's own territory and continued post-adolescent psychological development outside the family as a member of groups. Shapiro (2020) also notes that perspective on our "selves"—who we are, what matters to us, our interdependence with others, and our obligations to others—are acquired through repeated experiences in *democratic* groups. Here, "democratic" is shorthand for: the valuing and inclusion of each individual and their voice and the importance of each contribution to the welfare of the group. Based on the universal wish to belong and engage in meaningful relational experiences, groups are critical sites for powerful emotional sharing and learning.

However, groups can also often become repressive and emotionally chaotic settings, vulnerable to the development of hierarchical, authoritarian leadership, regressions among members—norms that inhibit creativity and problem-solving, emphasize conformity, and create scapegoats (Bion, 1961; Hopper, 2009; Hopper & Weinberg, 2018). Furthermore, groups without clear leadership, boundaries, and tasks can produce unconscious expressions of pathological orientations toward leaders or authority figures and the roles of members (Rice, 1965/2018; Kernberg, 2020). Regressive fantasies and overwhelming affects, carrying fragments of dissociated unmetabolized traumatic histories and pulls toward paranoid role enactments among members, can emerge, including those of the abuser, the victim, and the bystander. By containing facilitation and interpretation, these experiences can give access to what has been dissociated (both personally and in the community) and open opportunities for making meaning and changing our relationships with those histories (Davoine & Gaudilliere, 2005; Pivnick & Hennes, 2014; Pivnick, 2013, 2017). One potential outcome is that members make more realistic appraisals of their relationships to crimes of history, their places in the world, and their responsibilities to others and to their communities.

Rothberg (2019) also points to the importance of being part of groups in the process of re-owning connections to our cultural histories. For example, interacting with others in a group can offer increased awareness of one's fantasies of exemption from being an agent of harm, counterfactual data, and support for the emotional work involved in countering them. Groups also become creative sites for developing new approaches for collective action toward reparations and repairs. Similar to what happens in an effective individual therapy, a good group experience can elicit previously unformulated/dissociated or painful templates of family and group histories, thus creating the potential for (re)organizing narratives of the past and expectations for the future.

The experience of confronting one's own and others' implicated subjectivities can lessen denial, projection, and guilt, leading to revitalized engagements with one's citizenship and community. Because the exercise of citizenship is intrinsically relational, repeated collective actions to effect political decision-making are an essential element of what we have called *relational citizenship*, enacted in political terms *and* at interpersonal/intersubjective levels (Hassinger & Pivnick, 2022).

## Relational Citizenship

People are born into and grow up in groups (Tubert-Oklander, 2014; Shapiro, 2020; Dalal, 1998, 2017), the crucible for organizing the mutually constitutive relationship between self and others. These experiences become the stimulus and content for inherently relational multiple self-states. Multiplicity, the term used by relational psychoanalysts for the capacity for holding different, even contradictory self-states, is, as Bromberg (1998) asserts, a developmental achievement, similar to the achievement of an "interpretive stance" described by Shapiro and Carr (1991). Such engagement builds capacity for working with differences and conflict and, importantly, for experiencing the security and other satisfactions of belonging.

Politically, citizenship results from transactions between the state and the individual and confers both rights and duties (Fortier, 2017; Protevi, 2019). Akin to citizenship, group membership carries costs and benefits— on the one hand, the need for temporary adherence to group norms and relinquishing individual autonomy; on the other, the protective, esteem-enhancing features of being part of a valued collectivity. Experiences of membership and citizenship involve meaningful, affect-laden, value-driven *ways of being* in groups that privilege empathy and respect for others, recognition of all members' value and distinctiveness, mutual aid, and a sense of accountability to the group (Glassman, 2008).

In the intrapsychic and interpersonal registers, the experience of citizenship can be intersubjectively elicited via unconscious communications among members and manifested in the roles members take up in groups. We call the dynamic interplay of intrapsychic, interpersonal, and political aspects of identity *relational citizenship* (Hassinger & Pivnick, 2022). *Relational citizenship is the intersubjective experience of oneself as a responsible and generative citizen among citizens.* Inevitably involving internal struggle with competing identifications and loyalties, this psychic work supports increased empathy, self-authorization for leadership functions in the group, and mature participation in community life. *Relational citizenship* is premised on an implicit ethic of accepting implication for our interdependency and implication in one another's suffering (Butler, 2020; Layton, 2019; Tubert-Oklander, 2014; Fromm, 1958).[2]

## The Psychoanalytic Community Collaboratory

Our conceptualization of the psychological representation of self-as-citizen emerged at the same time we were working to articulate our perspective on our community-based psychoanalytic practices. We were inspired by our own experiences as consultants to and participants in a variety of community projects. As described in greater detail in our article on the community turn (Hassinger & Pivnick, 2022), one of us (Pivnick) was involved in developing art- and dance-therapy-based programs for hospitals and in the design of several history museums, including the National September 11 Memorial Museum, while Hassinger collaborated on the design and implementation of a number of international community-based programs focused on women's reproductive and mental health.

We launched the Collaboratory in 2014 to provide a context for exploring approaches to community-based psychoanalytic practice. The Collaboratory is a facilitated 12-to-14-week web-based seminar, project incubator, and experiential laboratory informed by relational and group psychoanalytic theories that highlight group process, multiplicity, intersectionality, historical trauma, enactment, and mourning. Each session is linked to a curriculum of readings, members' evolving projects, and group process observation and discussion.

Over its five iterations, Collaboratory participants from around the world have shared innovative projects and explored relevant interdisciplinary scholarship. The mix of nationalities, cultural identities, disciplines, and methodologies offer rich material for an evolving set of tools and practice principles. Discussions often delve into the nuts and bolts of the work itself, ranging from, for example, the shifting frame for psychoanalytic practice in the community to negotiating with various community stakeholders. Members explore challenges faced in the transition from "expert" to "collaborating citizen," such as the differences between being "psychoanalyst for the group" and "psychoanalyst in the group."

The Collaboratory's group methodology partakes of two traditions of psychoanalytically informed group leadership. The first, the Tavistock model, derives from the work of Wilfred Bion (1961) and focuses on authority relations in work group dynamics. We use a modified, less hierarchically organized version of his psychoanalytic thinking—to be discussed in the following sections. The second tradition utilizes the democratic-humanistic model developed by Urania Glassman (2008). The model is grounded in a view of democracy as "defined by particular standards of interaction that yield equality in relation to power, position, and resources" and humanistic values that "cast people in society as *responsible for and to one another*" (p. xix).

Humanistic values posit the inherent worth of every person, individuals' mutual responsibility for one another, and that people have a fundamental right to social conditions that support well-being. Democratic norms shape cooperative behavioral patterns and equitable distribution of resources. Put together, these values and norms view each member and facilitator as equal participants in the creation and maintenance of a democratic experiment that endeavors to bring about individual and collective change. Glassman's approach is inspired by Bion and other group theorists and offers a detailed, lucid roadmap for group facilitators. It is "experiential, experimental, existential, and interactional" (p. xxi).

Collaboratory participants create a temporary community in which the value of all voices and recognition of mutual implication in the struggles and successes of all are foregrounded. In the democratic-humanistic group, leadership, initially vested in the facilitator, is viewed as a function and a role that participants take up over time, based on their interests and expertise. In the Collaboratory, all contribute to the group's development, the evolving set of practice principles, and bibliographic resources. Members come to have a stake in each other's success. Within this inherently relational experience, inevitably freighted with historical trauma and culturally normative unconscious processes, members increase their capacities for multiplicity, empathy, and interpersonal perspective-taking that characterize relational citizenship and implicated subjectivity.

Through enacting evolving identification with the group and interdependency with other members, participants exercise their *relational citizenship* and engage in the psychic work required to move from an early exclusive focus on self-centered concerns to an identification with the group's task and mission and, further, to an experience of oneself as a beneficiary of and as a capable steward for the group. In some ways, parallel to the processes involved in exercising one's political citizenship, members come to feel themselves to be "citizens of the group" with benefits, responsibilities, and leadership functions.

## Critical Incidents in Group Work

In each Collaboratory, distinctive recurrent themes and *critical incidents* reflect the particular psychologies and interests of members, unconscious dynamics in the group, and influences of major events in the world. In each Collaboratory, after early positive identification with the facilitators is established (the basis of a working alliance), a normative crisis (or what we refer to as a *critical incident*) often erupts. This normative crisis can involve a challenge to authority relations that, if successfully resolved, leads to decreasing vertical, projection-based relations and increasing horizontal, peer-to-peer relations. *Critical incidents* reflect symbolic crystallizations of group defenses mobilized against anxiety and threats to the cohesion of the group, frequently including events outside the group.

These threats are revealed through changes in the quality of interaction among members, as well as absences, dreams, and parapraxes (Menzies, 1960; Foulkes, 1964; Shapiro & Carr, 2017; Glassman, 2008).

Hernandez-Tubert (2011) has observed that when society fails to act responsibly to contain the suffering of individuals and groups, traumatic levels of hopelessness often emerge. In these instances, the entire unconscious *group matrix*—dyad, group, family, institution—of communication and relationships can be affected. To help account for these developments in the Collaboratory, we rely on the aforementioned theories of Bion, Kernberg, and Hopper on unconscious regressive dynamics in groups (also a significant influence in Glassman's model) and their formulations of the "basic assumptions"—dependency, fight-flight, pairing, and incohesion—dynamics that reflect anxieties stirred intrapsychically, interpersonally, and in the larger social surround. Transgenerational traumas—the often dissociated "wounds of history"—also can be revived, pressing for repair and reconnection of broken relational links (Salberg & Grand, 2017; Vaughans, 2017; Apprey, 2004; Holmes, 2017).

In the next section, we will describe a *critical incident* from each of the second and fourth Collaboratories to illustrate the influences of traumatic community events on the experiences of participants, manifestations of the *Collaborative Third, relational citizenship*, and *implicated subjectivity* in the evolution of each group. In each vignette, we can see how grappling with one's implication in the suffering of the communities involved is associated with increased empathy and ultimately with the design of the projects (or Rothberg's "action") themselves.

Remarkably, each Collaboratory has coincided with one or more catastrophic political/cultural events. Here, we will focus on the 2017 Parkland School shooting in Florida and the 2020 surge in lockdowns and deaths that characterized the earliest phases of the worldwide Covid-19 pandemic. Emerging themes in each group reflected the psychological reverberations of these crises for individual participants and the group as a whole. As hoped, the exploration of enactments in the group became an important pedagogical tool. This form of experiential learning brings theory to life and facilitates participants' movement from dependency on the leaders in the group toward increasing self-authorization and productivity.

**The 2017 critical incident.** In 2017, the group included five women and five men, eight white and two Latinx participants. A week after the Parkland shootings, everyone expressed shock and despair in response.

Quickly, however, the discussion shifted away from Parkland to exploring tensions between participants' clinical and community-based identities. Violetta, a Latinx psychoanalyst, whose former analytic training had provoked feelings of inferiority and shame about working in community mental health, admitted to feeling insecure about how to be helpful to the Parkland community. Offering reassurances and a long list of ideas, the group seized on her insecurity, appearing to make her and Violetta doubt its "project." During a somewhat manic discussion, Violetta participated very little, seeming more disheartened.

Throughout, Ricardo, a Latinx graduate student and artist with limited access to internet resources, had been trying to connect by phone. For long stretches, he could neither be seen nor heard. Suddenly, the Zoom chat box exploded with messages from him. Like the proverbial Greek chorus, he called out from the margins, giving urgent voice to dissociated horror and grief over the murders in Parkland. Everyone else—facilitators and participants—were thunderstruck. In spite of efforts to show respect and compassion for one another's unique histories, only then did they notice Ricardo's absence. One facilitator pointed out the group's erasure of Ricardo and suggested that, in its intense focus on Violetta's anxieties, participants were engaged in collective defense against their own feelings of fear and helplessness, or what DiAngelo (2018) has labeled "white fragility." Slowly and painfully, members began to recognize the group's racialized/gendered erasure of Ricardo and projections of fragility and fear onto Violetta. By taking leadership and calling the group to attention, Ricardo enacted his relational psychic citizenship and awakened the group to its purpose.

During the next session, he presented his project—a tender film about a group of migrant workers who, for generations, journeyed from Mexico to Colorado and back. Several workers spoke passionately about their ancestors' cultural claim to the land, where colonial landowners and politicians stripped the people of rights and criminalized their border crossings. Members were deeply moved by his presentation. Later, with excitement and a sense of "being in this together," they discussed another member's "safe haven" project for undocumented immigrant university students. Several acknowledged their unconscious privileging of white voices that had pushed Ricardo into silence and rendered Violetta's anxiety a problem to solve. As this defensive splitting between BIPOC and white members gave way, a thoughtful exploration developed of how hegemonic whiteness had permeated our assumptions about what constitutes legitimate forms of and sites for practice. Participation increased, and members reengaged with their projects with greater depth and complexity. With an explicit mission to collaborate, the group provided a container for the members' multiple "groups-in-the-minds"—as in races, genders, ethnicities, sexual orientations, cultural histories, and so on (Shapiro, 2020). The atmosphere was charged with curiosity and creativity. Toward the session's end, with renewed confidence, Violetta shared her vision of a peer-based support project for Parkland families.

Over subsequent sessions, an intersubjective emotionally charged experience developed—one we call, with a nod to Benjamin's (2017) Moral Third, a *Collaborative Third* (Hassinger & Pivnick, 2022). In this shared state, participants identified with the group-as-a-whole and thus moved to a strengthened engagement with the group's task and mission. As teamwork improved, both creativity and productivity increased, and the sense described by Glassman that "we are good and able" was palpable (Glassman, 2008; Hassinger & Pivnick, 2022). The vignette illustrates how attending to the dynamic links between the psychic and social and the development of a *Collaborative Third* allow for increasing capacities for non-defensive reflection on and repair of inevitable enactments in the group's dynamics.

Participants' complicity with Ricardo's invisibility and Violetta's anxieties demonstrated how normative unconscious processes "reproduce inequality precisely where the link between the psychic and social has been disavowed" (Layton, 2020). When he signaled his erasure, Ricardo destabilized the grip of whiteness and avoidance, manifesting both his agency and responsibility to the group.

**The 2020 critical incident.** The 2020 Collaboratory included ten participants from the Northeastern and Midwestern US, Southeastern Australia, South Africa, India, Argentina, and Haiti, consisting of six white members and four BIPOC members. Participants brought project ideas that ranged from beginning a school for young women and new mental health delivery models for economically challenged communities in India, creating a program for training LGBTQ peer counselors in the US, providing psychological support services for immigrant populations in two US urban settings, designing arts-based witnessing projects that address intergenerational trauma in the US and Australia, and refining a plan for a curriculum for community-based practice in a US psychoanalytic institute.

Annihilation anxieties became apparent early in the group when, just after our first meeting, the Covid-19 virus exploded around the world. By the first week of March, the virus was rampant in Europe, the lockdown in the US had begun, and the virus was spreading quickly in South Asia and Australia. Extensive losses were disproportionately centered in communities of color and among the poor. In India and Australia, where devastating wildfires ravaged much of New South Wales, the outbreak of the virus led to widespread power outages, massive unemployment, and dislocation. Weakened infrastructure throughout South Asia and Australia aggravated the pressures of the Covid-19 lockdowns. In the US, hospitals and health systems were overwhelmed, and health care workers were dying in unexpectedly large numbers. Deaths already exceeded three times the losses of 9/11, and bans against communal mourning hit non-white communities particularly hard, leaving many traumatized without resolution to their bereavement. On May 25, George Floyd was killed in Minneapolis by a white policeman. Millions of people of all races took to the streets in grief and protested around the world.

From the start, Collaboratory members were very interested in one another and in our curriculum, but coping with the fall-out from Covid-19 and weakened infrastructures sometimes overwhelmed the formal agenda. Conversations were pulled toward sharing anecdotes about the struggle for survival many were experiencing. Within the first few weeks, we learned that the elderly father of one of the members was ill with Covid-19 and died. In addition, one of Billie's family members was assaulted by a stranger and required multiple neurosurgeries over the duration of the group. Billie was twice called to the hospital during our meetings. Frequent power losses meant that participants could suddenly go missing on the screen. Anxieties about adequate resources were palpable, as was disillusionment in political leaders.

As discussions focused more and more on horrific circumstances in many participants' communities, the group seemed to stall in concreteness and a collapse of symbolization. Throughout, attendance remained steady, and people referred to the group as an essential "life raft" that somehow kept us afloat together. At times, participants expressed increasing doubt about the value of their work and questioned the usefulness of a psychoanalytic perspective for addressing community challenges of this magnitude. Jane and Billie began to feel that we, too, had been clinging to the security-in-connection provided by the group. We realized then that the group had shifted from "work group" mode to basic assumption mode (Bion, 1961; Hopper, 2001). Our interpretation of this phenomenon helped members to return to a focus on their work together. The resolution of this critical incident depended on the facilitators' recognition that time had been lost (collapsed) in a collective "retreat" from the group's goals. When several members requested additional sessions—a departure from conventional psychoanalytic practice—the entire group agreed.

Not surprisingly, discussions next focused on challenging normative assumptions about psychoanalysis, psychoanalytic practice, and psycho-analysts themselves. Layton views these conversations as part of the nec-essary process of "dis-illusionment" (Layton, 2020) with dominance and constraints of concepts and practices; for example, the "frame," neutrality, and "internalist bias" (Dalal, 2002). A project with an indigenous Austral-ian community offered an excellent opportunity for engaging these themes because it demonstrated how the implicit Western assumptions of vertical authority structures and patriarchal values can create difficulty in arriving at consensual agreements about meanings and strategies.[3]

Shira, originally trained as an art therapist in South Africa, had moved to Australia, where she worked in community mental health clinics in small Indigenous seacoast communities. She had been recently dispatched to provide therapy to two boys who were having great difficulty with school performance. At their first meeting, under a tree outside the school, Shira felt caught inside a paradox she experienced as an ethical double bind. She found that what she expected as the basic conditions for therapeutic work—confidentiality, private spaces, individualized treatment plans—were almost impossible to establish or maintain out in the open, under the tree. But Shira was also acutely aware of her place in (and her implica-tion with) the complex web of institutional racism and historical abuses that perpetuated mistrust and alienation in the indigenous community. The anti-colonial, indigenous communitarian lens she had acquired while working in the field left her in conflict with her training, dominated by Western healing models that privilege the individual psyche, efface indig-enous wisdom, authorize professionals over community members, and undermine the psychic integrity and stability of the group.

Shira felt the heavy weight of the theft of indigenous lands and thou-sands of children over generations. Aware that families felt marginalized and threatened by the school's influence on their children, she knew as well that the two boys under her care—the "identified patients"—symbolically carried the stress and suffering in the larger community, reflecting a splitting of the patients from cultural history and community context. In order to gain the boys' and the community's trust, Shira knew she had to abandon an approach that focused only on the boys' problems in order to seek the collaboration of family and community, especially community elders who were recognized as custodians of cultural knowledge and lore.

Through weeks of conversation with elders, family members, teachers, and Collaboratory participants, Shira attempted to shift from a role as an "outside expert" to being a collaborator with community members. Soon, guided by the elders, a project was planned for an upcoming community day when parents and others would be in attendance. On the day of the visit, long tables covered with baskets full of clay were placed under trees. The two boys were at the table, surrounded by many other children, family members, and elders. The elders, known as uncles and aunties, offered a story in their Aboriginal language about the King of the Birds, who instructed his flocks, "no matter how small you are, you can maintain humility and succeed."

In response to this moral teaching, the other family members, with Shira's help, guided the children in making art from clay. The group of makers, with Shira, now as one of them, created hundreds of nests—containers for imaginary birds and other wildlife. The nests were collected in hand-carved wooden canoes and transported by truck to an exhibition at a local art show, planned as part of this process of community healing. What was first conceived as a therapeutic intervention for "underperforming" youngsters was transformed into a ritual aimed at embracing and 'owning': the boys, cultural restoration, and community repair (Pivnick and Hassinger, 2021). Throughout Shira's accounting of the project in the Collaboratory, participants were deeply engaged and emotionally moved. The Collaboratory had transformed from frightened "survivors on a life raft" to a thoughtful and creative task group of collaborators.

Subsequently, our discussions emphasized theoretical perspectives on working with arts-based methods. Manipulating materials by hand with others manipulating is inherently healing and empowering, as one is helped to metabolize non-narrativized trauma and potentially overwhelming affects (Charles, 2009). As co-created narrative is built through art-making, a sense of mastery over disorganization and fragmentation can solidify at both the individual and community levels (Hassinger & Berman, 2011). An experience of being held in the web of ancestors heightens both individual well-being and a sense of interdependency and mutual-aid in the community (Berman & Hassinger, 2012). Moreover, both therapists and witnesses experience increased empathy and sense of being implicated in, and responsive to, the suffering of others. The potential guilt, shame, and fear of contamination of the witness transforms in co-created intersubjective experiences of building a 'we' from 'us and them.' This experience permits a process of dis-illusionment with colonial hierarchies and practices; both white and indigenous community members are moved to consciously acknowledge normative unconscious assumptions contained implicitly in their "groups-in-the-mind."

In Shira's project, co-created art-making produced an experience of meaning-making (Pivnick, 1998, 2018), heightened identification with the community, and an increased sense of belonging and responsibility—or what we call *relational citizenship*. Collaboratory members pointed out the implicit patriarchal, vertical model of authority relations in psychoanalytic methodology and how it contrasted with the collectivist, networked, nonlinear, and intergenerational model illustrated in Shira's project. We also came to see that our experience of doubt about our efficacy and authority as leaders, as viewed through the lens of this vertical model, led us to temporarily misperceive what was happening in the group's dynamics. Earlier, we interpreted the absence of conflict to indicate possible technical mistakes (e.g., taking comfort in dependency dynamics on the "life raft together"). We viewed our sense of being in the "life raft" together as regressive and a reflection of a failure of (our) leadership.

Shira's presentation dramatically challenged this mode of thought by offering another way to understand self-in-community relations and a corresponding parallel process in the Collaboratory. It became possible to interrogate the individualistic premises about both authority in groups (as vested in the leader only) and in treatment/healing (relationally co-created but still dependent on the practitioner's expert status). It began to dawn on us that we had been involved/implicated in imposing a (re)colonizing enactment and reproduction of a hierarchical, patriarchal model of authority—a product of our normative unconscious as psychoanalytically trained clinicians. We had interpreted the "life raft" dynamics through a negative lens of classical Tavistock group relations theory and subsequently, as leaders, felt guilty and ashamed that we were unable to hold the group to its rules. Participants from Australia/South Africa (with perspectives derived from art therapy and indigenous healing traditions) and India (trained in

Foulksian group relations) offered important corrections by modeling non-Western, nonlinear models of membership, leadership, and authority as vested in cultural knowledge and values (Dalal, 2002). Indeed, leadership is a role anyone may take up in groups (Hayden & Molenkamp, 2002; Shapiro, 2020).

Being a citizen, like being a leader of a group, is not a reified identity or single state but an engagement in a constantly shifting dynamic process in which our internal worlds interact with the external world in a way that often reveals the psychological complexity of our multiple identities (Burka et al., 2007). Experiences in the 2020 Collaboratory included illustrative enactments of these shifting frames of reference when, for example, we realized that our group process shared many similarities with the community group of Shira's project and that, like Shira with her community collaborators, we were indeed also "in the boat" with all the Collaborators.

## Reflections and Conclusions

In each of the two *critical incidents* discussed, enactments reflected tensions associated with racial and existential anxieties, return of traumatic histories, and the shock of surrounding political and cultural crises. Emerging themes in each group were responses to psychological reverberations of these crises for individual participants and the group as a whole. Regressive pulls toward dynamics of exclusion, erasure, and "othering" associated with racial/ethnic differences sometimes threatened to derail the group's tasks. The exploration of enactments and group dynamics became an important pedagogical tool. Furthermore, cross-cultural and intergenerational interactions offered invaluable learning from which we learned about how we enact or defend against acknowledging our implication in the suffering of others.

These defensive "ways-of-being-in-community" are informed by what Layton (2006, 2019) has called "normative unconscious processes." Reflecting the social/political conditions, attitudes, values, and strictures of the time and place, these processes help organize how one behaves as a "raced" and "gendered" person, a person with ethnicity, class status, citizenship status, and relations with historical events and dehumanizing social and political arrangements such as chattel slavery and genocidal imperialism/nation building.

Layton observes that coercive normative unconscious processes, as well as counter-normative unconscious processes (like "de-identification"), express themselves through preferring the past over the future via compulsive reenactments. Multiple identifications, identities, power relations, and impacts of social histories of oppression are not additions to the psyche nor merely defending against something deeper but rather are found at the core of psychic life (Layton, 2020).

Indeed, over and over, as the group enactments were explored, albeit with some difficulty, participants described struggles among competing aspects of their identities, such as divided loyalties to the various racial/ethnic and sociopolitical groups to which they belonged. We found an example of how the past was preferred over the present when we persisted in using an authority model for interpreting the group process of the 2020 Collaboratory, despite not really being committed to it ourselves. It was only when "re-minded" by a group member's experience of something new and more adaptive that we were able to let go of our identification with colonialized images of what constituted the ideal analytic interpretation (Tubert-Oklander & Hernandez-Tubert, 2021).

Our certain experiences in the Collaboratory were illustrative enactments of what Frantz Fanon (1967) (after W.E.B. Du Bois, 1903) called the difficulty of living with a double-consciousness of one's dominant and subdominant identities. However, our experience also suggests that double-consciousness needs to be multiplied to describe the demands of the psychic work involved in negotiating multiple memberships in "groups-in-the-mind" with an emphasis on identifying our connection to and implication in the colonial roots of psychoanalysis. The Collaboratory offers a site and methodology for working with these dynamics as they play out in group and community life.

Stories from the Collaboratory highlight ways in which the emergence of members' relational citizenship marks the movement from regressive hierarchical group dynamics to shared responsibility and role flexibility in which members take on leadership and develop practices characterized by a valuing of mutual implication and accountability. These experiences have taught us how group and community engagements can serve as correctives to the splitting of the psychic and the social in our field.

## Notes

1 Although the conduct of play therapy is rarely considered part of the writing of history, play may bring to life meanings that have been left unformulated by traumatized adults in tragedy's aftermath (Beebe et al., 2013). This is especially true to the extent that the children carry vicariously what literary scholar Cathy

Caruth (2010) would consider their bereaved parents' unclaimed experienced. Winnicott interpreted this defensive maneuver as the child dramatizing the parent's displacement (Green, 2005). A similar dynamic can take place in intergenerational community trauma (Volkan, 2013; Pivnick & Hassinger, 2021).

2  Our concept of *relational citizenship* has been further informed by Eng and Han's (2006) exploration of the psychic challenges associated with assimilation desires and conflicting identifications for Asian American citizens. Referencing Klein's (1935) concept of the melancholic identification, Eng and Han view *psychic citizenship* as the resolution of continuous intrapsychic struggle with (implicitly relational) competing identifications in which the pain of racial and cultural marginalization is reduced by mourning the loss of good internal objects while still identifying with communities associated with those good objects. We link their psychic citizen to the intrapsychic-social realm and the domain of group and community dynamics. In this move, we have imagined an intersubjective *relational citizenship*. Intrapsychic/interpersonal management of multiple group identifications (*groups-in-the-mind*) strengthens capacity for negotiating authority relations, differences, power, and ideological commitments.

3  A more detailed account of this project can be found in Shein, R. (2021). Socially-engaged art therapy in an Australian aboriginal community: An art therapist's reflection. *International Advances in Art Therapy Research and Practice: The Emerging Picture, 248.*

# References

Apprey, M. (2004). From the events of history to a sense of history: Aspects of transgenerational trauma and brutality in the African-American experience. In B. Sklarew, S. W. Twemlow, & S. M. Wilkinson (Eds.), *Analysts in the trenches: Streets, schools, war zones* (pp. 45–55). The Analytic Press.

Banfield, E. (1967). *The moral basis of a backward society.* Free Press.

Bateson, G. (1972). *Steps to an ecology of mind.* University of Chicago Press.

Beebe, B., McCrorie, E., & Pivnick, B. (December, 2013). Poetry of 9/11: Trauma, grief, and imagination. *Clio's Psyche: Understanding the "Why" of Culture, Current Events, History, and Society* (Special Issue on Poetry and Psychohistory), *20*(3), 314–323.

Benjamin, J. (2017). *Beyond doer-done to: Recognition theory, intersubjectivity and the third.* Routledge.

Berman, K., & Hassinger, J. (2012). *Women on purpose: The resilience and creativity of the founding women of Phumani Paper.* DeskLink Publishing.

Bion, W. R. (1961). Experiences in groups and other papers. In *Experiences in groups and other papers* (pp. 1–191). Tavistock.

Bion, W. R. (2013). Attacks on linking. *The Psychoanalytic Quarterly, 82*(2), 285–300.

Boulanger, G. (2011). *Wounded by reality: Understanding and treating adult onset trauma.* Routledge.

Bromberg, P. (1998). *Standing in the spaces.* Psychology Press.

Burka, J. B., Sarnat, J. E., & John, C. S. (2007). Learning from experience in case conference: A Bionian approach in teaching and consulting. *International Journal of Psychoanalysis, 88*, 981–1000.

Butler, J. (2020). *The force of nonviolence*. Verso.

Caruth, C. (2010). *Unclaimed experience: Trauma, narrative and history*. JHU Press.

Charles, M. (2009, August 8). *Collage: Piecing together the fragments of traumatic memory*. Invited paper, APA.

Confino, A., & Fritsche, P. (Eds.). (2002). Introduction: Noises of the past. In *The work of memory: New directions in the study of German society and culture*. University of Illinois Press.

Connolly, M., Gobodo-Madikizela, P., Layton, L., Nichols, B., Pivnick, B., & Reading, R. (2022). What's repaired in reparations: A conversation among psychoanalytic and social activists. *Psychoanalytic Dialogues, 32*(1), 3–16.

Cushman, P. (2015). Relational psychoanalysis as political resistance. *Contemporary Psychoanalysis, 51*(3), 423–459.

Dalal, F. (1998). *Taking the group seriously*. Jessica Kingsley Press.

Dalal, F. (2002). *Race, colour, and the processes of racialization: New perspectives from group analysis*. Routledge.

Dalal, F. (2017). The analytic and the relational: Inquiring into practice. *Group Analysis, 50*(2), 171–189.

Davoine, F., & Gaudilliere, J. M. (2005). *History beyond trauma: Whereof one cannot speak, thereof one cannot stay silent*. Other Press.

DiAngelo, R. (2018). *White fragility: Why it's so hard for white people to talk about racism*. Beacon Press.

Du Bois, W. E. B. (1903). *The souls of black folk*. Penguin.

Eng, D., & Han, S. (2000). A dialogue on racial melancholia. *Psychoanalytic Dialogues, 10*(4), 667–700.

Fanon, F. (1967). *Black skin, White masks*. Grove Press.

Fortier, A. M. (2017). The psychic life of policy: Desire, anxiety and 'citizenisation' in Britain. *Critical Social Policy, 37*(1), 3–21.

Foulkes, S. H. (1964/1984). *Therapeutic group analysis*. Karnac Books. 1984 [Original publication, Allen & Unwin.

Foulkes, S. H. (1990/2018). *Selected papers: Psychoanalysis and group analysis*. Routledge.

Frie, R. (2017). History flows through us: Psychoanalysis and historical understanding. *Psychoanalysis, Self, and Context, 12*(3), 221–229.

Fromm, E. (1958/1992). The revolutionary character. In *The dogma of Christ and other essays* (pp. 147–168). Holt.

Frosh, S. (2001). Psychoanalysis, identity, and citizenship. In N. Stevenson (Ed.), *Culture and citizenship*. Sage Publications.

Freud, S. (1920). Beyond the pleasure principle. *S.E. 18*, 1–64. Hogarth.

Glassman, U. (2008). *Group work: A humanistic and skills-building approach* (2nd ed.). Sage Publications.

Green, A. (2005). *Play and reflection in Donald Winnicott's writings*. Karnac Books.

Hassinger, J., & Berman, K. (2011). Women on purpose: A model for cross-cultural, interdisciplinary collaborations. In G. Tsolidis (Ed.), *Identities in transition*. Interdisciplinary Press.

Hassinger, J., & Pivnick, B. A. (2022). The community turn: Relational citizenship in the Psychoanalytic Community Collaboratory. *International Journal of Psychoanalysis, 103*(1).

Hayden, C., & Molenkamp, R. J. (2002). *Tavistock primer II*. AK Rice Institute for Study of Social Systems.

Hernandez-Tubert, R. (2011). The politics of despair: From despair to dialogue and hope. *Group Analysis, 44*, 27–39.

Holmes, D. (2017). Culturally-imposed trauma: The sleeping dog has awakened: Will psychoanalysis take heed? *Psychoanalytic Dialogues, 26*(6), 641–654.

Hopper, E. (1982). A comment on professor M. Jahoda's "Individual and Group". In *The individual and the group* (pp. 17–25). Springer.

Hopper, E. (1985). The problem of context in group-analytic psychotherapy: A clinical illustration and a brief theoretical discussion. In M. Pines (Ed.) *Bion and group psychotherapy* (pp. 330–353). Routledge and Kegan Paul.

Hopper, E. (2000). From objects and subjects to citizens: Group analysis and the study of maturity. *Group Analysis, 33*, 29–34.

Hopper, E. (2001). Difficult patients in group analysis: The personification of (ba) I: A/M. *Group*, 25(3), 139–171.

Hopper, E. (2003). *Traumatic experience in the unconscious life of groups*. Jessica Kingsley.

Hopper, E. (2009). The theory of the basic assumption of in cohesion: Aggregation/massification OR (BA)I: A/M. *British Journal of Psychotherapy, 25*(2), 214–229.

Hopper, E., & Weinberg, H. (Eds.). (2018). *The social unconscious in persons, groups and societies: Mainly theory*. Routledge.

Jacoby, R. (1975/2017). *Social amnesia: A critique of contemporary psychology*. Routledge.

Kernberg, O. (2020). Malignant narcissism and large group regression. *The Psychoanalytic Quarterly, 89*(1), 1–24.

Klein, M. (1935). On the psychogenesis of manic-depressive states. In *Love, guilt and reparation and other works* (pp. 145–174). Hogarth.

Layton, L. (2006). Racial identities, racial enactments, and normative unconscious processes. *The Psychoanalytic Quarterly, 75*, 237–269.

Layton, L. (2019). *Toward a social psychoanalysis: Culture, character, and normative unconscious processes*. Routledge.

Layton, L. (2020). Intersectionality, normative unconscious processes, and racialized enactments of distinction. In M. Belkin & C. White (Eds.), *Intersectionality and relational psychoanalysis: New perspectives on race, gender, and sexuality* (pp. 171–191). Routledge.

Levine, D. (2017). *Psychoanalysis, society, and the inner world: Embedded meaning in politics and social conflict*. Routledge.

Losso, R., de Setton, L., & Scharff, D. (Eds.). (2017). *The linked self in psychoanalysis: The pioneering work of Enrique Pichon-Riviere*. Routledge.

Margalit, A. (2004). *The ethics of memory*. Harvard University Press.

Menzies, I. E. P. (1960). A case study in the functioning of social systems as a defense against anxiety. *Human Relations, 13*, 95–121.

Pivnick, B. A. (1998). Wriggles, squiggles, and words: From expression to meaning in early childhood and psychotherapy. In A. Robbins (Ed.), *Therapeutic presence*. Jessica Kingsley.

Pivnick, B. A. (2011). Enacting remembrance: Turning toward memorializing September 11th. *Journal of Religion and Health, 50*(3), 499–515.

Pivnick, B. A. (2013). What the living did: September 11th and its aftermath. In A. Adelman & K. Malawista (Eds.), *The therapist in mourning: From the faraway nearby*. Columbia University Press.

Pivnick, B. A. (2015). Spaces to stand in: Applying clinical psychoanalysis to the relational design of the national September 11 memorial museum. (Winner of the APA division 39 section five Schillinger memorial essay award). *Division/Review, 13*, 19–24.

Pivnick, B. A. (2017). Transforming collapse: Applying clinical psychoanalysis to the relational design of the national September 11 memorial museum. *International Forum of Psychoanalysis: Violence, Terror and Terrorism Today: Psychoanalytic Perspectives, Part II, 26*(4), 248–257.

Pivnick, B. A. (2018). Behind the lines: Toward an aesthetic framework for psychoanalytic psychotherapy. *Journal of Clinical Psychology, 74*, 218–232.

Pivnick, B. A. (2021). Recollecting the vanishing forms of 9/11: Twenty years of ruptures, ripples, and reflections. *Psychoanalytic Perspectives, 18*(3), 279–295.

Pivnick, B. A., & Hassinger, J. A. (2021). The child in the school, the school in the community, and the community in the child: Linking psychic and social domains in school violence prevention. *International Journal of Applied Psychoanalytic Studies, 2021*, 1–12.

Pivnick, B. A., & Hennes, T. (2014). Managing collapse: Memorializing September 11th through the co-creation of a memorial museum. In M. O'Loughlin (Ed.), *The ethics of remembering and the consequences of forgetting: Essays on trauma, history and memory*. Rowman & Littlefield.

Protevi, J. (2019). *Edges of the state*. University Minnesota Press.

Rice, A. K. (1965/2018). *Learning for leadership: Interpersonal and intergroup relations*. Routledge.

Rothberg, M. (2009). *Multidirectional memory: Remembering the holocaust in the age of decolonization*. Stanford University Press.

Rothberg, M. (2019). *The implicated subject: Beyond victims and perpetrators*. Stanford University Press.

Rozmarin, E. (2017). The social is the unconscious of the unconscious of psychoanalysis. *Contemporary Psychoanalysis*, 1–11.

Salberg, J., & Grand, S. (2017). *Wounds of history: Repair and resilience in the trans-generational transmission of trauma*. Routledge.

Samuels, A. (2004). Politics on the couch? Psychotherapy and society—possibilities and some limitations. *Psychoanalytic Dialogues, 14*(6), 817–834.

Samuels, A. (2016). *The political psyche*. Routledge.

Scharff, D. E. (2018). Pichon-Rivière and object relations theory. In *The linked self in psychoanalysis* (pp. 217–231). Routledge.

Shapiro, E. R. (2020). *Finding a place to stand: Developing self-reflective institutions, leaders and citizens*. Phoenix Publishing House.

Shapiro, E. R., & Carr, A. W. (1991). *Lost in familiar places: Creating new connections between the individual and society*. Yale University Press.

Shapiro, E. R., & Carr, A. W. (2017). Citizenship as development. *Organisational and Social Dynamics, 17*(2), 278–288.

Shein, R. (2021). Socially-engaged art therapy in an Australian aboriginal community: An art therapist's reflection. *International Advances in Art Therapy Research and Practice: The Emerging Picture, 248*.

Sullivan, H. S. (1953/1968). *The interpersonal theory of psychiatry*. Norton.

Tubert-Oklander, J. (2014). *The one and the many: Relational psychoanalysis and group analysis*. Routledge.

Tubert-Oklander, J., & De Tubert, R. H. (2004). *Operative groups: The Latin-American approach to group analysis* (Vol. 24). Jessica Kingsley Publishers.

Tubert-Oklander, J., & Hernandez-Tubert, R. (2021). *Psychoanalysis, group analysis, and beyond: Towards a new paradigm of the human being*. Routledge.

Ulanov, A. (2007). The space between pastoral care and global terrorism. *Scottish Journal of Healthcare Chaplaincy, 10*(2), 3–8.

Vaughans, K. (2017). To unchain haunting blood memories. In J. Salberg & S. Grand (Eds.), *Wounds of history. Repair and resilience in the transgenerational transmission of trauma* (pp. 226–239). Routledge.

Volkan, D. (2013). Large-group-psychology in its own right: Large-group identity and peace making. *International J of Applied Psychoanalytic Studies, 10*(3), 210–246.

# Chapter 10

# Awakening to the Political—Or Is It All an Undream?

*Matt Aibel*

I remember the shock when John McCain chose a manifestly unfit politician, Sarah Palin, to be his presidential running mate in the summer of 2008. I was heading into my second year of psychoanalytic training in New York City. The prior year, our governor, Eliot Spitzer, had resigned in scandal. Barack Obama would soon enough become the first black man elected president. None of these major political events were mentioned, let alone discussed, in any aspect of my analytic training experience. At an institute social function, I eagerly asked a senior faculty member what she made of Palin. She demurred and, in a move familiar to anyone who's ever been in treatment with a classical analyst, turned the question around: what did *I* think?

What I thought was that no one at my institute seemed at all comfortable discussing anything political, despite its being a primarily relational institute (and that faculty member professed to be a relational analyst). Greenberg and Mitchell's (1983) elucidation of the mind as formed in a wider relational matrix beyond just mother and father had long pointed toward a more social psychoanalytic theory, but it seemed something still kept relational analysts from extending this understanding to the sociopolitical sphere. Obama's inauguration telecast was viewed amid deep pleasure and cheers in a conference room adjacent to my classroom, yet all the analysts and candidates watching seemed implicitly to understand that nothing about the election ought to be discussed as if to do so would problematically sanction political talk in an analytic institute. Nowhere else, on that day or afterward, did I hear any conversation about the election or the political surround. I was confounded. Was there no rightful place for

DOI: 10.4324/9781003265146-10

politics in psychoanalytic training or treatment? I don't recall ever talking politics in my own supervision or training analysis. Was it, in fact, taboo?

It seemed a strange lacuna.

My post-training self-directed psychoanalytic reading focused on what felt to me to be of more immediate concern, namely, my continuing desire to clarify the extent to which my personal history and characterological proclivities were (over)determining my theoretical stances. While politics caught my analytic attention, it remained off to one side, a curiosity: relevant but less immediate to my concerns than my narcissistic injuries, self-doubts and determination to develop my analytic skills. Echoing aspects of Freud's metapsychology, I was more occupied with Oedipal issues than with interrogating sociopolitical impacts. The privilege from which I benefitted as a straight white cisgender male helped to structure and permit this prioritizing. The security of my circumstances fostered the stability of my psyche: I was afforded a stable enough social positioning that I could compartmentalize thoughts about sociopolitical impingements and interpellations, relegating them to secondary or tertiary status, my wonderings about politics more curiosity than existentially compelled preoccupation.

Enter Donald Trump, a character so patently, monumentally absurd and so grotesquely emblematic of America's dark leanings and flawed character that not even Jerzy Kosiński, author of *Being There* (1970), had dared imagine him—though Philip Roth, in *The Plot Against America* (2004), sort of had. Stunned, horrified and grieving over his election, I found my erstwhile political wonderings now galvanized into an urgent engagement. Shrugging over what was happening "out there" while going about my business no longer felt defensible. Too much was at stake. I no longer felt insulated from implications. This coup de politique smacked deep into my psyche, heart and kishkes. Undertaking focused research, I discovered that, in spite of the silence on the topic throughout my training, there was, in fact, a history and a burgeoning literature, with roots in Freud, Adorno and the Interpersonalists, notably Fromm, addressing many of the questions I'd wondered about and many others I hadn't formulated. I located precedents for socially informed psychoanalytic work conducted during periods of discombobulating political turmoil. Yet I wondered if something new was called for in our particular harrowing political moment. Had American democracy been under such internecine threat at any other time since the Civil War? America was not the only country flirting with, if not already endorsing, strong-man authoritarianism: a disturbing tectonic shift to the right was occurring worldwide. In the context of more frequent extreme weather events resulting from climate change, plus ever-increasing economic disparities, existential threats felt imminent; a dread about end times could be discerned, which increased dramatically when the coronavirus pandemic began (Samuels, 2020). Was the world in its death throes? And if so, of how much use was an analytic attitude? Simultaneous to these unnerving national and international dynamics, new trends were emerging in relational psychoanalytic theory and practice, coalescing around heightened sensitivity to and deeper appreciation of the psychological impacts of oppression with respect to race, ethnicity, culture, class, gender, sexual orientation and other axes of identity. These vital new impulses suggested that the relational turn was undergoing significant ideological evolution toward a more genuinely social psychoanalysis (Hollander, 2017; Aibel, 2018, 2019; Layton, 2019, 2020).

My questions about the place of political discourse in psychoanalytic treatment no longer stemmed just from intellectual curiosity but now from felt necessity. What was I to do with patients whose politics might be in direct opposition to mine? In an era of such fiercely pitched hyperpartisanship, would such an analytic pair inevitably succumb to the same aggressive complementarity and us/them power operations which so quickly sink almost any attempt to engage in political conversations across the partisan divide? Could an analyst maintain her therapeutic commitments, offering an analytic attitude of curiosity, empathy and respect toward her patient's subjectivity while simultaneously holding on to her sense of personal integrity? If a patient's political commitments, in essence, threatened the well-being of all non-white, non-straight, non-Christian, non-citizen non-males, and quite possibly the functioning of American democracy (Snyder, 2017) and the habitability of the planet (Orange, 2017), ought there to be a particular clinical stance by which to interrogate that patient's political allegiances? Was it analytically sound to diagnose such a patient's politics as pathological and then work to ameliorate this condition? Did clinical work have any role to play in helping heal the nation, or were such concerns misplaced, overblown or anathema to providing credible psychoanalytic treatment?

From a different vertex, what of the trap of falling into collusive self-satisfaction or righteous indignation along with patients whose politics resemble their analyst's? This is the more likely scenario, after all, for liberal analysts working in big cities like New York (Aibel, 2018). Another conundrum: what to make of patients whose narcissistic preoccupations, privilege, or cynicism resulted in their not at all addressing the election beyond a cursory acknowledgment of it? Isn't this indifference or avoidance a legitimate site for analytic inquiry?

It seemed reasonable to acknowledge that political affiliations, beliefs and commitments are essential aspects of our self and other representations. Further, the political surround is an undeniably consequential factor in our difficulties in living. These psychic realities thus confer legitimacy upon politics as a focus of analytic attention. After all, we can neither help ameliorate patients' suffering nor widen and deepen their understanding of their lives if we don't help them discover how their and our embeddedness in particular historical and sociopolitical arrangements shapes, limits and deforms them and us (Aibel, 2018; see also Cushman, 1995, 2015; Layton, 2004; Hollander, 2017). We must therefore attend to our patients' and our own larger sociohistorical resonances and repositories, as well as our respective social locations.

As our Interpersonal forebearers (i.e., Sullivan, Horney, Fromm) had argued, social factors are not extra-analytic (see Lionells et al., 1995; Howell & Itzkowitz, 2016). More recently, Layton summed up this position this way: "Gender, race, class, and sexual orientation are not add-ons to psychodynamics; they *constitute* psychodynamics" (2004, p. 248). The same can be said of political identity (Aibel, 2018). Guralnik states that the personal and the political are "an inevitable and ineradicable aspect of [each other]" such that "the discourses of sociopolitics and individual subject do not compete, but rather weave together" (2016a). Once we recognize how inextricably interwoven our individual psyches are to our sociopolitical surround, we begin to appreciate how illogical and internally inconsistent it is to deem political considerations off-limits in psychoanalytic inquiry. The sociopolitical is an irreducible register of experience and psychic organization which deserves the same analytic consideration we bring to any other aspect of psychic experience.

The real reasons behind the received wisdom of psychoanalysis' marginalization of political discourse, I discovered, lay in an intriguing psychosocial history that began with Freud's conflicts over the role of the sociocultural in his theories of mind and pathology (Aibel, 2018; see also Layton, 2020). From the start of psychoanalysis, it could be said, identification with marginality and cultural trauma was largely suppressed (Tummala-Narra, 2016) and due consideration of the impacts of the political surround dissociated. A depoliticized self and a depoliticized psychoanalysis were legitimated for deeply personal rather than theoretically sound reasons (Aibel, 2018; see also Layton, 2004; Kuriloff, 2014; Philipson, 2017). This striking conclusion opens up the field for reintroduction or reclamation of sociopolitical inquiry and analysis in our clinical work, harkening back to the radical aspects of Freud's project (Danto, 2007; Zaretsky, 2015; Layton, 2019) and the appreciation of sociocultural impacts from the interpersonal tradition (Philipson, 2017).

As well, we are becoming alert to the interpellations of Big History (Guralnik & Simeon, 2010; Guralnik, 2016b) and the impacts and interpenetrations of the trans-generational transmission of trauma (Harris et al., 2016; Grand & Salberg, 2017; Salberg & Grand, 2017). Historical sociocultural/political traumas live on in the psyches and environments of victims' descendants. Cordoning off these traumas may facilitate a clean clinical picture that permits a sharper focus on Oedipal dynamics, but the resulting picture is oversimplified, false. It does (iatrogenic) damage to the integrity and fullness of the patient's psychic truth. A relational sensibility recognizes such wider forces as being crucial shapers of identity and internal structure. This understanding undoubtedly complicates our work. It gets messier, unwieldy, ever more kaleidoscopic—more like life. We are restoring missing dimensions and thus encountering a fuller clinical picture.

Traditional psychoanalytic thinking "reduces political content to family drama" (Layton, 2005, p. 4). For example, Greenson states that when a patient speaks of events in the social surround, even those "of great political magnitude, if the external situation does not lead to a personal, internal situation, a resistance is at work" (1967, p. 64). Bettelheim once dismissively "declared that antiwar demonstrators were simply acting out an Oedipal conflict" (Osnos, 2011, p. 56). From a relational perspective, we can hear political content as symbolic communication—of internal conflict, attachment issues, transference or any other unconscious content—*as well as* an expression of reasonable, deeply rooted anxiety about the actual state of the external world (Barry, 2022). One register does not preclude the other; there is room for both to be operative.

Samuels turns the old-fashioned reductionistic view on its head, suggesting that when a patient raises political issues, they provide "an amplification" of more so-called personal or intrapsychic issues: "thin material becomes more ample, a low volume that made it hard to hear gets turned up" (2004, p. 46). This keen observation may lower the anxiety of the clinician deciding whether or not to pursue political dimensions of clinical material since focusing on the political does not necessarily mean the more so-called intrapsychic dimensions go unattended. In Samuels' experience, political discussion aids the rest of our work; it's another register of it, refracting the same psychic issues. When a patient of mine recently remarked, "You and I both know that Americans are turned against each other right now," I heard the comment both as a legitimate, well-considered expression of a civic-minded progressive citizen's pained disappointment over the state of our nation's disunion and as an unconscious communication about his own currently strained marriage—"both/and"—giving me a clinical choice as to which register to privilege. In the event, given the specific trajectory of our process and following the contours of an unobtrusive relational stance (Grossmark, 2018), I chose to make no interpretive comment, letting the resonances linger.

A relational, two-person model encourages engagement of political themes for still other reasons. In a co-constructed treatment, our similarities and differences across all domains are ripe for analytic unpacking, negotiation and collaborative meaning-making. Hoffman's (1998) dialectical constructivism makes space for the analyst to speak freely to and even challenge a patient's politics (see Hoffman, 2013), predicated on the understanding that the analyst's decentered subjectivity is as prone to blind spots as the patient's. Hoffman's sense of ironic authority (1992) courts freedom in the context of uncertainty or radical humility, bearing in mind both the fundamental dyadic asymmetry and the fundamental commitment to keeping the teleology of any intervention for the patient's benefit. The humbler relational analyst seeks and actively recruits the patient's collaborative input. The patient is free, even encouraged, to challenge or disagree with her analyst's beliefs, though this may be much easier said than done. If complementary political positions begin to emerge, the analyst might remark, "It seems like we may have differing viewpoints here. What should we do? How might we handle this? What does or doesn't feel safe to you?" (April Feldman, personal communication, 2017). Soliciting our patient's agency in such a manner is a hallmark of relational technique.

While there is not yet a wealth of literature on the challenges of working with patients whose politics significantly and powerfully differ from those of the therapist, clinical investigation in this area has been expanding in recent years, driven in no small part, of course, by the rise of Trumpism in the United States. If it's in the room, it's in the treatment, and Trump supporters have been in the room. Political differences have always been present in American analytic dyads, but as noted, they have historically been sidestepped or interpreted solely in terms of patients' object relations. Further, in our highly polarized political environment, ideological differences of all stripes have become increasingly fraught. As a result, many American clinicians have at last found themselves confronting the types of tricky, even perilous dynamics that colleagues abroad, especially those in war-torn or strife-ridden countries, have contended with for years. While it's not a given that we will be more reactive to a patient's politics than to any other aspect of their character, it's hard to deny the strong magnetic pull into the vertex of opposing binaries for any analyst paying attention to the paroxysms of our current world.

Case reports of relational analysts working with patients whose political allegiances counter their own often describe iatrogenic wounding, contentious ruptures and dysregulating enactments. Patients who feel criticized, judged or othered by their analysts become deeply offended (Hendelman, 2018) or even moved to eruptions of near violence (Rozmarin, 2009). Some treatments end over such untenable tensions; others may be worked through to facilitative resolution. Still, others may continue in an unsatisfactorily wan or circumscribed manner, "in the truncated way that treads carefully around . . . political worldview and identity" (Tublin, 2017a, p. 75) in order to avoid further ruptures. I suspect avoiding a contentious area in this manner limits the dyad's optimal relational freedom in ways both obvious and subtle and only causes the unresolved issue to fester.

A pathway I keep returning to in my thinking is that left-wing analysts might typically conceptualize our patients' right-wing politics as pathology in need of a cure. Having in mind a private treatment plan of this nature, though, is clearly problematic: our patients do not come to us because they are seeking to overcome their limiting political beliefs. They don't have a problem with their beliefs; *we* do (Tublin, 2015; Aibel, 2020). We might contend (as some analysts do; see below) that certain political beliefs lead to poorer mental health outcomes. Yet a danger in proceeding from this formulation is that if we believe a patient's political beliefs are pathological, we may engage in overzealous interventions that could play out like totalitarian re-education mandates conceived of as enlightenment (Aibel, 2020). I suspect many liberal analysts hope or imagine, whether consciously or not, that eventually, as they get healthier, our right-wing patients will shift their beliefs to the left (see Sandberg, 2017). How comfortable are we admitting to such a protocol? How might we hold our political commitments more lightly when engaging with patients whose politics are to the right (or, let's not forget, to the left) of our own? I find it helpful to recenter around this core analytic understanding: when sitting with our patients, we track their utterances in terms of everything we have come to know about their developmental histories, object worlds, organizing principles, identifications and internalizations, as well as the distress and suffering that initially brought them to us. This deep contextual knowledge allows us to situate patients' politics as but one manifestation of their complex, multiply determined psyches. We do not want to ignore the real-world implications of their politics, yet we need not take their beliefs (only) at face value. Our analytic sensibility moves to the forefront; to the extent that we cognize being with a "suffering stranger" (Orange, 2011), our civic self may quiet down. We allow ourselves to become less literal, listening with an ear attuned to symbolic meanings and unconscious resonances, alert to multiplicity, primary process and dream logic. We court reverie and move into potential space. This disposition, after all, lies at the core of our work. With patients toward whom we have strong negative countertransference, we are often able to shift into a listening mode that allows us to make empathic contact with all kinds of challenging material. Encountering and dwelling with patients' distressing and disturbing thoughts, feelings, images, memories, fantasies and behaviors—or our own—we may feel rotten, appalled, disgusted, crazy and sad. We also sit with patients whom we may regard as *better* than we are in some respects—superior in ethics, bravery, generosity, compassion, intelligence, looks—in which case we may need to reckon with our envy and insecurity. (This may be so for left-of-center analysts working with more progressive or radical patients.) We know how to contemplate such differences in multiple dimensions and how to account for reactive countertransferences. We strive to recruit genuine curiosity, sometimes a kind of fascination, in the search for psychoanalytic understanding. With this in mind, sitting with strong political differences that would ordinarily exercise or incite us may not necessarily be such a different matter. Altman, reflecting on this challenge, reminds us:

> That's the tricky thing that I think we, as psychoanalysts, get a lot of experience in doing—not giving up our own point of view, but at the

same time finding a way to resonate with the other person's point of view, so that they feel understood. And if they feel understood, then they're more likely to feel free to resonate with your point of view.

(Altman et al., 2004, p. 9)

Of course, as any left-leaning analyst who has worked with Trump-supporting or right-wing patients may readily understand, invoking this attitude may be far easier said than done.

Another thorny reality that problematizes Altman's point is that relational psychoanalysis is not a morally neutral endeavor. It arrives with a politics already, and its undergirding values are primarily progressive. Beginning with the liberatory impulse animating Freud's work, as well as the socialist politics that informed some of his close colleagues (e.g., Adler, Jung, Jacobson), aided by the deconstructed hierarchical structure of Ferenczi's mutual analysis, and continuing with the Frankfurt School's and Fromm's leftist critiques, psychoanalysis in its first decades could be regarded as radical, "a site of resistance" (Harris, 2009, p. 139) to social conformity and traditional notions of authority. Following ego psychology's postwar ascendancy with its emphasis on adaptation and "the need to . . . seek security" (Shapiro, 2000, p. 305; see also Aron & Starr, 2013; Cushman, 1995, 2005), the resurgence of a radical politics is discernible (Aron, 1996; Aron & Starr, 2013; Kuchuck, 2021; Samuels, 2021; Avila-Espada, 2021). The 1980s relational turn was created by a cohort of clinicians who had come of age in the late '60s counterculture. Influenced by the critical and postmodern discourses of feminism, gender studies, queer theory, deconstruction, African American and colonial studies, they moved their psychoanalytic theories further left.

We can limn liberal values constituting relational theory: empathy, care and the notion of fairness as defined by equality (Tublin, 2017b); an ethical humanitarian sensibility (Avila-Espada, 2021) or radical ethics (Orange, 2015, 2017, 2020); the democratizing, egalitarian impulse to decenter authority, whether in terms of the *I-thou* relationship's structuring of equality and mutuality (Buber & Kaufmann, 1970), Hoffman's ironic authority arising out of a social-constructivist view of process (1992, 1998, 2013), or relational theory's deep interest in the variable impacts of the analyst's subjectivity upon the patient. These all stand in marked contrast to the comparatively authoritarian stance deriving from classical analysis' hierarchical power structure. More: our faith in the merits of dependency and the virtues of vulnerability, in contrast to right-wing politics' investment in independence and invincibility, and our nurturing of patients' agency and desire (Gentile, 2016a, 2016b, 2020). In these and other respects, relational theory instantiates aspects of a subversive anti-authoritarianism, despite our embeddedness in late-capitalist era neoliberalism (Hollander, 2017). Cushman's body of work (e.g., 1990, 1995, 2015) argues that we therapists do not speak from outside the system; we are players who have chosen sides, a point Botticelli (2004, 2018) and Tublin (2017a, 2017b) both strongly elaborate. Contemporary relational theory is implicated as a purveyor of a politically progressive ideology.

This reality has significant implications for the way that relational analysts conceive of the goals of our work. Characterizing his work as part of "the political turn" in relational theory, Samuels asks, "Isn't it the task of therapy to facilitate people in stopping thinking like the state wants them to think, just as we try to facilitate judicious freedom from persecutory, authoritarian and judgmental parental introjects?" (2017, p. 679). Layton asks, "Should a concern for the social world be a criterion of health?" (2005, p. 5), and Hollander inquires, "Do we reflect with our patients about the impact of our disordered social reality upon our psyches?" (2017, p. 435). These authors all argue that patients' relationships to the polity are a key aspect of mental health and are therefore important sites of analytic work.

Others take a more measured position on this question. Rozmarin argues for a theoretical and clinical stance of "ambivalent activism" (2007a, p. 386). He suggests that, given the unresolvable "dialectic of self and other" (2007b, p. 330) that pervades the inherently "conflicted discourse" (2007b, p. 327) of psychoanalysis, the optimal clinical position is one of "deliberate ambivalence" (ibid.). Jacobs, considering "whether we should have as a goal for the patient to be more interested in the world, be more altruistic, have more of a feeling for society, and so on," likewise argues for a balanced approach. He notes that it may be "a sign of growth and health for some patients . . . a movement away from narcissistic concern to a kind of feeling for others," but he is reluctant to make this "a standard of health" out of deference to patients "who need simply to live their lives with a certain kind of privacy . . . a kind of more private world [apart from] the social network. . . . We can't describe that as an illness," he cautions (Altman et al., p. 30).

Tublin and Botticelli, both of whom are very politically conscious, express outright wariness with the type of interventions Layton and

Hollander propose. They feel we ought to be very careful about injecting our politics into our patients' treatments. Tublin flatly states he has no interest in influencing a patient's politics; he avers that his interest is simply in helping patients to love and to live with more satisfaction (2020). Botticelli remarks,

> I don't see analysis as a place to try to bring people around to more right-minded ideas about anything. I'd have no trouble refraining from questioning or challenging my patient's beliefs, let alone trying to bring them over to my way of viewing things.
>
> (personal communication, 2021)

I wonder whether it is possible to make such clear distinctions. Sandberg, stunned to discover that a long-time patient, "a man I thought I knew" (2017, p. 383), voted for Trump, confesses that "it is not so easy to metabolize the feelings of anger, betrayal, and sadness I feel" (p. 382). Sandberg regards his patient's choice of candidate as indicative of some degree of analytic failure, leaving him with the shameful "feeling that the good work I had done with this man was not good enough" (p. 383). We know that Trump voters can be loving people: some of them raised us, sat at our Thanksgiving table and married our children. Still, how confident can we be in our patients' expanding capacities for loving and living with more satisfaction if their lives are simultaneously organized around projecting their disowned badness onto despised others, supporting a hateful, harmful demagogue, turning away from truth, science, good faith and anything remotely resembling an ethic of care (Gilligan, 1982)? So long as they express and enact their fear and loathing, desperation and pain in these ways, I, too, would have a hard time feeling good about my work with such patients. The distinction that Tublin and Botticelli seek to draw seems to me to rely upon ignoring or compartmentalizing this inconvenient truth.

The idea of attributing problematic, even pathological characteristics to Trump voters, and really, Republican voters more broadly, as Sandberg and I do—and I would venture to say, Layton and Hollander do as well—likely troubles Tublin, though he is by no means sympathetic to Trump's agenda (2017b). Tublin (2017a, 2017b) proposes that the liberal hegemony in relational psychoanalysis creates significant problems we must confront, limiting the robustness of our theory and presenting inherent challenges to conservative patients (and, I might add, to the presumably few conservative analysts) who likely feel the protective need to conceal their marginalized, even despised politics, thus omitting a key aspect of their subjectivities.

For dyads in the U.S., the feeling that "only one can live" (Benjamin, 2018) is reinforced by our embeddedness in a principally two-party political system wherein, structurally speaking, political victory may very well determine the very survival of our way of life. Tublin (2017a) insightfully argues that the zero-sum game of America's two-party system, predicated on non-recognition and, more pointedly, *negation* of the other side, effectively constrains the liberal analyst from conferring relational recognition upon a conservative patient, a significant predicament. "Political identity," Tublin observes, "is intrinsically and inescapably adversarial" (2017a, p. 71).

Courting "radical openness" (Hart, 2017), then, to political perspectives not simply different from but in fact antithetical to our own, may feel theoretically aspirational at best. Or given the relational orientation's widespread embrace of recognition theory (Benjamin, 2018), it may feel theoretically impossible. We may become sadistically judgmental and othering of a patient whose politics we abhor, as previously established. Or if we allow the patient to express political beliefs that aim to constrain or deny our legitimacy, rights, safety or very existence without challenging them, we may feel masochistically self-negating (Hendelman, 2018). Novelist Robert Jones Jr. (2005) poignantly expresses the limits of a tolerant, let alone embracing, stance toward an annihilating politics: "We can disagree and still love each other, unless your disagreement is rooted in my oppression and denial of my humanity and right to exist."

So then, how on earth might we hope to recruit an analytic attitude with patients whose politics thus inflame us? How might we orient ourselves so that we do not seek to rid our patients of politics we find destructive? Nor fall prey to the sinking feeling that we are colluding with a politics we find repugnant? Nor avoid the topic altogether until the hour mercifully expires, leaving us mired in bad-analyst-feeling (Epstein, 1987)? I have a few strategies I find potentially facilitative, though I don't pretend they magically resolve the conundrum.

It sometimes helps us sit more dispassionately with patients if we think of their political commitments as manifestations of their underlying values. Social psychologist Jonathan Haidt (2008, 2012) asserts that there are but five major principles that organize moral systems across cultures (see also Saletan, 2012; Tublin, 2017a). The differences between us and them, then, consist not of opposing sets of values but rather of which values among a common set we differentially prioritize. Viewing differences through this matrix may sponsor more fluidity in our thinking, helping us intuit and recognize something worthy, human, something of ourselves, in the other. Tracing out and clarifying a patient's (or our own) values might open up analytic space in a way that avoids the foreclosing that can happen if we seek to directly unpack or challenge a patient's political ideology. Seeing beneath political positions to their moral underpinnings in this way might help us metabolize, with apologies to Winnicott, Haidt in the countertransference.

I find it useful to keep in mind my fallibility (Orange, 2006, 2009). My beliefs, opinions and actions are rife with internal inconsistencies; my values are often more assumed than thoroughly worked out, more aspirational than lived. It's humbling to consider how seldom I actually follow through with donations to causes I profess to support, how few political protests I have, in fact, attended over the past five or so years—a number, to be sure, but far fewer than I feel I ought to have. I fall short, my virtuous politics sometimes merely signaled. I don't always have the courage of my convictions, and I recognize ways that I'm implicated in late-capitalist neoliberal society (Aibel, 2020). Bearing this in mind, I can regard patients whose politics I find problematic or even abhorrent through a softer lens. We're all fallible and imperfect by virtue of being human. As Shakespeare put it, "Lord, what fools these mortals be!"— ourselves among them (Aibel, 2014).

In an effort to avoid splitting when working with right-wing patients, left-wing Chilean analyst Doñas seeks to locate his "micro-fascist-within" (2018, drawing on the work of Deleuze & Guattari, 1976), which he identifies as the intolerant inner oppressor. Doñas strives to cultivate relational freedom for himself by finding "psychic common ground" with such patients through "a common sense of alterity" (p. 531). When sitting with a politically conservative patient, I translate Doñas' idea into an American idiom by seeking to recognize and make contact with my inner Republican. This is the part of me that might argue that the ends justify the means, which favors me and my family (i.e., "loyalty") over the communal good, that in the past assumed the poor were responsible for their abject economic plight. These are not mere thought experiments; they are uncomfortable truths. Acknowledging them helps me maintain empathic contact with, even provide recognition to, patients who express what I otherwise regard as inferior, degraded but recognizably human parts of themselves.

But whereas I feel shame about my self-interested qualities, many Trump supporters are unabashedly, aggressively shameless in trumpeting self-interest, intolerance and venality as points of pride. Indeed, some argue this is the whole psychological point of Trumpism (Ducat, 2017). I recognize that my excoriation and even repulsion toward most, if not all, right-wing values, coupled with my certitude about the superiority of my liberal values, exacerbates and helps create the impudence that defensively animates many Trump voters. This liberal self-righteousness leads many Republicans, not just Trumpers, to wear "deplorable" (Hillary Clinton's one-time descriptor) as a badge of honor. In this way, my unempathetic othering of those holding "wrong" or even "insane" beliefs perpetuates a political feud and increases the resulting chasm. Striving to keep in mind my contradictoriness and complexity (I contain multitudes, and they're not all reputable) helps mitigate against this tendency.

Another technique to better contain ourselves while hearing triggering political material is to hear it as if the patient is sharing a dream. This approach, introduced by Ferro (2002, 2009) and further developed by Ogden (2004) and Bass (2021), helps bring dimensionality to material we might otherwise be inclined to hear concretely, opening our imaginations to other registers of the patient's experience, allowing us to access reverie, metabolize beta elements (Bion, 1962, 1963, 1965) and listen for unconscious experiences and self-states (Bromberg, 1998; Bermudez, 2019).

In my dream, people are hopelessly split between two tribes. It's like a Dr. Seuss story. They represent completely opposite, utterly incompatible philosophies for living. They are called, well, Democrats and Republicans. Suddenly there's some sort of outside threat, and it seems they might all come together: *e pluribus unum*. Then, an orange baby-blob-thing, cold and fiery, spitting, sneering, bulging, appears. It starts fulminating, tells lie after lie, each more outlandish than the last. The people start cheering and jeering. Now it's a sporting match: banners, protests, punching, crying, shock, awe. I awaken, bathed in sweat.

Needless to say, a patient aligned with Republican ideology will have a very different version of this dream. I've slipped into the trope of dream reporting, but this is very much the point. Suddenly, polarizing material that is challenging to sit with opens into the imaginative space of dreamwork (see Bermudez, 2019, 2021 for reflections on social dreaming), helping us ask a different set of questions of the political material. What affect is aroused in the patient? In me? What other vistas in her psychic landscape open up for us? Who represents her disowned, repressed or dissociated self? Do the two tribes represent a tension within her? What about the orange-blob-thing; who might he (it) be to her, to me?

Still, for analysts ourselves traumatized by the toxicity of our political surround, can such techniques really encourage us to respond with genuine curiosity rather than repulsion to beliefs with which we vehemently disagree? Or are these approaches merely an interesting set of mental gymnastics that become inaccessible in the press of the clinical moment when so much is at stake for our lives, our communities, our planet? In this terribly fraught political moment, how much complexity and multiplicity can we hold? How far can our analytic attitude extend?

An inconvenient, potentially provocative aspect of all this is something we often hesitate to say aloud in analytic circles, although I suspect many of us fervently believe it: the values of the American left—for the past 40 years at least—typically *are* more just and fair, more aligned with the true meaning of equality. The left's commitment to social justice— as some key examples, the work of anti-racism, including commitments to equity and reparations as means of ameliorating historical and ongoing racism; the (re)establishment of an economic safety net for those in poverty, including universal health care, affordable childcare and a higher minimum wage; ending police brutality, most of it directed against people of color—are, I maintain, commitments of a higher moral order.

Still, I acknowledge, this is *my* truth. I leave room for my blind spots and limits of understanding. I seek to hold my convictions in dynamic tension with the humility I know I must recognize. There are matters I don't understand—not fully, maybe not at all. I am hardly above reproach; I am a beneficiary of an unjust society in an unjust world. When doing clinical work, I try to hold these dialectics in mind.

How all this impacts my clinical stance on a case-by-case basis remains an open question. A core part of the relational sensibility is a commitment to recognizing how the analyst's subjectivity, including our beliefs and biases, informs the countertransference and influences the analytic field and the patient. We do our best to track these impacts in order to acknowledge, account for and limit our potential for positioning ourselves in injurious stances toward our patients. We sometimes share our clinical dilemmas with our patients, offering something along the lines of what

Feldman (personal communication, 2017) suggested earlier: "It seems like we may be on opposite sides of the political aisle here. What do you imagine this means for us? Can we navigate this?" Given the extraordinarily polarizing tensions of this political era, maybe this is the best we can do.

Returning to Doñas' work on the "micro-fascist-within" (2018), I discovered that I initially misunderstood his intention. Finding a point of empathic contact with the other's complementary view and locating the "enemy" or inflexible ideologue within are certainly useful. But Doñas is after more than simply flipping the analyst's perspective to the opposite pole of the binary; rather, he aims to transcend the binary, arriving at an "opening where there is no 'I' and no 'you'" (2021, p. 3), a wholeness perhaps more familiar to the mystics, yet somewhat akin to Eshel's (2019) "analytic oneness." Envisioning intersubjectivity as potentiating "a common sense of alterity, a shared human experience that can bridge the oppressed and oppressor both within, but especially between, subjects" (Doñas, 2018, p. 531), he invokes a process of accessing "radical imagination" in order to move from "a binary psychic fracture" (p. 528) to an expansive psychic realm borne of lived relational experience. Citing Laing (1967), he calls this "a new politics of the experience" (Doñas, 2018, p. 531).

Many case reports traversing sociopolitical themes sooner or later recruit the notion of impossibility. In her work with a Trump-supporting patient, Hendelman (2018) despairs, "I cannot find the psychoanalytic third" because "to do so feels like a deep betrayal of my inner core" (p. 482). Discussing González's (2020) exploration of a politically fraught transference/countertransference, Doñas (2020) highlights "the experience of impossibility" (p. 414). Tublin (2017a) notes that the analyst:

> must be prepared to do something that may feel impossible . . . to reflect upon his own most basic political assumptions and . . . his own defining values . . . [and] consider negotiating his non-negotiables (Pizer, 1998), the values he would otherwise never think to question.
>
> (p. 76)

Faced with the seemingly insurmountable task of engaging impassioned political differences and finding (or fighting) our way through to some sort of dyadic transformation, we may come to hopelessness or despair. Yet a psychoanalytic sensibility demands that we continue. As Bass and Moss suggest, "at precisely this moment, this moment of despair, when nothing I have seems to me to be useful, right here is where work as a psychoanalyst begins" (2012, p. 29).

Hendelman (2018) states that the patient must ultimately become more important to us than who is right. I wonder if we might regard this prioritization as a psychic sacrifice or surrender (Ghent, 1990) we make in service to our patient's growth, the type of transformation of ourselves that allows our patients to change (Slavin & Kriegman, 1998). Can we love our patients this much? Or does our steadfast commitment to our progressive values make this impossible? In a paradox familiar to analysts, acknowledging the impossibility of a situation allows something else to become possible. Doñas encourages us to "think the impossible" (2021). In his undream, "To admit the impossible is therefore to pave the way for the experience of 'becoming' . . . and to allow the creation of renewed meanings" (2020, p. 410). Committing to the analytic process in this way, an outcome that seems unimaginable or impossible may yet emerge.

I close by offering a personal reflection demonstrating the amplification effect that Samuels observes, the "both/and" proposition whereby voiced political material stands irreducibly for itself as a legitimate locus of patients' concern over their social surround, as well as the always surprising clinical truth that it also simultaneously recruits and expresses more "personal" family-of-origin issues. My gradual political awakening across the years has been a result of lived experience, academic education and professional training, and ongoing critical reflection on my personal values. This, however, is but half the story. I am a child of divorce, a trauma at age nine that irrevocably rent the fabric of my family and tore me into two (or far more) pieces. With no amicable parting or conscious uncoupling, my parents' separation and divorce were marked by the same rancor, dysfunction and entrenched inability to reach across the aisle that has plagued America's congressional bodies in recent decades. Like the Democrats and Republicans, my parents were unwilling or unable to set aside their competing narratives, recriminations and agendas to jointly focus on the common good of their offspring. It was an uncivil war and a house divided against itself could not stand. Nor did living between two houses (bicamerally, as it were) appreciably improve my or my siblings' pursuit of happiness.

Little wonder, then, that I, like many therapists in the making, always sought to focus upon how opposite sides might abide each other, seeing beyond their pain and anger to forge a common, generative purpose beyond the rehearsing of their respective grievances—a longed-for reinstantiation of the moral law of the third (Benjamin, 2004, 2018). Benjamin's complementarity theory, wherein "only one can live" (2018), describes a reality I painfully lived and, in many respects, internalized.

So the plight of a liberal psychoanalyst faced with the seemingly impossible task of cultivating an empathetic understanding of the political worldview of a conservative patient, in the context of our no-holds-barred, take-no-prisoners political era, especially within a two-person relational psychoanalytic model wherein the analyst can neither ignore nor truly hide his own subjectivity, is naturally a source of fascination for me—a philosophical, ethical and clinical quagmire and a technical conundrum. Its pathways have occasionally loomed as threatening and triggering to me but always mysterious, puzzling and compelling. So my interest in this topic has not simply been the product of intellectual curiosity. As Stolorow and Atwood (1979) have argued, all theory is autobiography (Olney, 1980, paraphrasing Paul Valery; see also Maroda, 2021). Whenever I read, write, present, teach, discuss, ponder and work clinically with matters of political differences (and, as well, similarities), I am not only wrestling with intriguing matters of theory and praxis, but I am also seeking to rework my personal preoccupations.

Awakening to the myriad complexities of competing and colliding political worldviews and the resultant doer/done-to dynamics (Benjamin, 2004), which so often lead to othering, subjugation, violence, destruction and existential threat, is a crucial clinical task we are increasingly called to develop in this highly polarized and politically ill era. It's increasingly clear that if we are to offer patients robust treatments based on a therapeutic action of recognition, bringing analytic curiosity to all forms of difference as well, then we must develop the same comfort and familiarity with socially and politically inflected psychic experience, and the varying positions within society that our patients and we inhabit, as we strive to bring to all narratives of personal pain and suffering.

## References

Aibel, M. (2014). Response to commentaries. *Psychoanalytic Perspectives*, *11*(2), 188–197.

Aibel, M. (2018). The personal is political is psychoanalytic: Politics in the consulting room. *Psychoanalytic Perspectives*, *15*(1), 64–101.

Aibel, M. (2019, February 5–10). *How to steer the treatment through the current political storm: We have a course for that.* Presentation. National Meeting, American Psychoanalytic Association.

Aibel, M. (2020, March 1). *Partisanship: Navigating the volatility of politics in the consulting room.* Presentation. Annual Conference, Suffolk Institute for Psychotherapy and Psychoanalysis.

Altman, N., Benjamin, J., Jacobs, T., & Wachtel, P. (2004). Is politics the last taboo in psychoanalysis? A roundtable discussion. *Psychoanalytic Perspectives, 2*(1), 5–37.

Aron, L. (1996). *A meeting of minds: Mutuality in psychoanalysis.* The Analytic Press.

Aron, L., & Starr, K. (2013). *A psychotherapy for the people: Toward a progressive psychoanalysis.* Routledge.

Avila-Espada, A. (2021). *Facing the mourning of our world as we lose ourselves to it: A relational reflection for action as an ethical requirement.* Presentation. Symposium, International Association for Relational Psychoanalysis and Psychotherapy, online.

Barry, E. (2022, February 6). Climate change enters the therapy room. *The New York Times*, p. A1. www.nytimes.com/2022/02/06/health/climate-anxiety-therapy.html

Bass, A. (2021). Unmasked: Personal transformations, frame alterations, and making the conscious unconscious during the traumatic times of the COVID and other plagues. *Psychoanalytic Perspectives, 18*(3), 347–357.

Bass, A., & Moss, D. (2012). On keeping thought erotic: Some problems in contemporary theory and practice. *DIVISION/Review, 6*, 29–33.

Benjamin, J. (2004). Beyond doer and done-to: An intersubjective view of thirdness. *Psychoanalytic Quarterly, 63*, 15–46.

Benjamin, J. (2018). *Beyond doer and done to: Recognition theory, intersubjectivity and the third.* Routledge.

Bermudez, G. (2019). Community psychoanalysis: A contribution to an emerging paradigm. *Psychoanalytic Inquiry, 39*(5), 297–304.

Bermudez, G. (2021). *Dreaming psychoanalysis forward: Toward a sociocentric psychoanalysis contributing to deliberative democracy.* Unpublished manuscript.

Bion, W. R. (1962). *Learning from experience.* Tavistock.

Bion, W. R. (1963). *Elements of psycho-analysis.* Heinemann.

Bion, W. R. (1965). *Transformations.* Tavistock.

Botticelli, S. (2004). The politics of relational psychoanalysis. *Psychoanalytic Dialogues, 14*(5), 635–651.

Botticelli, S. (2018). How do we talk about justice in psychoanalysis? The case of Palestine. *DIVISION/Review, 18*, 24–26.

Bromberg, P. M. (1998). *Standing in the spaces: Essays on clinical process, trauma, and dissociation.* The Analytic Press.

Buber, M., & Kaufmann, W. A. (1970). *I and thou: Martin Buber* (W. A. Kaufmann, Trans.). Charles Scribner's Sons.

Cushman, P. (1990). Why the self is empty: Toward a historically situated psychology. *American Psychologist, 45*(5), 599–611.

Cushman, P. (1995). *Constructing the self, constructing America: A cultural history of psychotherapy.* Perseus Publishing.

Cushman, P. (2005). Clinical applications. *Contemporary Psychoanalysis, 41*(3), 431–445.

Cushman, P. (2015). Relational psychoanalysis as political resistance. *Contemporary Psychoanalysis, 51*(3), 423–459.

Danto, E. (2007). *Freud's free clinics: Psychoanalysis and social justice, 1918–1938.* Columbia University Press.

Deleuze, G., & Guattari, F. (1976). *Rhizome [Introduction].* Éditions de Minuit.

Doñas, V. A. (2018). The undream: When the clinical (becomes?) political. *Psychoanalytic Dialogues, 28*(5), 528–534.

Doñas, V. A. (2020). The message of a bottle: A discussion of "Trump cards and Klein bottles: On the collective of the individual." *Psychoanalytic Dialogues, 30*(4), 408–416.

Doñas, V. A. (2021, October 23–24). *These are not nos-otros: The paradox of integrity.* Presentation. Symposium, International Association for Relational Psychoanalysis and Psychotherapy.

Ducat, S. J. (2017, December 17). Trump's pathology is also his brand. *The Psychoanalytic Activist* [Website]. Retrieved December 31, 2017, from https://psychoanalyticactivist.com/2017/12/17/trumps-pathology-is-also-his-brand/

Epstein, L. (1987). The problem of the bad-analyst-feeling. *Modern Psychoanalysis, 12,* 35–45.

Eshel, O. (2019). *The emergence of analytic oneness: Into the heart of psychoanalysis.* Routledge.

Ferro, A. (2002). Superego transformations through the analyst's capacity for reverie. *Psychoanalytic Quarterly, 71,* 477–450.

Ferro, A. (2009). Transformations in dreaming and characters in the psychoanalytic field. *International Journal of Psychoanalysis, 90,* 209–230.

Gentile, J. (2016a). *Feminine law: Freud, free speech, and the voice of desire* (with M. Macrone). Karnac Books.

Gentile, J. (2016b). What is special about speech? *Psychoanalytic Psychology, 33,* 73–88.

Gentile, J. (2020). Time may change us: The strange temporalities, novel paradoxes, and democratic imaginaries of a pandemic. *Journal of the American Psychoanalytic Association, 68,* 649–669.

Ghent, E. (1990). Masochism, submission, and surrender: Masochism as a perversion of surrender. *Contemporary Psychoanalysis, 26*(1), 108–136.

Gilligan, C. (1982). *In a different voice: Psychological theory and women's development.* Harvard University Press.

González, F. J. (2020). Trump cards and Klein bottles: On the collective of the individual. *Psychoanalytic Dialogues, 30*(4), 383–398.

Grand, S., & Salberg, J. (Eds.). (2017). *Trans-generational trauma and the other: Dialogues across history and difference*. Routledge.

Greenberg, J. R., & Mitchell, S. A. (1983). *Object relations in psychoanalytic theory*. Harvard University Press.

Greenson, R. R. (1967). *The technique and practice of psychoanalysis*. International Universities Press.

Grossmark, R. (2018). *The unobtrusive relational analyst: Explorations in psychoanalytic companioning*. Routledge.

Guralnik, O. (2016a, May 9–22). *Subjectivity and the collective: Encountering the political in psychoanalysis*. Colloquium. International Association for Relational Psychoanalysis and Psychotherapy.

Guralnik, O. (2016b). Sleeping dogs: Psychoanalysis and the socio-political. *Psychoanalytic Dialogues, 26*(6), 655–663.

Guralnik, O., & Simeon, D. (2010). Depersonalization: Standing in the spaces between recognition and interpellation. *Psychoanalytic Dialogues, 20*(4), 400–416.

Haidt, J. (2008). The moral roots of liberals and conservatives. *TEDtalk*. www.ted.com/talks/jonathan_haidt_the_moral_roots_of_liberals_and_conservatives?language=en#t-1093263

Haidt, J. (2012). *The righteous mind: Why good people are divided by politics and religion*. Pantheon Books.

Harris, A. E. (2009). The socio-political recruitment of identities. *Psychoanalytic Dialogues, 19*(2), 138–147.

Harris, A. E., Kalb, M., & Klebanoff, S. (2016). *Demons in the consulting room: Echoes of genocide, slavery and extreme trauma in psychoanalytic practice*. Routledge.

Hart, A. (2017). From multicultural competence to radical openness: A psychoanalytic engagement of otherness. *The American Psychoanalyst, 51*(1), 12–27.

Hendelman, L. A. (2018). Political divide in the consulting room. *American Journal of Psychoanalysis, 78*, 478–487.

Hoffman, I. Z. (1992). Some practical implications of a social-constructivist view of the psychoanalytic situation. *Psychoanalytic Dialogues, 2*(3), 287–304.

Hoffman, I. Z. (1998). *Ritual and spontaneity in the psychoanalytic process: A dialectical-constructivist view*. The Analytic Press.

Hoffman, I. Z. (2013). Response to Layton: Considering the sociopolitical context of dialectical constructivism. *Psychoanalytic Dialogues, 23*(3), 287–295.

Hollander, N. C. (2017). Who is the sufferer and what is being suffered? Subjectivity in times of social malaise. *Psychoanalytic Dialogues, 27*(6), 635–650.

Howell, E. F., & Itzkowitz, S. (2016). *The dissociative mind in psychoanalysis: Understanding and working with trauma*. Routledge.

Jones Jr., R. [@SonofBaldwin]. (2005, August 18). We can disagree and still love each other, unless your disagreement is rooted in my oppression and denial of my [Tweet]. *Twitter*. https://twitter.com/SonofBaldwin/status/633644373423562753

Kosiński, J. (1970). *Being there*. Harcourt Brace Jovanovich, Inc.

Kuchuck, S. (2021). *The relational revolution in psychoanalysis and psychotherapy*. Confer Books.

Kuriloff, E. A. (2014). *Contemporary psychoanalysis and the legacy of the Third Reich: History, memory, tradition*. Routledge.

Laing, R. D. (1967). *The politics of experience and the bird of paradise*. Penguin Books Ltd.

Layton, L. (2004). Dreams of America/American dreams. *Psychoanalytic Dialogues, 14*(2), 233–254.

Layton, L. (2005). Commentary on roundtable: "Is politics the last taboo in psychoanalysis?" *Psychoanalytic Perspectives, 2*(2), 3–8.

Layton, L. (2019). Transgenerational hauntings: Toward a social psychoanalysis and an ethic of dis-illusionment. *Psychoanalytic Dialogues, 29*(2), 105–121.

Layton, L. (2020). *Toward a social psychoanalysis: Culture, character, and normative unconscious processes* (M. Leavy-Sperounis, Ed.). Routledge.

Lionells, M., Fiscalini, J., Mann, C., & Stern, D. B. (Eds.). (1995). *Handbook of interpersonal psychoanalysis*. The Analytic Press.

Maroda, K. (2021). *The analyst's vulnerability: Impact on theory and practice*. Routledge.

Ogden, T. H. (2004). This art of psychoanalysis: Dreaming undreamt dreams and interrupted cries. *International Journal of Psychoanalysis, 85*, 857–877.

Olney, J. (1980). Autobiography and the cultural moment: A thematic, historical and bibliographical introduction. In J. Olney (Ed.), *Autobiography: Essays theoretical and critical* (pp. 3–27). Princeton University Press.

Orange, D. M. (2006). For whom the bell tolls: Context, complexity, and compassion in psychoanalysis. *International Journal of Psychoanalytic Self Psychology, 1*, 5–21.

Orange, D. M. (2009). Attitudes, values and intersubjective vulnerability. *International Journal of Psychoanalytic Self Psychology, 4*, 235–253.

Orange, D. M. (2011). *The suffering stranger: Hermeneutics for everyday clinical practice*. Routledge.

Orange, D. M. (2015). *Nourishing the inner life of clinicians and humanitarians: The ethical turn in psychoanalysis*. Routledge.

Orange, D. M. (2017). *Climate crisis, psychoanalysis, and radical ethics*. Routledge.

Orange, D. M. (2020). *Psychoanalysis, history, and radical ethics: Learning to hear*. Routledge.

Osnos, E. (2011, January 10). Meet Dr. Freud: Does psychoanalysis have a future in an authoritarian state? *The New Yorker*. www.newyorker.com/magazine/2011/01/10/meet-dr-freud

Philipson, I. (2017). The last public psychoanalyst? Why Fromm matters in the 21st century. *Psychoanalytic Perspectives, 14*(1), 52–74.

Pizer, S. A. (1998). *Building bridges: The negotiation of paradox in psychoanalysis*. The Analytic Press.

Roth, P. (2004). *The plot against America*. Houghton Mifflin Company.

Rozmarin, E. (2007a). The other is everything: A response to Adrienne Harris's and Bruce Reis's discussions of "An other in psychoanalysis." *Contemporary Psychoanalysis, 43*(3), 386–398.

Rozmarin, E. (2007b). An other in psychoanalysis: Emmanuel Levinas's critique of knowledge and analytic sense. *Contemporary Psychoanalysis, 43*(3), 327–360.

Rozmarin, E. (2009). I am yourself: Subjectivity and the collective. *Psychoanalytic Dialogues, 19*(5), 604–616.

Salberg, J., & Grand, S. (Eds.). (2017). *Wounds of history: Repair and resilience in the transgenerational transmission of trauma*. Routledge.

Saletan, W. (2012, March 23). Why won't they listen? [Book review.] *The New York Times*. www.nytimes.com/2012/03/25/books/review/the-righteous-mind-by-jonathan-haidt.html

Samuels, A. (2004). Politics and/of/in/for psychoanalysis. *Psychoanalytic Perspectives, 2*(1), 39–47.

Samuels, A. (2017). The "activist client": Social responsibility, the political self, and clinical practice in psychotherapy and psychoanalysis. *Psychoanalytic Dialogues, 27*(6), 678–693.

Samuels, A. (2020, May 3). *Covid and climate: Apocalypse and alternatives*. London Climate Change Festival. www.youtube.com/watch?v=WXg9cEb08Z0

Samuels, A. (2021, September 17). *Psychotherapy and politics: A cutting edge and transformative contribution—or a narcissistic total waste of time only of use to the therapists*. Analysis & Activism, Online.

Sandberg, L. (2017). Shame and the question of responsibility. *Psychoanalytic Dialogues, 27*(3), 382–383.

Shapiro, S. A. (2000). The unique Benjamin Wolstein as experienced and read. *Contemporary Psychoanalysis, 36*(2), 301–341.

Slavin, M. O., & Kriegman, D. (1998). Why the analyst needs to change: Toward a theory of conflict, negotiation, and mutual influence in the therapeutic process. *Psychoanalytic Dialogues, 8*(2), 247–284.

Snyder, T. (2017). *On tyranny: Twenty lessons from the twentieth century*. Random House.

Stolorow, R. D., & Atwood, G. E. (1979). *Faces in a cloud: Subjectivity in personality theory*. Jason Aronson.

Tublin, S. (2015, June 25–28). *Non-negotiable political identity, recognition, and negation*. Presentation. Annual Conference, International Association for Relational Psychoanalysis and Psychotherapy.

Tublin, S. (2017a). Political identity and countertransference. In J. Petrucelli & S. Schoen (Eds.), *Unknowable, unspeakable, and unsprung: Navigating the thrill and danger of living amidst truth, fantasy, and privacy* (pp. 71–80). Routledge.

Tublin, S. (2017b). Partisanship in the psychoanalytic community: Navigating the conflicting roles of citizen and analyst amid Trump-era polarization. *Contemporary Psychoanalysis, 53*(4), 505–515.

Tublin, S. (2020, March 1). *Political partisanship and psychoanalysis*. Presentation. Annual Conference, Suffolk Institute for Psychotherapy and Psychoanalysis.

Tummala-Narra, P. (2016). Discussion of "Culturally imposed trauma: The sleeping dog has awakened. Will psychoanalysis take heed?" Commentary on the paper by Dorothy Evans Holmes. *Psychoanalytic Dialogues*, *26*(6), 664–672.

Zaretsky, E. (2015). *Political Freud: A history*. Columbia University Press.

# Chapter 11

# Parental Implication and the Expansion of the Child Relational Therapist's Clinical Imagination

*Laurel Moldawsky Silber*

## Reflection

I believe my imagination was given some freedom in my childhood to think about the subject of parents, which I have continued to think about throughout a personal and professional lifetime. I recall my father saying to me when I was a kid, "We are different parents to each of you" (I have three siblings). I don't remember the circumstances or why he said it, but I remember the perplexity. What in the world did he mean? They were the same people. I had to think, but were we, and were they really? The freedom to set things in motion, to have to think beyond what is in front of you, or on the surface, was in statements like that, and perhaps in the jazz he played on the piano. What was parental subjectivity? How is it different and the same? And how do children find their agency, to value and resist transmitted experience? My father spoke to me like he thought I might understand what he meant. It is to his memory that I dedicate this chapter.

## Introduction

Parents co-create procedural life with their children and, as such, are implicated in transmitting trauma to the next generation. When it is trauma that is transmitted, it has a disorganizing influence on the intersubjective space of the parent and child and on the child's self-development. The transmission, enacted primarily within the implicit procedural realm, can essentially be hidden in plain sight. Children communicate their difficulty deciphering an incoherent transmission through their behavior, symptoms and play. The likelihood of recognizing the import of intergenerational

DOI: 10.4324/9781003265146-11

transmission of trauma to the child's troubles is much reduced when parental subjectivity is left out of the child's psychotherapeutic intervention.

The historical and current challenge to addressing the intergenerational transmission of trauma in clinical work with children is part of a larger story about childism. This chapter will foreground the discussion of parental implication in clinical work with children by noting the influence of childism within the culture and, specifically, within the psychoanalytic culture. The expansion of the child therapist's clinical mind involves overcoming resistance both within and outside the field, as well as within the case itself. Parental subjectivity, taken out of a vault, so to speak, can help solve real developmental problems.

## Cultural Context for Parenting or the Absence of a Holding Environment

When adults transition to parenthood, they look around themselves for support. They seek help to create a nested space. The evocation of vulnerability attuning to a new baby and the increased sense of responsibility is part of the many changes experienced in the transition. As our classic nursery rhyme "Rock-a-Bye Baby" replays through the ages, it reflects this truth: without the infrastructure, the baby and mother are precarious: "When the bough breaks, the cradle will fall and down will come baby, cradle and all." We seem to both know and disavow this. The infant's helplessness and relative dependence throughout childhood and adolescence implicates parents and society in their care. Our recent witnessing of migrant children, separated from their parents, and placed in cages at the border of the United States and Mexico, enacts much that is broken in our society. As Nicholas Kristof (6/5/21) opines in *New York Times* editorial, *Turning Child Care into a New Cold War;* "Families desperately need help. In other countries, they get it. In the United States they get empty homilies about the importance of family." The many reasons for this are beyond the scope of this chapter. However, it bears mentioning the childist context within the United States, one that doesn't securely hold the parents or their child's developmental/dependency needs in mind. Consideration of a parent's implicated subjective state within this cultural space is more fraught.

Reflecting on the embeddedness of families in their cultural surrounds, consider Mark and Shapiro's circuitous view of influence within the dynamic system: "Our subjective experience stretches out into the world," they write, "only to fold upon itself again. Physical and psychological events unfold and re-enfold recursively upon themselves, revealing self-similar patterns at multiple levels of organization" (2021, p. 483). Linking across systems of thought to Rothberg's social/philosophical/political concept of implication, we see how he refers to the implicated subject as being "'folded into' (implicated in) events that at first seem beyond our agency as individual subjects" (Rothberg, 2019, p. 1). Rothberg infuses the topic of responsibility with a multigenerational long view. He points out that implicated subjects may not have originated the wrongdoing, but they indirectly inhabit and, therefore, participate in perpetuating it (Rothberg in Knittel & Forchieri, 2020, p. 8). As such, (un)developed systems of care, consistent with a patriarchal, capitalist and racist society, infuse cultural attitudes about vulnerability and responsibility that, in turn, structure and inform parenthood. Parents are embedded in a system; there is "no such thing as a baby" (in reference to Winnicott's [1965] famous quote) because there is a baby and caregiver, and there is no such thing as a parent because there is a parent in an attachment and cultural context.

## Psychoanalytic Context for Work with Parents

At another level of organization, within the discipline of child psychoanalysis, work with parents has had a complicated history. The risk of professional disparagement was a disincentive to openly address the subject of parental influence in working with children. For example, when Winnicott presented his work with a two-and-a-half-year-old patient and her parents in the classic case, *The Piggle* (1977), he referred to the work as "psychoanalysis shared." He said it was "not casework or family work it was psychoanalysis shared" (see Silber in Masur, 2021). I believe Winnicott, who appreciated paradox, was straddling an implicit and explicit boundary within the professional psychoanalytic culture at the time. My sense was that he was trying to remain included and perhaps potentially expand the boundary for what was an acceptable practice in child analysis. He was essentially saying that including the parents in the work, working within the reality of the child's dependency, should not downgrade the work. It was still psychoanalytic, just dyadic, a precursor to relational child analytic work.

Bowlby, another child analyst developing his theories on attachment at around this time, received a strong rebuke from the British Psychoanalytic Society. Resisting the objections, he developed attachment theory, and subsequent research was undertaken (Ainsworth et al. [2015], Hesse and Main [1999], Lyons-Ruth [2002, 2003], Schechter [2017], Slade [2005], Steele [2018] and others) outside of psychoanalysis, within academic psychology. The bridge back to psychoanalysis, slowly incorporating the import of attachment research, supported the paradigm shift to relational psychoanalysis.

Simultaneous to these theoretical debates and professional controversies, in 1964, the American Psychoanalytic Association (APA) voted against having the newly forming American Association for Child Psychoanalysis create a section within its organizational framework. It was renamed the Association for Child Psychoanalysis (ACP) in 1965 and was independent of APA. Anna Freud expressed her surprise that adult analysts were not interested in the analysis of children: "The analysts of adults remained more or less aloof from child-analysis, almost as if it were an inferior type of professional occupation." And she maintained,

> for those of us who are committed to child-analysis and concerned for its future, there was no alternative but to go it alone . . . there was always the hope that, at some future date, the result of our efforts might be recognized and incorporated belatedly into the organizational framework.
>
> (1972, pp. 153–154)

How did the divisive organizational structure work out? The number of child analysts has decreased over the years. Hoffman et al. referred to the child and adolescent field as an "endangered specialty for many decades" (2009, p. 911). The exclusion of ACP, within psychoanalysis, like the fate of the mythical child Oedipus, did not work out well.

The history of psychoanalysis has been marked by controversy regarding parents, attachment and systems thinking. To unpack contradictions, support the research and thereby improve the science of psychoanalysis, it was necessary to leave (be forced out of) organizational child analysis. The one-person classical model, upholding the flawed concept of neutrality (or lack of influence) at one time revered as pure gold in adult psychoanalysis (Lewis & Starr, 2013), was not in the best interests of the child. It was also not in the best interests of the parent or parent-child relationship. The explosion of infancy (Beebe & Lachmann, 2014; Tronick, 2007), attachment (Lyons-Ruth, 2002; Slade, 2005; Steele & Steele, 2018; Tronick, 2007; Schechter, 2017) and neuroscience research (Cozolino, 2010; Solms, 2018) acknowledged explicitly what we all knew implicitly: the critical importance of attachment figures to the child's self-development. Leaving the child alone on the treetops or mountaintops, as the fables go, was indeed precarious.

Mentalization theory (Fonagy et al., 2002) took hold in the fertile integrative space of psychoanalysis and attachment research. The focus of attention shifted to the intersubjective space—that is, how internal mental states are represented between self and other.

The clinical mind manages many more moving parts in the shift to "both/and" thinking, reconfigured to a nonlinear systems frame. The expanded theoretical shift is consistent with the medium of play and the notion of multiplicity encapsulated in relational thought and in the concept of implication. The psychoanalytic ideal of purity, sharing a conceptual frame with white supremacy, is decolonized. Decolonizing development (Tummala-Narra, in press) instantiates the psychoanalytic ideal of freedom and opens the way to take up the more nuanced and complicated subject of implication in child relational work. Along these lines, the organization of psychoanalysis has been implicated in minimizing work with parents and maintaining a nonreflective stance regarding their accountability.

Child analyst Diane Siskind defined "working with parents" (which was also the title of her 1997 book) as a neglected topic. She found it surprising "that this topic has failed to be represented as a complex and important treatment issue, one requiring a theoretical framework and careful discussion of its clinical application" (1997, p. 4). Siskind introduced her subject by asking questions about the meaning of the silence on a topic within a field that seeks expansion of knowledge. She found the shirking from complexity or depth odd and felt the reason for the omission obscure. Arietta Slade, a psychoanalytically informed attachment researcher who has done much to build the bridge between the attachment theory and psychoanalysis, conjectured about "ghosts in the psychoanalytic nursery" (2014). I, too, have found the silence on this topic puzzling and explored implicit bias (Silber, 2015). However, one aspect, as it relates to this discussion, is the following: the classical theory was insufficient to hold the many parts of the work. A one-person, linear model delimited the focus and left the subject of implication in transgenerational trauma for parents and children unexplored. It was a subject area, one Fraiberg et al. (1975) referred to as "ghosts in the nursery," that unequivocally declared the necessity of bringing clinical attention to what had been so elusive. The inevitable transmission of the past trauma, parental ghosts, was identified. How to address it? Where is the theory to hold the complexity? This problem is linked to Rothberg's seeking clarity in a related circumstance:

> Because the position of the implicated subject has largely remained unnamed and unexplored, our accounts of trauma, violence and power also remain incomplete; theorizing implication helps us explain how historical and contemporary forms of violence can be simultaneously pervasive and persistent, and yet so difficult to pin down and eradicate.
>
> (Rothberg, 2019, p. 33)

In the circumstance of parental subjectivity, the shift to a nonlinear dynamic system frame expanded the thinking to include the parents and the cultural surround of the child in the thinking and process. The problem, newly considered, of trauma's afterwardsness, its "second generational effects" (Hesse & Main, 1999) or "traumatically skewed intersubjectivity" (Schechter, 2017), took up space for exploration. New questions could be asked: For example, what is the texture of the child's context when there is transmitted parental trauma? What do the children say about it, and how do they say it? How is the problem communicated through their play and behavior?

## Parental Implication in the Intergenerational Transmission of Trauma with the Child's Mind in Mind

Conceptualizing the adult with a kind of responsibility that is both direct and also indirect, with self-states shaped by both the past and present, and engaged in co-creating and transmitting procedural life with and for a new generation, opened the space for broader consideration. This shift led to further questions like "What aspect (among the multitude) within parental subjectivity becomes important to focus on in relationship to their child?" A theoretical shift to mentalization supported by Tronick's (2007) "dyadic expansion of consciousness model," focusing on interactive processes

(Beebe & Lachmann, 2014; Schechter, 2017; Lieberman, 1999), widened the clinical focus.

Implicated parental subjectivity is no longer eclipsed in psychodynamic theory or practice. A clinical sensibility that is mentalizing the parent's vulnerability and responsibility, simultaneous to the child's subjective and developmental position, requires multiple levels in which to seek links across, within and between. It is reductionistic to polarize a child as vulnerable and a parent as responsible. With more nuanced empathic abilities, more dimensions are considered as we respond to the real clinical challenges in an asymmetrical bidirectional relationship. The clinical imagination is given expanded consciousness.

It is to this position, the consequential opening of the child therapist's mentalizing capacity for playing at the fulcrum of parent and child intersubjectivity, that this discussion turns. "Implicated position" (Rothberg, 2019) clarifies the need for more nuanced thinking about the parent's use of self in the work with and for their child. The child therapist explores the interrelatedness across time and place in order to more adequately formulate and address contributions to present troubles in family relationships.

The child's subjectivity is in play, flowing within and between the mental states of others to whom they are scaffolding a self from and with. As part of the therapeutic intervention with the child, a more nuanced assessment via participation in the child's play simultaneous to work with the parents allows for the processing of multiple dimensions. How enigmatic are the messages for the child? How are they struggling to make sense of contradictions? How are they adapting within the parent-child interaction, as well as apart from the parent? In other words, in the process of developing a therapeutic relationship with the child, what emerges as distinct from their ongoing relationship with their parent? To what extent are there "degrees of freedom" (Moldawsky Silber, 2012) to experience agency in self-construction within the intersubjective spaces? How is experience mentalized, symbolized in play, and how linked across the intersubjective space(s)? How is the therapeutic relationship integrated into the existing structure of family relationships? What is involved in creating more openness within and across other minds in the attachment system? Access to the subjectivities of those attached to the child is necessary to explore these pertinent clinical questions.

The intergenerational transmission of trauma serves as a special kind of complication to child development. Adults can both be internally preoccupied with trauma and raise children. In folding in trauma theory with psychoanalysis, we know an adult's mental state is organized to defend access to painful sequelae of trauma. The trauma's aftermath includes both the experience itself—possibly in fragments of psychic imagery and affect—and the defensive action to contain it. The parents' dissociative defenses serve the purpose of maintaining an emotional distance from their memory. However, the circumstance of parenting catapults the adult into a most evocative "present remembering context" (Stern, 2004, p. 197) of their own childhood trauma. The parent is both a victim being triggered (Coates, 2012) and, in this context, a perpetrator inadvertently implicated in harming their child. The parent's behavior is experienced as incoherent by the child in this circumstance, which is destabilizing to the child and the relationship. The parent is confused and uncomfortable—frightened and frightening (Hesse & Main, 1999)—and both are made helpless (Lyons-Ruth, 2002) by the transmitted trauma. This is the "second generational effects" of trauma (Hesse & Main, 1999). The parent's behavior is the result of their internal preoccupation, something the child has no knowledge of and the parent is defending against knowing. "Haunting ghosts" serves as an apt metaphor for the gaps in the narrative due to fear and unformulated experience. The child clinician can stumble on and become curious about the gap(s), potentially "busting" some ghosts (Moldawsky Silber, 2012) making their way into the next generation.

What is the parent's responsibility for dissociated dynamic content? Renn, a psychoanalyst who integrates neuroscience into his thinking, elaborates on the role of dissociation in disorganizing the memory system. In his book on this subject, *The Silent Past and the Invisible Present*, Renn states,

> Dissociation does not erase traumatic memories, but severs the links among the different memory systems. As a consequence, aspects of the past or periods of ongoing experience become detached from conscious awareness, and the dissociated traumatic experience is encoded and stored in the systems of implicit/procedural memory as sensory fragments with no linking narrative.
>
> (2012, p. 28)

The intergenerational transmission of trauma forms not only the parent's internal landscape—the severed links and sensory fragments—but also impacts the coherence of the child's living relational context. In a parent's quest for meaning-making, the co-constructed enactment with the next generation contributes to a child forming a "false self" (state).

The child therapist pivots between the minds of parent and child, bringing therapeutic attention to linking the parts that resist connection across and within the minds populating the intersubjective space. With the new generation's "invitation" (symptomatic behavior), a parent's internal organization is challenged to reorganize in response to their child's present need to be recognized. An opportunity to re-remember and re-represent memories experienced as painful at one time emerges in parenting the next generation. The retrieval of memories, sometimes generation(s) removed from the traumatic events, creates new possibilities in the interaction, increasing degrees of freedom.

The responsibility to modify the second-generation effects of past trauma places parents in a vulnerable position. The child's subjectivity, as expressed through the immediacy of their play gestures and metaphors, symptoms and confusion, calls attention to the effects of a parent's past trauma on the present generation. Accountability for parental implication involves retrieving painful disorganized non-conscious memories. In accomplishing this psychologically courageous feat, forgiveness can potentially emerge in the wake.

The implicated parent who chooses to reflect on the "non-reflectable" ignites a host of associated psychological tasks: tolerating a sense of sadness and guilt/shame over their own role in perpetuating pain, re-regulating pain associated with retrieving childhood traumatic memories, mourning loss differentiating from patterns associated with the way they were parented and imagining new uncharted ways of family life. In recontextualizing traumatic memories, the parent is empowered to forgive their ancestors, themselves and their child. Further clarity involves owning ancestral mistakes made and expanding to incorporate a fuller appreciation for the complexity of the present and of their child. The clinician's mentalization, holding and linking the past and the present, formulated and unformulated, implicit and explicit, the parent and the child and the cultural surroundings, can support changing ghosts into ancestors (Loewald, 2000a). The family narrative takes on more texture and meaning.

## Clinical Illustration #1

In one instance (further described in Silber, 2017), after a 12-year-old confronted her father in a family session, articulating the way he scared her, the father then requested some individual sessions. There, he proceeded to explain that when he was the age of his child, his father was arrested and sent to prison. It was something he didn't feel comfortable discussing with his daughter at that moment. It was also something he had not shared in the therapy. He then proceeded to describe the painful experience that still haunted him, one he had no idea was haunting her. For example, as the oldest in his family, he felt responsible for his younger sibling when they lost their father. He could see his quick criticism of his daughter (the oldest), reminding her at any "infraction" of her influence on her younger siblings, as a passing of a pressure he felt in the context of his childhood trauma. The hurt and anger he felt regarding his father's infractions infused his anxious parenting. Subsequent to this therapeutic process, he chose to write a family story which he shared with me. It was his way of finding new meaning and recontextualizing experience. The father's "implication making tendency" (Stern, 2004, p. 30) is described by Stern as "imposing a form to what is happening, something done without thinking or really listening." The procedural knowledge barrels down the implicit generational highway without pause to notice or mark the boundary of the new generation. "The past," Stern notes, "can eclipse the present by casting so strong a shadow on it that the present can only confirm what was already known and can add little more. It is essentially effaced" (Stern, 2004, p. 28). This daughter resisted this tendency; she wished for a future she had something to do with. She needed her experience to make sense and did not wish to be folded into his story.

The affective shift in the father-daughter relationship was noteworthy: she had begun the family work sitting with her back to the family, getting up and slamming the door on her way out of the middle of a session, claiming everything was always being blamed on her. Meanwhile, her younger sibling, crouched behind the sofa, sent paper airplanes with notes that said, essentially, we better get out of here. The older daughter's behavior (i.e., the door slam) reflected the anger, helplessness and wish to break the form of the past in the present moment. This is not to suggest that it was all necessarily understood at the moment in which it was happening. It felt as chaotic as it sounds. This kind of maladaptive behavior on the part of the child is typically met with a punitive response, and the message and opportunity for meaning is missed.

Subsequent to her father's follow-up individual sessions, his daughter, in turn, requested some sessions of her own. After she discussed her experience directly with her father, his shift in the ability to mentalize her was felt by her. Her attention was newly brought to the concerns she was having in relation to her peers, and she wished for some space to sort out her concerns. She sat up straight on the couch with a direct gaze and shared her thoughts. It is very reassuring to a child that if they "rock the cradle," it does not fall down and become destroyed. The repair process freed her up to place more value on her own experience.

Stern refers to this kind of moment with the Greek word *kairos*: "as a moment of opportunity, when events demand action or are propitious for action . . . transcending the passage of linear time, yet also containing a past" (Stern, 2004, p. 7). I have referred to moments like these as ghost-busting (Moldawsky Silber, 2012). Therapeutic action at the convergence of generations offers a moment of *kairos*. A father began to see the form the past was taking in his present interaction with his daughter, and he shifted with the new perception. The door that he had slammed psychically and his daughter physically slammed was an enactment. Once the dust settled, like the fate of transitional objects and experience, the form was no longer defensively needed; the interaction was no longer the same. The fearful witness, her sibling, could relax his guard. Something new emerged.

## Clinical Illustration #2

As another example, a teenage daughter in a family session told her father not to lean so far into her personal space when he spoke to her. She asked him to "please, stop doing that." He was puzzled and thought she was distracting him from listening to what it was he wanted to say. She was drawing our attention to the implicit relational form of the interaction rather than the content. Parents often assert, "you are not listening to me," to which one could insert, what are they listening to? In other words, who is not listening to what? We paused, and I wondered with him why he thought she might want her personal boundary better observed. He sat back and thought about it. My position as a third in this interaction was meaningful for opening this up. She felt she could take her experience seriously (not always so available in the asymmetry of the relationship) and call his attention to this behavior. The therapeutic support earned in the work prior to this moment shifted her sense of the possibility of being heard. In response, he was able to recall his father's physically abusive style of discipline, complete with the invasion of his and his brothers' boundaries. What was being transmitted in the procedural realm had to do with what fathers do to/with their children: they intimidate. This was unpleasant for him to think about. His gesture to his daughter was not a replica of his father's behavior. It was different, and it was made all the more differentiated by the present moment, by the reflective activity in which they were both able to engage. The discussion followed the changed state of the relational form. He was unaware of having this effect on his daughter, and to recognize the way fathers were represented in his mind and, therefore, in his behavior was a revelation to him. It only became visible to him when his daughter called attention to it, thus bringing the procedural knowledge into conscious awareness. His daughter's experience was not disavowed by her and, now, not by her father. He recalled being afraid of his father and how important it was to stand up to him. When she spoke up to her father, she did not know where it would go. It was a leap of faith, with some hopefulness, vitalized by the therapeutic setting, its meaning made only in the aftermath.

## Temporality and Systems

In the course of normal development, generational boundaries are negotiated and renegotiated as part of registering the passage of time. Transmitted transgenerational trauma of all kinds interferes in this process. The dissociated traumatic memories, static and by definition unintegrated, obstruct the recontextualization of experience. In this instance, past, present and future are jumbled and less differentiated. The curious detaching from the present to expand the view of the moment is akin to Antiguan author Jamaica Kincaid's observation in her essay from *A Small Place*. For emphasis, Kincaid notes the special kind of focused attention required as "the invention of a silence" for the purposes of reclaiming the existence of time in her island community beset by colonial and post-colonial racial trauma (Kincaid, 1988, p. 53). The use of the term "invention" appreciates the breaking of the form and, in so doing, the relationship to time and place. This is similar to Stern's further elaboration of *kairos*, which was understood as an "opportunity to register difference, including temporality, illuminating boundaries in the paradoxical moment" (in Stern, 2004). It is an awakening to the present moment, and moreover, it changes how one views the past.

A parent's perceptual transformation, articulating the generational differences, comes through seeing themselves through the eyes of their child—a present way into a past otherwise unavailable to consciousness. Parents generally feel blown away by this. In other words, a piece of what is recognized and transcended is the parents' own fear from their childhood, now apprehending their child's fear, one generation removed. When supported, parents have felt proud of their children for reflecting on the incoherence of "procedures-for-being-with" they passed on without conscious notice. A child (to be discussed further in vignette #4) produced a drawing in which a boat is sailing along the ocean water. The drawing was folded and contained a sea monster within the water, essentially under the boat (the one you cannot see unless unfolded). In addition to this child's other drawings of ghosts, symbolically, one can consider his attempt to reconcile the duality of experience, blurry in and on the water, influencing his present moment. As the child attempts this kind of therapeutic reflection, taking seriously what is felt and unthought about, a pivot to the parent's subjective experience can "illuminate the boundaries" and bring needed clarity. The child's effort to fold in the felt confusion offers an opportunity for opening up the parent's implicated subjective state.

The shift in the parents' perception can be sudden, even ruthless, and not always in a "good way." There have been a few instances of suicidal thoughts and gestures on the part of parents who are undergoing a transformative re-representation of their internal systems of thought. However, in my clinical experience, the passage has generally been traversed with no lasting injury, although one child was left with a scar near her eye (the result of self-harm), reflecting the embodied sense of danger, the shift into seeing/knowing what had heretofore been kept from view.

Major change happens in ways not always so straightforward or obvious. "The modification of the past by the present does not change 'what objectively happened in the past,' but it changes that past which the patient carries within him as his living history" (Loewald, 2000b, p. 144). How that history is "carried within," assembled and/or embodied, communicated in the interaction, and within the system can emerge and potentially shift in novel ways.

Loewald referred to time dimensions forming a kind of nexus, fragmenting and/or linking past, present and future. He elaborated his description of nexus by stating that modes of time are not held in mind so linearly but rather as "modes of time which determine and shape each other, which differentiate out of and articulate a pure now" (Loewald, 2000b, p. 143). The nonlinear shape of time can include transmitted fragments influenced by the degree of reliance on dissociation (in connection to Renn's comments, included earlier). The "implication-making tendency" becomes a bidirectional event with the next generation, ignoring the boundaries of time, co-creating a psychic equivalence. The transmission of trauma becomes the next generation's trouble, a space where a third person, a child therapist, may intervene, marking a boundary—first by locating it and then by troubling it.

Loewald's (2000b) concept of internal nexus, similar to the assembly of fractals in systems thinking, leads to a question about how the third person, the child therapist, might develop a *mirror-nexus-in-mind* regarding the attachment of minds across the generations? Can the clinician, as a witness to the current experience of past trauma, imagine a new intergenerational perspective? Can the child feel less threatened about maintaining the attachment to the parent (and self) while simultaneously taking ownership of what they see/know/feel? Can links be made in the new present moment with the child therapist's intergenerational mentalization (i.e., holding them both in mind)? Can the child resist the haunting, insist a ghost be formulated and then feel real?

## Clinical Illustration #3

The following vignette is in the context of supervising a child therapist who worked with an adolescent girl and her mother. A supervisee described her adolescent patient's struggles with her mother's intrusiveness, complicating the adolescent's sense of security and confidence. In forming a felt connection to the adolescent through individual psychotherapy sessions, the therapist could mentalize the struggle she was having. Her patient's mother's behavior was indeed impeding her daughter's development. As the therapist/supervisee pivoted to a session with the mother, she reported feeling "sweaty" in session, trying to keep all the parts in mind. The therapist's internal process, the zigzag between experiences, holding them both in mind, was challenging.

Reflecting on the mother in supervision, we began to appreciate the mother's many struggles and past sexual abuse history, which was activated by her experience of parenting a daughter during her teenage years. In seeing the link between the enactment and the mother's anxiety, and the daughter's anger, present and past, the supervisee found she could "lean in" and give the mother space to imagine her experience. The "perpetrator" or "transmitter" was also a victim with unprocessed trauma. The therapist was holding the mother's past history in mind, her present fear and the daughter's experience of misattunement, as well as the loneliness of both of them. Through the therapist's emphatic "lean in," the mother's past experience was both de-shamed and valued in the shared consideration. The silence on the subject gave way to the mother wondering if she might be transmitting her "trauma armor" (her words) to her daughter in her many anxious questions and monitoring (including having placed a video camera in her daughter's room—not subtle, in other words). In her daughter's therapist, the mother found someone to help her look inward at a time when she was so fearful. The psychic equivalence was upended, creating a space for otherness. The therapist had served as an external nexus for this mother and daughter, reworking the connections within and between. The mother could observe her behavior and consider the impact on her daughter as the therapist held open the possibility, expanding maternal subjectivity. The therapist/supervisee noticed a substantial shift in the mother and in the daughter subsequent to this work.

## Further Discussion

Perhaps solving the Sphinx's riddle "What goes on four legs in the morning, two legs in the afternoon, and three legs in the evening?" benefits from a triadic expansion of consciousness (in reference to Tronick's "dyadic expansion of consciousness" 2007) in the circumstance of transgenerational trauma (child-parent-therapist).

Speaking of triads, the Oedipal myth can be read in multiple ways. One way is seeing it as a cautionary tale regarding what happens when the parent avoids tolerating and reckoning with the ways they are implicated in the lives of the younger generation. A parent's fear and avoidance, as the myth portrays, can be deadly. Oedipus' father, Lauis, had no intention of reflecting on his past and no understanding of the necessity. Lauis responded to the fear of the increased vulnerability and responsibility that comes with parenthood by putting his child on a mountaintop to die. The things he fearfully imagined were the things that scripted the enactment. The child, Oedipus, ultimately punished himself by blinding himself, embodying the non-reflection of the family story. It is a myth about the intergenerational costs of ignoring the parent's implicated subjective state. It served as the formative centerpiece for child development in the classical model of psychoanalysis and was enacted in the practice of child analysis. Parental reflection, necessary to protect the child from the second generational effects of trauma, was, for the most part, a missed opportunity. Breaking the bough, severing the attachment and maintaining unlinked fragments protect from consciously knowing and feeling the increased vulnerability and responsibility. The boundaries of time and generation remain muddled and confused, rattling the next generation.

Hirsch, a professor of comparative literature and gender studies, discussed what she referred to as post-memory in the context of second-generation Holocaust trauma (Hirsch, 2012). Post memories, similar to this discussion of transmitted trauma, culminate with the question: whose memory is whose? A memory is described as implanted in the next generation and therefore linked conceptually to psychic equivalence.

## Clinical Illustration #4

A nine-year-old boy, Bobby (mentioned earlier in relation to the boat drawing and further elaborated in Silber, 2020), came into a session with his parents after treatment had evolved over a two-year period. He had made progress with his symptoms, eating disorder and separation anxiety, and they were all considering the possibility of his attending a sleepaway camp. Bobby was fearful and resisted being "forced" into anything. He began to build a ramp with blocks on the drawing table as his parents were talking about this. The ramp became more elaborate with a truck that had magic markers taped on either side of it, like wings. He placed many army men at the base of the ramp, and the truck was sent down the ramp knocking everything over. By that point, Bobby and I had built an infrastructure of metaphoric communication. In his words, "there you go relating again." Children (as well as adults) regulate surprise at their discovery of knowing more than they thought they knew. I again "related," or rather observed, "that perhaps he felt that his feelings were going to be run over?" That he would not be heard? The next session was planned to further our discussion. The mother, who had in the past shared her childhood experience of her mother forcing her to eat, came in and said she had thought about our discussion the week before and wanted to say that, though she was encouraging the camp, she was most interested in what her son had to say. The mother shifted in the pause offered through the child's play communication of a truck careening down a ramp (fueled by fear?). Such communication helped her to pause and reconsider. The mother, who had shared her childhood story with Bobby present, felt supported to further reflect and change the implicit relational space. She differentiated from her mother: she took the bid and played with him.

Carrying a past traumatic (disorganized) memory is similar to Winnicott's (1974) concept of "fear of breakdown." The fear from past experience abides, bringing anticipatory anxiety to the present, which is connected to a prior event. The feared experience can be constructed from more than one generation and influence more than one generation. In other words, the parent's fear, overshadowing the present, misattributed to the child, culminates by extension to a *fear of my child's breakdown*. The child can become essentially caught in reworking and differentiating from the parent's memory. Bobby began to recognize that his mother's fear was connected to her experience with his grandmother (attributed to him). With her help, the blurry, ghostly felt experience was formulated. It made sense to him and helped differentiate their subjective experiences that had been bound up with each other. Bobby had substantial grief surrounding this process, but with familial support, he mourned.

## Further Discussion

The therapist can be critical to the renegotiation of the dysregulated state that accompanies the retrieval of traumatic memories and their associated affects. It may be the child's dysregulation that can signal confused feelings in an intergenerational enactment, seeking new meaning and boundaries. In this way, the child can initially be feared as a perpetrator who is activating memories in the person to whom they are also dependent. In parent-child interaction, internal ruptures can beget external ruptures. The inside is linked to the outside, with confusion spiraling between.

One pre-adolescent child directed the sign of the vampire at me as she and her father walked into the consulting office to convey how dangerous the work at this particular juncture was felt to be (this work was described in Moldawsky Silber, 2012). The forbidden passage was renegotiated, and when this child became an adolescent, she shared that she felt this work had saved her life. A generation later, she brought her seven-year-old son to the office. She explained that her son asked if he could see the doctor who had helped her with big feelings when she was a child. As a parent, she felt she was missing something, and in the new generational perspective, she sought help to rework what had been so difficult then and, with a new configuration, now. When the parent recontextualizes the dynamics, they become acquainted with a feeling of empowerment, which results from being instrumental in creating a safer environment for their child.

In play therapy, a child becomes empowered through organizing their feelings. It is this preliminary work, which allows the child to differentiate and register their implicit relational knowing as valid. With this increased sense of self-efficacy, knowing what he knew, a son sought to "break the silence" (his words) with his father. When the child found the courage to speak about what was felt but unspoken, he explained to his father the hurt he felt was "mental." It got the father thinking. The father requested some individual parent sessions to sort this out. He was able to see how different a father he was to his son than his father had been to him. The father was able to explain that he was proud of his son. He could have never done, with his father, what his son was able to do with him. In the act of listening to his son, he was differentiating from his past. He was instantiating the difference to his father. The father made a trip to visit his mother to learn more about his deceased father, the child's paternal grandfather. In sharing what he learned about his father with his son, his son came to know of him rather than live a version of the experience of being fathered by him.

## Multiple Systems Implicated in the Developing Child

Pediatrician Nadine Burke Harris, author of *The Deepest Well*, summarized the multiple systems implicated when there is childhood adversity:

> Twenty years of medical research has shown that childhood adversity literally gets under our skin, changing people in ways that can endure in their bodies for decades. It can tip a child's developmental trajectory and affect physiology. It can trigger chronic inflammation and hormonal changes that can last a lifetime. It can alter the way DNA is read and how cells replicate, and it can dramatically increase the risk for heart disease, stroke, cancer, diabetes—even Alzheimer's.
>
> (Harris, 2018, p. xv)

Complementing the discussion was Dr. Nadine Burke's self-reflection:

> I caught a glimpse of what it might be like to lose the ability to be the parent we all want to be . . . my mother did not have the network of

support . . . the benefit of two decades of research on toxic stress and the impact on her children . . . I believe we can rewrite the story of adversity and break the intergenerational cycle of toxic stress.

(Harris, 2018, p. 221)

This base of knowledge could inform the building of an infrastructure of support systems and could indeed keep "boughs" from breaking. The challenge seems to be in illuminating the silence around parental and societal implications in the disavowal of an ethic of care or childism.

It is to the arts that the collective seeks support for this kind of breaking of and inventing a reflective silence. In Morrison's words, her work, in reference to racially transmitted trauma,

must bear witness and identify that which is useful from the past and that which ought to be discarded; it must make it possible to prepare for the present and live it out; and it must do that not by avoiding problems and contradictions but by examining them.

(2019, p. 331)

The child/family therapist can draw inspiration from Morrison's placing emphasis, in a collective sense, on bringing contradictions to light, similar to Winnicott's position of not seeking to resolve paradox but to clarify these as they come to be known. The attention culminates in expanding the form of the narrative. Transmitted trauma, at a societal and/or individual level, is dissociated experience affectively sealed with shame and fear, both distorting and minimizing the present and making impossible the envisioning of the future. Children, in pursuit of understanding themselves and their place in the world, familiarly and culturally, seek openings (within the power structure) for recognition. When trauma is confusing the affective landscape, they seek support to resist the fear to gain developmentally needed clarity. If given the opportunity, they change and enliven the intergenerational dialogue.

## Conclusion

The inclusion of parental subjectivity in relational child work expands the clinical imagination. The ways parents are implicated in the transmission of trauma to the next generation are brought into specific focus. The child therapist's mentalization involves linking across the intergenerational minds forming a nexus of thought and process necessary to reorganizing the attachment relationship. This chapter included brief clinical vignettes illustrating the transformative moment which could not have occurred without the subjectivities of child and parent in the treatment process. In the asymmetrical bidirectional parent-child relationship, the child is supported to find agency to resist transmitted experience, and a parent comes to recognize the ways they are implicated in the transmission. The therapeutic action flows within and between the multiple nonlinear parts: responsibility and vulnerability, fear and grief, past and present, implicit and explicit memory systems and developmental levels. The family narrative is reconsidered, parts held out become formulated and ancestors are memorialized with a living history, enriching and expanding the present moment. The attachment system is contextualized within a larger systems frame riddled with childism and racism. A child's recognition process, emerging through the shadows of transmitted history, is felt as a courageous intergenerational achievement.

Post reflection: Childhood includes cracking a number of codes. For some children, their psychic life depends on it. May we use our imagination and give them a hand?

Appreciation goes to Marjorie Bosk, PhD, and Timothy Wright, PsyD, faculty at IRPP, for their help in articulating these ideas and collaboration in the teaching of them. And to the editors, Rachel Kabasakalian-McKay and David Mark, for expanding the dialogue both in the institutional life of IRPP, in this volume and in their comments on this chapter. And to Michal Meyer, PhD.

## References

Ainsworth, M., Blehar, M., Waters, E., & Wall, S. (2015). *Patterns of attachment: A psychological study of the strange situation*. Routledge.

Beebe, B., & Lachmann, F. (2014). *The origins of attachment; Infant research and adult treatment*. Routledge.

Coates, S. (2012). The child as trigger; Commentary on paper by Laurel Moldawsky Silber. *Psychoanalytic Dialogues, 2*(1), 123–128.

Cozolino, L. (2010). *The neuroscience of psychotherapy: Healing the social brain*. W. W. Norton & Company.

Fonagy, P., Gergely, G., Jurist, E. L., & Target, M. (2002). *Affect regulation, mentalization, and the development of the self*. Other Press.

Fraiberg, S., Adelson, E., & Shapiro, V. (1975). Ghosts in the nursery: A psychoanalytic approach to the problems of impaired infant-mother relationships. *Journal of the American Academy of Child Psychiatry, 14*, 387–421.

Freud, A. (1972). Child-analysis as a sub-specialty of psychoanalysis. *The International Journal of Psycho-Analysis, 53*, 151–156.

Harris, N. B. (2018). *The deepest well; Healing the long-term effects of childhood adversity*. Houghton Mifflin Harcourt.

Hesse, E., & Main, M. (1999). Second-generation effects of unresolved trauma in nonmaltreating parents; Dissociated, frightened, and threatening parental behavior. *Psychoanalytic Inquiry, 19*(4), 481–540.

Hirsch, M. (2012). *The generation of post memory: Writing and visual culture after the holocaust*. Columbia University Press.

Hoffman, L., Karush, R., Garfinkle, M., Roose, S., & Cherry, S. (2009). A cross-sectional survey of child and adolescent analysts in New York City. *JAPA, 57*(4), 911–917.

Kincaid, J. (1988). *A small place*. Farrar, Straus, and Giroux.

Knittel, S. C., & Forchieri, M. (2020). Navigating implication: An interview with Michael Rothberg. *Journal of Perpetrator Research, 3*, 6–19.

Kristoff, N. (2021, May 6). In editorial entitled, turning child care into a new cold war. *New York Times*.

Lewis, A., & Starr, K. (2013). *A psychotherapy of the people: Toward a progressive psychoanalysis*. Routledge.

Lieberman, A. F. (1999). Negative maternal attributions: Effects on toddler's sense of self. *Psychoanalytic Inquiry, 19*, 737–756.

Loewald, H. (2000a). On the therapeutic action of psychoanalysis, (1960). In *The Essential Loewald: Collected papers and monographs* (pp. 221–256). University Publishing Group, Inc.

Loewald, H. (2000b). The experience of time, (1972). In *The Essential Loewald: Collected papers and monographs* (pp. 138–147). University Publishing Group, Inc.

Lyons-Ruth, K. (2002). The two-person construction of defenses: Disorganized attachment strategies, unintegrated mental states, and hostile/helpless relational processing. *Journal of Infant, Child, Adolescent Psychotherapy, 2*(4), 107–119.

Lyons-Ruth, K. (2003). Dissociation and the parent-infant dialogue: A longitudinal perspective from attachment research. *Journal of the American Psychoanalytic Association, 51*(3), 883–911.

Marks, T., & Shapiro, Y. (2021). Synchronicity, acausal connection, and fractal dynamics of clinical practice. *Psychoanalytic Dialogues, 31*(4), 468–486.

Moldawsky Silber, L. (2012). Ghostbusting transgenerational processes. *Psychoanalytic Dialogues, 22*, 106–122.

Morrison. (2019). *The source of self-regard*. Alfred A. Knopf.

Renn, P. (2012). *The silent past and the invisible present; Memory, trauma, and representation in psychotherapy*. Relational Perspective Book Series, 54. Routledge.

Rothberg, M. (2019). *The implicated subject: Beyond victims and perpetrators*. Stanford University Press.

Schechter, D. (2017). On traumatically skewed intersubjectivity. *Psychoanalytic Inquiry, 37*, 251–264.

Silber, L. (2015). A view from the margins: Children in relational psychoanalysis. *Journal of Infant, Child, & Adolescent Psychotherapy*, 14345–14362.

Silber, L. (2020). Reimagining humpty dumpty with play's therapeutic action. *Journal of Infant, Child, and Adolescent Psychotherapy*, *19*(2), 182–198.

Silber, L. (2021). Child analysis is shared: Holding the child's relational context in mind. In C. Masur (Ed.), *Finding the piggle; Reconsidering D.W. Winnicott's most famous child case*. Phoenix Publishing House.

Silber, L. (2017). Playing in the intergenerational spaces. In B. Seitler & K. Kleinman (Eds.), *From cradle to couch*. International Psychoanalytic Books.

Siskind, D. (1997). *Working with parents: Establishing the essential alliance in child psychotherapy and consultation*. Jason Aronson, Inc.

Slade, A. (2005). Parental reflective functioning: An introduction. *Attachment & Human Development*, *7*, 269–281.

Slade, A. (2014). 'Ghosts in the psychoanalytic nursery': A response to Lieberman and Harris. *Psychoanalytic Dial*, *24*(3), 282–286.

Solms, M. (2018). Neurobiological underpinnings of psychoanalytic theory and therapy. *Frontiers in Behavioral Neuroscience, 4*.

Steele, H., & Steele, M. (2018). *Handbook of attachment-based interventions*. Guilford Press.

Stern, D. (2004). *The present moment in psychotherapy and everyday life*. W. W. Norton & Co.

Tronick, E. (2007). *The neurobehavioral and social-emotional development of infants and children*. Norton Books.

Tummala-Narra, U. (in press). Can we decolonize psychoanalytic theory and practice? *Psychoanalytic Dialogues*.

Winnicott, D. W. (1965). *The maturational processes and the facilitating environment: Studies in the theory of emotional development*. Karnac Books.

Winnicott, D. W. (1974). The fear of breakdown. *International Journal of Psychoanalysis*, *1*, 103–107.

Winnicott, D. W. (1977). *The piggle: An account of the psychoanalytic treatment of a little girl*. Hogarth Press of Penguin Books.

## Chapter 12

# Implication as Central to a Relational Stance

## Vulnerability, Responsibility, and Racial Enactment

*Rachel Kabasakalian-McKay and David Mark*

We are all caught in a moment of reckoning; in the world around us, the vast and worsening disparities between poor communities and wealthy ones are more and more apparent as we endure the ravages of a global pandemic. The destruction of the climate, no longer a hypothetical worry but a reality with increasingly catastrophic consequences, is swirling around us. And in the United States, the foundational crime of our nation, in which the bodies, minds, and lands of Black and indigenous people have been violated, suppressed, and plundered, has risen again to the forefront of our collective consciousness, met with the sober realization of how our current social arrangements perpetuate racial inequities, how much work we have still to do.

How do we position ourselves, individually and as a field, in this fraught but deeply consequential moment? And which elements of our theories might carry us forward and unite our efforts as psychoanalysts with our commitments to social justice and which might be holding us back?

An idea that has struck us as of great use in regard to these questions is that of *implication*, as developed by social theorist Michael Rothberg (2019). Linking his work to other theorists in the humanities, Rothberg takes up social structures of inequality, oppression, and violence in a novel way that seems especially relevant for thinking about race and racism in the United States. In addition, we see Rothberg's conception of implication as a particularly good fit with crucial elements of a relational clinical sensibility, as we will discuss.

Implicated subjects, in Rothberg's words, "occupy positions aligned with power and privilege" and as such "contribute to, inhabit, inherit, or benefit from regimes of domination but do not originate or control such

DOI: 10.4324/9781003265146-12

regimes" (2019, p. 1). This conception allows us to consider more deeply how we are implicated in harms we are neither actively pursuing nor intending, but in which we are nevertheless participants. To be implicated, in Rothberg's view, means we cannot be outside of a situation of harm; we may not have brought it about, we may not approve of it, but we are *folded within* it.

While foregrounding implication as an inevitable mode of participation and of "the implicated subject" as a category distinct from victim and perpetrator, Rothberg also distinguishes ways in which we are implicated differently in different contexts and may occupy several positions simultaneously. To be implicated is thus a feature of particular social, structural, or relational configurations rather than a stable aspect of identity. He introduces the term "complex implication" as a way to make room for the multiplicity of identities, as well as both current and historical experiences. One may be a victim or descendant of victims in some contexts, for example, while also implicated in others.

It should be underscored that the introduction of the implicated subject position is not intended to do away with the categories of victim and perpetrator; naming the actions of perpetrators and the suffering of victims is the foundation of considering greater complexity, not an erasure of this crucial recognition. Rather, the idea of implication is offered as a way to expand the space for us to consider our deep involvement in the lives and circumstances of others, even without our awareness or intent. Rothberg writes,

> A theory of implication allows us to retain our sense that situations of conflict position us in morally and emotionally complex ways and yet still call out for forms of political engagement that cut through complexity to remain on the side of justice.

> (p. 19)

Implication, in both senses described above, evokes what Benjamin (2004, 2018) describes as Thirdness. The *implicated subject* refers to a third position, neither perpetrator nor victim, but implicated; neither "good" nor "bad" but "un-good" (Benjamin, 2018). In Thirdness, the complementarity of doer and done-to yields to mutual recognition, in which each one can hear and grasp the other's experience. Crucially, this does not mean that complexity of positioning relieves us of the burden of acknowledging and acting from awareness of our implication. Just the opposite is true: the idea of implication makes clear that we are responsible for acting in response to injustice from which we benefit, or injuries we have inflicted through commission or omission, even as we are also injured or vulnerable, in other domains.

## Vulnerability and Responsibility

We are all "folded within" (Rothberg, 2019, p. 1) larger, often traumatic events, as well as within structures of power and injustice; there is no outside place to stand—however well-intentioned we may be; we are all connected to what happens to others. While this aspect of Rothberg's theory emphasizes our inescapable participation—and thus, responsibility—his idea of "complex implication" speaks to how we may be both victims in some situations and in some respects, and beneficiaries, or even perpetrators, in others. This facilitates our holding the tension inherent in occupying more than one position and thus expands the space for considering the multiplicity of identifications and affective experiences that are brought to bear in both intimate and large-scale interactions. From this perspective, we can more readily see vulnerability and responsibility as coexisting, even inextricably linked, rather than canceling one another out. Relational psychoanalysis provides the matrix within which to elaborate the ways holding this tension is crucial in interpersonal engagement, including within therapeutic dyads.

Layton (2009) has linked the weakening of this vital tension with the reigning neoliberalism, pointing out that the relentless message that everyone is on their own and needs to take care of themselves has dulled both our sense of our own vulnerability and our responsibility to others. She has noted that our implication in the suffering of others is inherently tied to the fact that we are all vulnerable; this is the foundation of empathy, and both retaliation and withdrawal can be understood as defenses against vulnerability. We may understand Layton as arguing that in eschewing awareness or tolerance of our own vulnerability, we actually move further from our responsibility to others, a compelling and deeply humane argument.

Stephens (2020, and reprinted in this volume), in a deeply consequential contribution to the literature, puts forward a relational conception of White double-consciousness in a way that seems to us not only compatible with but an intersubjective elaboration of Rothberg's implicated subject position. Integrating the writings on Black double-consciousness of Du Bois (1903/1994) and Fanon (1986/1967) with contemporary inter-subjectivity theory, Stephens elaborates a position of a White double-consciousness. In the context of racialized relating, she sees the capacity for double-consciousness as akin to Bromberg's ideal that we may see ourselves as others see us, even when that is not at all what we wish to have seen, without losing a sense of one's own worth. It is the "both/and," holding these alongside one another, that Stephens, evoking the words of Bert Williams, a turn-of-the-20th-century Black performer about whom she has written extensively, terms "getting next to ourselves." This "both/and," in our reading of Stephens, as of Rothberg and Benjamin, allows for each subject to hold vulnerability, including injury, shame, and the wish to have one's benign intentions recognized, alongside the openness to how one is being experienced as harming or unyielding.

Stephens describes two events, separated by a period of ten years, from her experience as a faculty member in two very different college settings, in which painful, racially charged incidents reverberated through the entire college community. As she reflected, "in the end, no one came through unharmed" (p. 205), despite the fact that "most if not all of the players involved . . . were well-meaning people trying to find their way through a thicket of individual emotions and feelings, and interpersonal confrontations and reactions that were highly distressing, destabilizing—traumatizing, really" (p. 205).

The first incident was ignited when a White staff member referred to a group of Black students as "you people" while arguing with the students to vacate a room they had reserved ten minutes before their allotted time expired in order to make way for a subsequent meeting. The phrase "became the lightning rod for a complex encounter involving issues of race and class in a fractious confrontation between working class White, female, administrative staff and middle to upper class, Black, undergraduate students" (p. 204). We imagine that viewing this painful encounter through the lens of Rothberg's idea of "complex implication" might facilitate each person's capacity to do what Stephens imagines: to "get next to ourselves"—that is, to undertake a form of emotional work to find the truth, find another version of our "selves" in the others' projection onto us (see also Hart, 2017), and thereby hold an awareness of both vulnerability and responsibility in the situation.

In considering the second incident, it is Rothberg's category of the implicated subject itself that may help *us* "get next to ourselves," as we consider (and can easily identify with) the problematic positioning of a group of faculty as they became engaged in what began as a racial enactment among students. The situation began when a White student emailed a racist joke to other students, whom he assumed (incorrectly) were all also White. The faculty, once they were made aware of what had happened, encouraged the Black students to talk to the White students about how they experienced the initial email. The Black students found this request, or expectation, on the part of the faculty insensitive, once again asking the students of color to take the risks and do the work of explaining themselves, as well as an abdication of responsibility on the part of the faculty (p. 205). We imagine (perhaps because, as therapists, we can all too easily slip into this position) that the faculty, who probably saw themselves as helpful or benign figures in this conflict between the Black and White students, felt injured, misunderstood, and unfairly judged. For the faculty, the version of themselves as "benign" and "helpful" stood, more or less, *outside* the conflict among the students as if they themselves were not deeply implicated in this incident. From such a position, we imagine the faculty were not perceived as feeling, *in a personal way*, sufficiently vulnerable *or* responsible. The Black students were likely to perceive this lack of feeling implicated so that requests, let alone expectations, from them, especially requests that entail interpersonal risk, were apt to be experienced by the students as an upsetting, if not galling, abdication of responsibility by the faculty.

## Vulnerability and Responsibility in the Analytic Relationship

A central challenge for us, as analysts, is to deepen the awareness of our own vulnerability as it is emerging in the relationship (Levine, 2016) while retaining our fundamental responsibility to the other. The concept of implication may speak to the challenge of holding these simultaneously, even as the intensity deepens. In the most ordinary, even benign-seeming enactments, the analyst retreats into being ever more helpful and "good" to preserve the illusion of being less vulnerable that this position can confer. "I am not vulnerable or weak or useless, I am the helpful one." In this, the patient can feel gaslighted and more alone with the feelings of being bad or shameful (Davies, 2004, 2014).

A common way in which the failure to hold vulnerability and responsibility can emerge is when what is happening in the relationship is piercing most sharply into areas of the analyst's own woundedness (Harris, 2009). When we feel unfairly accused, shamed, or told how cruel or unhelpful we are being (e.g., Bromberg, 2003; Hart, 2006), to give some examples, it can be especially hard not to retaliate or withdraw. While the professional role may help stabilize us in such moments, and necessarily so—reminding us of our greater responsibility in the situation and guarding against extremes of retaliation or withdrawal—too much of a retreat into the seeming safety of that position then risks draining affect and aliveness from the encounter, as well as leaving the patient alone in feeling shameful vulnerability.

As the relational sensibility has been deepened and elaborated over the past 30 years, there has been an increased appreciation of the most powerful transformational moments as marked by mutual vulnerability and a shared sense of participation, moments of "radical equality" (Mark, 2018). In such moments we, as analysts, surrender the safety of the professional perch and come closer, bearing our own vulnerability while able to see how we have contributed to what has left our patients feeling ashamed, injured, or misrecognized. Along with this has come the realization that an over-reliance on roles and rules can stifle creativity, intimacy, and vitality (e.g., Hoffman, 1998). This realization has transformed and deepened the way we, as therapists, think of responsibility in the clinical situation, which in turn alters the way responsibility feels. Much the way the *fact* of implication alters the way responsibility *feels* in the political realm (it is not merely abstractly "right" or "good" to be responsible; implication makes it feel imperative in a personal way), implication alters the way responsibility feels in the therapeutic situation (it is not merely a fulfillment of one's role to be responsible; the implicated analyst feels it specifically and personally). Our responsibility to our patients is not fundamentally a matter of roles; rather, our responsibility in a relational approach lies primarily in our commitment to participating in a deepening personal relationship, an unfolding process of opening up to another, a commitment that often requires a necessarily uncomfortable process of seeing oneself through the eyes of the other (Bromberg, 2011; Hart, 2017; Stephens, 2020). Clinging too tightly to the protections of the professional role can constitute a deep deprivation: taking away from the patient as well as the analyst opportunities to feel we are allowed to know the other "where they live emotionally" (Aron, 1999, p. 252).

We are responsible and vulnerable both. We are implicated. Perhaps paradoxically, it is the analyst's capacity to bear our vulnerability (hurt, shame, sadness, fear) and find a way to share something of this with our patient that often represents our deepest responsibility to this same person. It is in these moments in which a basic need of the patient—to have and to be "a partner in thought" and a "mutual witness" (in Don Stern's, 2009, language)—is satisfied and in which both care for and faith in the other can be demonstrated.

## Social identities and action

The concept of the "implicated subject" is essentially a political one, centering on collective responsibility and action, social identities, and history, all of which have traditionally been marginal concepts, if that, in many varieties of psychoanalysis. This has, nevertheless, been changing over the past few decades.

Layton (2009; Layton with Leavy-Sperounis, 2020), for many years, has argued that analysts have colluded with a capitalist worldview by artificially separating the individual from the social. Even in many versions of relational theory, despite its inherently social nature, the analytic relationship—the dyad—has often been described as if it existed in a neutral social-political space. In the words of Jones (2020), compatible with Layton's position in this regard, "[i]t is as though the very act of being immersed in contemporary psychoanalytic thinking and training includes the psychologizing away of social inequality" (2020, p. 81).

Layton (Layton, with Leavy-Sperounis, 2020) and Jones (2015) are part of a growing chorus of psychoanalytic writers (e.g., Altman, 1995; Yi, 1998; Eng & Han, 2000; Leary, 2000; White, K. P., 2002; Suchet, 2004, 2007; Gump, 2010; Cushman, 2015; White, C. 2015; Evans Holmes, 2016; Tummala-Narra, 2015; Grand & Salberg, 2017; Hart, 2017; Vaughans, 2017, 2022; Fors, 2018; Powell, 2018; González, 2020; Knoblauch, 2020; Sheehi, 2020; Stephens, 2020, 2022; Harris, 2022; Levine, 2022) arguing that in nurturing the illusion of two individuals meeting as if outside of history, psychoanalysis has colluded in a denial of the ways we cannot but bring the raced—as well as gendered, classed, and differently abled—versions of ourselves to how we see and engage with one another. In the intensive focus on the individual, the salience of one's identity as a part of a group or groups is minimized (González, 2020), both masking power differences and consigning important aspects of identity and belonging to the margins of the work. Eng and Han (2000) years ago pointed to the erasure of the social as also erasing the political and, in so doing, misreading intrafamilial and intergenerational conflict within families who have been subjected to trauma based on racism and xenophobia as if this traumatic context were not enormously shaping of psychic experience. Arguing for the importance of attending to the analyst's capacity to reflect on her own social location and racial identity, Yi (1998) points out that "analysts' racial background and associated cultural values are an important part of their subjectivity and influence their therapeutic endeavors, from their views of human nature to their choice of techniques to therapy goals" (1998, p. 258). Jones (2020), emphasizing the central role of racism and its continuously unfolding traumas, writes of the need not to separate consideration of transference from the "Real World experiences" of the analyst and analysand (p. 77) where race is concerned. Although these authors are writing from different theoretical positions within the field of contemporary psychoanalysis, each speaks to the necessity to consider cultural and racial identity as central, and racism and its attendant violence as real elements of trauma not only historical but pressing heavily on what is unfolding within the relational present.

The writing of these and other contemporary analytic theorists has begun to address how we, patients and therapists, are implicated, often differentially, within the larger culture, specifically within structures of inequality. An inescapable aspect of this implication involves social identity, that of ourselves and of our patients. Furthermore, as many of these theorists have persuasively argued, these social identities have more power and influence and operate more deeply, less consciously, than psychoanalytic theory has traditionally understood. In short, social identities have increasingly come to be understood as central to *who we are*.

This trend converges with another core feature of relational thought, a focus on "real-world experiences," including and especially forms of trauma. Relational theory concerns what people do to and with each other, which is to say, real actions. Furthermore, unlike some versions of field theory (see Stern, 2013a, 2013b), relational theory is *both* intersubjective *and* interpersonal. That is, the analytic situation involves not only two subjects (who generate intersubjective phenomena) but two whole people.

"Who we are" includes not only our social identities and not only our minds and our bodies but also includes what we do with and to each other. Our actions inescapably implicate us, as analysts, in our treatments. Benjamin's (2018; and this volume) focus on acknowledgment, about taking responsibility for the things we have done to the patient, makes this implication clear. In addition to restoring the Third—affirming the other's sense of the way things ought to go, of what is right and just—as Benjamin's acknowledgment is intended to do, spelling out what we have done to, and with, our patients can generate a deeper kind of intimacy, one that has the power to increase a patient's self-acceptance and self-respect.

## Fantasy and the Analyst as Lightly Implicated

A young white woman in her late teens had been suffering from a puzzling combination of physical symptoms. Unable to identify a medical cause, her parents decided to try psychotherapy. Her therapist was struck immediately by how sharp her mind seemed, how engaging she was, and at the same time, how much these symptoms were getting in the way of her living a fuller life. In one session, she described a very upsetting event that had taken place: a family friend, a much older man, had gotten her into a private place with no one else around and tried to convince her to have sex with him. But what was really most upsetting to her, she explained with obvious distress, was that when she tried to tell her father what happened, he didn't believe her. Instead, he suggested that she must have imagined that this was really what the friend had meant.

Unlike her father, the therapist was willing to believe that the experience with the older man had taken place. However, with unshakable conviction regarding the power of Oedipal fantasies on the human psyche, he concluded that she was defending against the strength of her own desires. Reasoning it out to himself, her therapist noted her distress with her father's disbelief as a sign that she had not truly been upset by the come-on from this man, that she had wanted it in some way. In the therapist's words, "[i]t was justifiable to suspect that there was something concealed, for a reproach which misses the mark gives no lasting offense" (Freud, 1901, p. 46).

Freud's work with "Dora," from which this vignette was taken, has long provided one window into the complicated relationship that psychoanalysis has had with external, interpersonal reality, and with the inescapable fact of power in social life (see Bernheimer & Kahane, 1985, for a collection of essays on Dora's case and feminism), and therefore also with implication. After all, implication refers to "the action or state of being involved in something." The analyst, in the original psychoanalytic model, was understood to be minimally involved, either as a specific person or a carrier of social hierarchies and therefore barely implicated. In the first place, the analyst's primary activity, interpretation, was understood to be from outside the interaction and was also understood to be experienced as such—if the person was analyzable—by the patient. In this regard, Freud's position on an inaccurate interpretation was parallel to his position on Dora's father's "reproach"—that is, an interpretation that is inexact, inaccurate, or just plain wrong—exerts no suggestive influence upon the patient (Freud, 1917, p. 452). "Whatever . . . is inaccurate" in the analyst's interpretation "drops out in the course of the analysis" (Freud, p. 452); like father's "reproach . . . which misses the mark," it ultimately doesn't affect the patient. Furthermore, an analyst who regards themself as outside the interaction does not feel personally implicated in what transpires in the analytic situation and is similarly less likely to be aware of their own vulnerability to their patient.

Freud's question is not "Who am I?" but "Who do I represent?" within an Oedipal scenario. With this question, the analyst is merely lightly implicated, and thus, "who we are"—incorporating our social identities, our personality or character, and our actions, what we actually do with our patients—is relegated to an unimportant and superficial position. We can hear this light implication in Freud's speculation about what it might have been that drove Dora's transference. Transference occurred "because of the unknown quantity in me which reminded Dora of Herr K. . . . What this unknown quantity was I naturally cannot tell. I suspect it had to do with money or with jealousy of another patient" (Freud, 1905, p. 119). He can't tell what it is about the situation (he has been employed by her father in a patriarchal culture, in a bid to "cure" her of her insistence on her sexuality or subjectivity as her own) or him (including what he actually has done with her, thought about her, or felt toward her) that is motivating Dora's antipathy toward him. Within this frame of reference, we can understand how he would let the matter rest there; it simply does not matter.

In the focus on intrapsychic fantasy (i.e., the Oedipus complex), analysts couldn't see what seems so obvious to us now, that qualities of interpersonal relatedness such as basic care and taking one's experience seriously, particularly in relation to a significant other, matter deeply. The failure to take Dora's experience seriously influenced more than her relationship with her analyst. The idea that a young woman would be profoundly upset by her parents not believing her when she described intrusive sexual advances (the first when she was 14) from an adult man she'd known for most of her life was not only hard to believe for Freud, but it proved that the opposite must be true: she would only have been upset by her father's dismissive response, suggesting she was "imagining" something that had happened to her if she had wanted the sexual advance to happen, and then was anxious about her own conflicting desires. Of course, in taking this position, Freud became further implicated with Dora, repeating the precise response that so distressed her from her father and then compounding it. Where her father questioned her interpretation of reality, Freud did not just challenge her naming of her own emotional experience but asserted, based on theory, that it had to be the opposite and was confounded by his patient's steadfast resistance to this interpretation.

For Freud, to accept the truth of what his patient was telling him had happened *and* her subjective report of her distress risked the elegance and power of his theoretical edifice. And here, perhaps more than in his own relationship with Dora or his knowing that it was her father who could influence future referrals and the physician's standing in the community, we can see Freud's vulnerability, for which his theory left little room.

## Trauma and the Analyst as Deeply Implicated

While the *implicated subject* is not a psychoanalytic term and comes from a different realm of social practice and discourse, there has been a history of useful dialogue between psychoanalysis and cultural studies when it comes to thinking about trauma. Until fairly recently, perpetrator, bystander, and victim constituted the triad of positions that were commonly referred to when describing traumatic events, whether individual or collective. In both the academic fields and in the psychoanalytic literature, the dissatisfaction with the term "bystander" has been evident in the variety of alternate concepts that have been proposed (e.g., "failed witness," "beneficiary"). It is quite possible that the frequency with which conflicts may collapse into the victim-perpetrator binary has something to do with the inadequacy of the "third" term. It is in this space, between perpetrator and victim, that Rothberg's term, implicated subject, is so valuable. In the political realm, implication, particularly the notion of complex implication in which we all occupy multiple subject positions, is a capacious idea, opening the possibility of new coalitions of people to work toward common projects of social justice (Rothberg, 2019, p. 20). Furthermore, to the degree we are implicated subjects and not perpetrators, we are held to account but with more room to think—to think about how we are implicated, to think about the grievous harm done to others and what we can do about it—than if we are perpetrators (Connolly, 2021.[1])

From a clinical trauma perspective, the analyst is a deeply implicated subject, one who is "folded into" (Rothberg) the traumatic scenario—sometimes inhabiting the position of victim, sometimes perpetrator, sometimes failed witness. As Ferenczi (1949) came to appreciate, it is crucial for the analyst to be able to acknowledge reality with respect to the enormous shaping impact of real traumatic events on a person's psyche. And as he made clear, in treating patients with trauma, we will inevitably in some way participate in a repetition of the trauma, often well before either person knows what is happening. For Ferenczi, both participants emerge as vulnerable, even as the analyst's inevitable implication is brought to the fore. Indeed, it is entirely possible that Ferenczi—working alone as a therapist in the area of trauma—became stuck in the perpetrator position. This might have led him, out of the need to flee from the unbearable sense of extreme guilt that rightfully belongs to the perpetrator, to the lengths he went to in his mutual analysis with R.N. (Ferenczi and Elizabeth Severn, or "R.N.," took turns on the couch, analyzing each other; see Ferenczi, 1995). The idea of the analyst as "implicated subject" might have stabilized him enough to recognize his responsibility—not merely his responsibility in the general sense as therapist, but in the personal and specific sense of actual things he did, thought, and felt that genuinely harmed Severn—while, at the same time, tempering his perpetrator guilt enough to think more clearly about what could actually be done to repair.

Despite Ferenczi's attempts, it was not until the early 1990s, with the publication of Davies and Frawley's (1994) landmark work, that psychoanalysis could consistently reconcile the pervasiveness of childhood sexual abuse with a no-less rich appreciation of complexity and paradox within the human psyche. It is not coincidental that Davies and Frawley were writing within the then-newly emergent relational tradition, heir to two of Ferenczi's most powerful insights: real trauma happens and matters, and the analyst cannot help but be caught up in re-injury. Further, acknowledging both of these truths, both in the abstract plane of theory and in the all too sharply felt space of therapeutic enactment, is crucial to both therapeutic action and restoration of what Benjamin (2004, 2018) has referred to as the moral third—a conviction that injury can be seen and lawful relatedness restored. Because relational clinical work is grounded in these principles, there is a natural (but far from automatic) foundation for grasping one's implication, both in fraught moments and more generally across the arc of a treatment. Each of these two elements—first, seeing the pervasiveness of real trauma and grasping the necessity to one's patients of such trauma being named and, second, the inevitable participation of the analyst in enactments that may be extraordinarily painful for each person while they are taking place—has been richly elaborated in our literature. Each of these is central to grappling with implication. We suggest as well that distinctly personal aspects of the analyst, especially as they are made accessible to one's patient, are central to how we may understand and inhabit implication, including holding both vulnerability and responsibility, as well as the possibility for intimacy and relational growth.

Regarding the ubiquity of trauma, Davies and Frawley's work opened the door to being able, within our field, to both name and elaborate on the role of other kinds of trauma, including developmental or relational trauma (Bromberg, 2006, 2011), and the powerful and elusive effects of historical traumas transmitted through generations (Salberg & Grand, 2017; Silber, 2012). Vaughans (2017) address especially the intergenerational transmission of the horror of enslavement of Black people within the "collective memory of slavery by those who endured it" (2017, p. 228) and the subsequent generations of their children while stressing that the national response in the aftermath of slavery's official ending is part of the inherited trauma. Jones (2015) writes of the enslavement of Black Americans as a trauma affecting all of us, "scarr[ing] the psyche of both Blacks and Whites with the intergenerational transmission of the belief that dark skin and all other socially defined features of Blackness signify a difference that is inherently/genetically inferior" (2015, p. 723). The causes of trauma—social, historical, and idiosyncratic to each individual—compound one another and may be felt in multiple painful and complex ways within the treatment relationship.

## Intersubjectivity and the Analyst as Thoroughly Implicated

Acknowledging both historical trauma and the real impact of the analyst's unconscious participation in the treatment relationship has meant that our implication with our patients can come to be known and spoken of in ways that transcend the bounds of older versions of the analytic frame. From this perspective, in contrast to versions of psychoanalysis closer to Freud's, the analyst is more deeply implicated from the start. If in the classical model and its closest heirs, it is the patient who generates "data" via free association and the analyst who makes sense of it via interpretation, intersubjectivity in the analytic situation means—at the very least—that the patient's narratives, thoughts, and feelings, which emerge in the session, are co-created. The analyst is therefore involved in the generation of "psychoanalytic data"; just as the patient, at least in some versions of intersubjectivity, is involved in its interpretation (see Atlas & Aron's, 2017, delightful play on Ferro's analogy of the analyst as cook; and also McGleughlin, 2020, for a comparison of inherently dyadic relational approaches in contrast to Bionian approaches to intersubjectivity).

Beyond a state of involvement, implication connotes that one is "folded into" something larger (Rothberg, 2019, p. 1). Precisely how we are folded in depends on which version of intersubjectivity we orient to. In versions of post-Bionian field theory, for example, there is an emphasis on this something larger, the field itself, rather than two distinct (if infinitely complex) people. For example, Ferro (2020), in his response to McGleughlin (2020), writes that the current emphasis in Bionian field theory is to "attend to the field in which the analyst, patient, and their diffractions all equally become its characters" (2020, p. 148). He contrasts this with relational theory, which is concerned with two actors.

It is precisely the "two actors" part of relational theory that we wish to draw out. Relational versions of intersubjectivity have contained a tension between the intersubjective as field and the very specific interpersonal. On the one hand, intersubjective by nature connotes what is more fluid, in the sense not just of less bounded structures but of a movement out of two-ness in surrender to a Third (Benjamin, 2004, 2018)—a lawful relatedness where both parties can find one another in the wake of a rupture. On the other hand, relational analysts have stretched the bounds of the degree of the analyst's emotional participation resulting in a profoundly intimate form of interpersonal relatedness; it is between two separate, specific, and unique people. Thus, in the communication of unconsciouses of which Bass (2015) writes, there is a powerful personal degree of participation as there is in projective identificatory processes (Davies, 2004) and a discovery that one's own emergent intensely personal feeling is also the patient's dissociated overwhelming affect (Bromberg, 2006). We are implicated in both dimensions: as Benjamin (2018) has established, in accord with Ferenczi, we will inevitably wound our patients in just the ways they are most vulnerable, but our willingness to acknowledge this comes from seeing our own implication and speaking from that place. We would add, however, that it is in the register of the deeply personal that the analyst's vulnerability and responsibility come even more to the fore.

In this register, the analyst is implicated as a specific flawed person, both an active agent and a uniquely responsive subject. This forms a thread throughout the relational literature: we are not merely objects of transference, and we function as initiators as much as receptors; that is, we are subjects whose feelings, reveries, intentions, and missteps reflect ourselves and our patients in whose presence these are stirred. Seen through this lens, the vulnerabilities of the therapist are her own, and she may injure when the patient's projections or entreaties come too close. In these moments, too exclusive reliance on understanding the therapist as only responding, rather than sometimes initiating or intensifying the enactments, can mean not grasping that something is *really happening, now*, that involves two people, each vulnerable and one with greater responsibility for keeping the process safe enough. There is a power in having one's partner in interaction stop, listen more intently, and slowly grasp what it is that she has done that has affected you in a particular way. To acknowledge having caused harm in this case is not only to say that one has failed to contain or responded to provocation with retaliation (Winnicott, 1969) or withdrawal, but to allow the bewilderment, shame, and fear of not knowing for a bit just what one has done, and hanging in (Bromberg, 2006) and learning about it with and often from one's patient. To participate fully, to see one's implication in relation to the other, entails holding one's own vulnerability and the responsibility to this other person.

Benjamin's writing (1990, 2018) is central to both a theory and an ethos of subject-to-subject relating within psychoanalysis. She writes of what is both a longing and a developmental achievement, as well as a quality of relatedness between any two persons that must be continually reestablished—*mutual recognition* (1990). This mutuality is not coerced but is inherent in the nature of recognition: in order for me to feel recognized by you—meaning, to feel you are really grasping something central to my experience, that you really get me in some essential way—I have to be able to recognize you as a separate other who has subjectivity of your own from which this capacity, effort, and desire to recognize me originates. This is no minor achievement; it often has the feel of a small and sometimes sweatily achieved miracle when it is realized. If it is not easy really to grasp the other's experience, it is that much more challenging to do so when the other is reacting to something in us that we are not aware we are doing. The ways in which these unseen hotspots within patient and analyst may inflame one another are at the heart of relational writing on enactments. In perhaps its most transformative moments, mutual recognition emerges as one person—usually, but not always, the therapist—grasps and owns implication in relation to the other and communicates this in a meaningful way. This is often the "sweatily achieved" part; the miraculous part is in the way this opening of oneself, as one acknowledges how one has harmed the other, often leading to a reciprocal opening by the other person. Acknowledging implication has the power to deepen intimacy and recognition in a unique and powerful way.

Because of the nature of such unconscious enactments, we cannot escape repeating the injury our patients come to us to have healed (Ferenczi, 1949), but what we can do, Benjamin asserts, is to acknowledge this. This speaking of what has happened in the procedural heat of enactment, including the acknowledgment by the analyst, is essential in restoring a sense of lawfulness in human relating, allowing the felt sense of the "moral third" in the dyad. The Third, in Benjamin's conception of this vitalizing idea, is both process and structure: it is the place we can get to when two people are able to move out of the locked horns of complementary engagement, in which each feels "done to" by the ("doer") other. In complementarity, each feels vulnerable; each rejects the dreaded implication of blame, shame, and guilt. As we read Benjamin's descriptions of dyads moving from impasse into the Thirdness of mutual recognition (a mode of relating continually lost and regained), we can see how when the analyst is able to hold her own vulnerability alongside her responsibility, bearing her implication, this opens the possibility of both parties shifting.

As we have written about this (McKay, 2019), mutual recognition, as a quality of relatedness that goes beyond empathy, is characterized by a sense of grasping who this other person is in the moment when she is stretching herself to be able to see what you need her to, including what she has done that has left you feeling so missed. It is not only experiencing the acknowledgment of implication but feeling how the person who is offering this has had to shift in response to what you have needed her to understand.

The distinction between empathy and recognition seems important in considering implication, as the terms are often used interchangeably (e.g., Knoblauch, 2020), which can obscure important differences even as they often overlap. Layton (Layton, with Leavy-Sperounis, 2020), following Butler, argues that "acts" of recognition depend upon social norms and power structures and thus contain within them the oppressive dimensions of such structures. We are suggesting that the radical spirit of mutual recognition is advanced when the ways in which the interactions have been enacting these oppressive structures are part of what is recognized.

In this regard, we turn to recent work by González (2020), who offers a tremendously important additional lens, grounding the social very concretely in directly lived experience. Psychoanalysis, he points out, has tended to leave out the "groupal dimensions of subjectivity." Thus, González explains, gender, which had been regarded within psychoanalysis as a matter of same-sex identification with one's parent (with the larger social forces seen as carried by the mother or father), "is much more an effect of complexly layered identifications within and to ensembles, rather than to individuals" (p. 390). When we consider that both therapist and patient have a huge number of such "ensembles" (relatives, cultural communities, groups of friends at different stages of life, professional associations, etc.) that are both within us (constitute us) and with which we interact in the external world, the ways in which the analyst becomes implicated—particularly when there are power differentials involved—in relation to the patient's pain and struggles becomes infinitely complex.

We are struck by the way in which González's theorization of the multiple ensembles we each carry can be brought into dialogue with Rothberg's idea about the multiple positions one can occupy in regard to varying forms of oppression. We are not only continually engaged with our ensembles but have powerful feelings aroused when something—a word, a joke, an offhand comment, for example—evokes the ways in which those ensembles have been victims, perpetrators, or otherwise implicated. In such inevitable but unpredictable moments, we—as analysts—are implicated as distinct, complex, and unique persons who carry multiple social and "groupal" identities. We—patient and analyst both—are one and many, simultaneously, with one another.

## Psychoanalysis, Race, and Implication

Until very recently, there has been little space within psychoanalysis to think about race and racism, much less to dwell on one's own implication. This, as many authors have recently observed, despite the fact that we are supposed to be able to look at what is most difficult to look at, what is swept under the carpet but exerts more power the more it is disavowed. As the field finally tunes into listening more intently to those within our midst (Altman, 1995; Yi, 1998; Eng & Han, 2000; Leary, 2000; White, K. P., 2002; Suchet, 2004, 2007; White, C. 2015; Jones, 2015, 2020; Tummala-Narra, 2015; Evans Holmes, 2016; Hart, 2017; Vaughans, 2017, 2022; Grand & Salberg, 2017; Powell, 2018; González, 2020; Knoblauch, 2020; Sheehi, 2020; Stephens, 2020, 2022; Harris, 2022; Levine, 2022)[2] who have been calling our attention to this crucial dimension, we start to have the language to deepen our ability to conceptualize both subjectivity and intersubjectivity as including considerations of racial and other "groupal" (González, 2020) dimensions, as well as racism among other forms of insidious oppression.

Jones (2015) calls us to look at the ways in which our intersubjective experiences within the analytic field are stunted by the systems of oppression that contain us and that we then construct the field itself so that what is disavowed cannot enter. Such hierarchies of identity, she writes, "constitute a loss, in fact create it. They systematically prevent the other's reality from coming into view by threatening dangers and risks" (p. 723). Brickman (2017) calls our attention to how modes of thought deeply ingrained in our field serve to reinscribe racist ideologies in all their insidiousness. None of us can be unshaken by these challenges, which call for us to revisit some of our most cherished beliefs about how our mode of therapy proceeds, what is evoked in the analytic relationship and our field more broadly.

In order for us to allow the other's reality to come into view, the analyst must be able to reflect on and make use of her own racial locations—actual and perceived. Psychoanalytic training has a history of either totally disregarding the need for such reflection or, particularly for analysts of color, discouraging it. Thus, only relatively recently have authors such as Suchet (2007) begun to write of the need to "unravel" whiteness in psychoanalysis, while Jones (2020) writes of the pressures she has felt "to suspend the experience of myself as a black woman in order to occupy the space of analyst" (p. 78).

The therapist's—especially the white therapist's—quality of listening and care must be different when a space can be held open, including the fact that the therapist has benefited from structurally racist arrangements. The category of implicated subject helps pry open a space in which the therapist cannot be a neutral witness or bystander to the patient's feelings about racism or a racial enactment; at the same time, by helping prevent the situation from rapidly devolving into one where the therapist's guilt (perpetrator) or wounded innocence (victim) takes center stage (even, if that will inevitably occur in some heated moments), the concept of the implicated subject helps keep "the space of thirdness" (Benjamin, 2004, 2018) open long enough for new thoughts and feelings to emerge. Stephens's (2020, and this volume) elaboration of the need to cultivate the capacity for White double-consciousness deepens and makes more explicit how we may understand and work with implication where race is concerned.

While we were moving toward the conclusion of our initial draft of this paper, we were fortunate to read a series of papers in *Psychoanalytic Dialogues* (Knoblauch, 2020; Hartman, 2020; Sheehi, 2020) that considered a powerful moment in the work of a White (Knoblauch) therapist with a Black patient, whom he called Waverly. At the moment described, Waverly is talking with his therapist of many years about the distress stirred in him as he contemplates a move from one NYC neighborhood to another. He is living with a partner, who is excited and all in to make this move. However, the second neighborhood—unlike the one where Waverly has made his home up until now—is marked by the absence of Black people, a fact that evokes deep and complex anguish. As they are talking, Knoblauch replies in one moment with a particularly off (we would suggest meaningfully dissociated) "helpful" direction—might Waverly list the pros and cons of the two neighborhoods? Waverly replies first with a look of disbelief, concern, and irritation (p. 303) and then speaks to the sharp truth emerging in the moment—that his therapist does not know what it is like to walk as a Black man in a neighborhood not known as one in which Black people live. Knoblauch is struck by the truth of this and feels suddenly and painfully aware of his racial privilege and how he has failed Waverly at this moment—how much he has missed not only Waverly's experience of walking in his body in a racist world but how much his own White subjectivity has contributed to his missing his patient in such a deep way at this moment. Waverly (who confirmed the description as written by Knoblauch) watches his therapist really grappling with what it is that has just happened, the harm he—Knoblauch—has just committed. Then, something shifts in the session. As Knoblauch writes, "[i]n a strange way outside of the theory and practice in which I have been trained, this *lack of recognition* (or mis-recognition) catalyzes an opening" (p. 304). As something is mis-recognized, something else is opened; as Sheehi notes in her discussion of Knoblauch's paper, "the lived and embodied material reality of the present" (p. 327) is held by both participants.

To our reading, this seems to describe precisely the way recognition comes to be created between people when empathy is insufficient (McKay, 2019); that is, mutual recognition is characterized especially by those moments in which one person misses the other and then has to struggle not only with the miss but how it landed *and* where it came from. And it is in the second person's holding the space along with the first that this willingness to see how one has failed comes to matter deeply to the other. As we understand it, Knoblauch—a committed, thoughtful White person who thinks a great deal about race and his own Whiteness—was likely dissociating the affect associated with his own implication in what it means to move freely between neighborhoods, as he describes in the early part of the paper. He doesn't want to know, at that moment—to feel deep in his bones—how he is implicated, how maybe he himself really likes that second neighborhood being described, as Waverly's partner seems to. And in pushing away the guilt and shame that we imagine that would evoke for Knoblauch, he asks a question that lands like a thud.

What happens then is crucial: Knoblauch is willing to grasp, first, that he has really failed Waverly. He feels it personally, like a punch to the gut from his own fist. He is ashamed, and he bears this. And he is able to hold both the ways this is deeply, intimately, consequentially personal for Waverly, for himself, and for their connection—clearly a very strong one—and the ways in which his coolly reaching for a "rational" tool, listing the pros and cons, is an enactment of a racist power dynamic. In trying to flee from his implication in a racist system in which his own body would be welcomed, unremarkably, in a space where his patients would be both viewed as dangerous and actually be endangered, he enacts the very thing he is trying to escape from. While racial enactments may be inevitable, what happened next has to be worked for: as Knoblauch faces, in Waverly's presence, his implication in both the intimate miss in the intersubjective space and the injustice in the larger world they both inhabit and as Waverly allows himself, as hurt as he feels, to stay open to his therapist, the two together create a moment of mutual recognition that allows the power dynamic between them to shift.

We understand such moments in relational work as moments characterized by a feeling of "radical equality" (Mark, 2018). These moments are perhaps more elusive in dyads where racial or other marked differences in social power are present, in part because they demand that the therapist be willing to see himself not only as a flawed person, though that is necessary but as incorporating within himself the very oppression that he consciously hates and wishes to disavow.

## Conclusion

We are in a moment of reckoning with the ways in which aspects of our theories, our institutions, our ways of training, and even our understandings of what constitutes recognition (González, 2020; Knoblauch, 2020) bear the freight of racialized oppression. The imperative to examine and shift how we constitute our training and our theories, as González (2020) and others call us to do, makes a powerful argument for our thinking to the outside: we cannot change how we think and relate without changing the institutions that hold and shape us. We are focusing here on the ways in which we embody the outside within and between us, the enactments this engenders both instantiating the larger forces of oppression and also offering sites for transformation. In this, there is a specific form of hope. We are making a case for ways in which work between two people, in which both can look together at how they meet within a social fabric, can both transform the fabric, in some small way, and help bring into being moments of recognition that are both intimate and specific. To bear implication, whether it is in a singular moment of missing the thing the other most needed us to see or it is in the enormity of the ways we enact the systemic oppressions that run deeper in us than we want to believe, is what each of us can do, with our patients, with each other, in the consulting room and in the world.

## Notes

1  See also Nichols and Connolly (2020), writing on the political, moral, and also psychological case for reparations.
2  In the time we have been working on this project, there has been a reckoning within our field, so that the list of relevant papers has fortunately become much, much longer than is captured here.

## References

Altman, N. (1995). *The analyst in the inner city: Race, class, and culture through a psychoanalytic lens*. Routledge.

Aron, L. (1999). The patient's experience of the analyst's subjectivity. In S. Mitchell & L. Aron (Eds.), *Relational psychoanalysis: The emergence of a tradition*. The Analytic Press.

Atlas, G., & Aron, L. (2017). *Dramatic dialogue: Contemporary clinical practice*. Routledge.

Bass, A. (2015). The dialogue of unconsciouses, mutual analysis and the uses of the self in contemporary relational psychoanalysis. *Psychoanalytic Dialogues*, *25*(1), 2–17.

Benjamin, J. (1990). An outline of intersubjectivity: The development of recognition. *Psychoanalytic Psychology*, *7*(S), 33.

Benjamin, J. (2004). Beyond doer and done to: An intersubjective view of thirdness. *The Psychoanalytic Quarterly*, *73*(1), 5–46.

Benjamin, J. (2018). *Beyond doer and done to: Recognition theory, intersubjectivity and the third*. Routledge.

Bernheimer, C., & Kahane, C. (1985). *In Dora's case: Freud-hysteria-feminism*. Columbia University Press.

Brickman, C. (2017). *Race in psychoanalysis: Aboriginal populations in the mind*. Routledge.

Bromberg, P. M. (2003). Something wicked this way comes: Trauma, dissociation, and conflict: The space where psychoanalysis, cognitive science, and neuroscience overlap. *Psychoanalytic Psychology*, *20*(3), 558.

Bromberg, P. M. (2006). *Awakening the dreamer: Clinical journeys*. Routledge.

Bromberg, P. M. (2011). *The shadow of the tsunami: And the growth of the relational mind*. Routledge.

Butler, J. (2004). *Precarious life: The powers of mourning and violence*. Verso.

Connolly, M. (2021).

Cushman, P. (2015). Relational psychoanalysis as political resistance. *Contemporary Psychoanalysis*, *51*(3), 423–459.

Davies, J. M. (2004). Whose bad objects are we anyway? Repetition and our elusive love affair with evil. *Psychoanalytic Dialogues*, *14*(6), 711–732.

Davies, J. M. (2014). *Empathy, impasse, complementarity and therapeutic change: Adventures on the dark side of psychoanalysis.* Paper presented at the Irving Shulman Symposium, Widener University, Chester, PA.

Davies, J. M., & Frawley, M. G. (1994). *Treating the adult survivor of childhood sexual abuse* (Vol. 1). Basic Books.

Du Bois, W. E. B. (1903/1994). *The souls of black folk.* Dover Publications, Inc.

Eng, D. L., & Han, S. (2000). A dialogue on racial melancholia. *Psychoanalytic Dialogues*, *10*(4), 667–700.

Evans Holmes, D. (2016). Culturally imposed trauma: The sleeping dog has awakened. Will psychoanalysis take heed? *Psychoanalytic Dialogues*, *26*(6), 641–654.

Fanon, F. (1986/1967). *Black skin, White masks* (C. Lam Markmann, Trans.). Pluto Press.

Ferenczi, S. (1949). Confusion of the tongues between the adults and the child— (The language of tenderness and of passion). *International Journal of Psycho-Analysis*, *30*, 225–230.

Ferenczi, S. (1995). *The clinical diary of Sándor Ferenczi.* Harvard University Press.

Ferro, A. (2020). A discussion of "the analyst's necessary nonsovereignty and the generative power of the negative." *Psychoanalytic Dialogues*, *30*(2), 146–149.

Fors, M. (2018). *A grammar of power in psychotherapy: Exploring the dynamics of privilege.* American Psychological Association.

Freud, S. (1953). Fragment of an analysis of a case of hysteria (1905 [1901]). In *The standard edition of the complete psychological works of Sigmund Freud* (Vol. VII).

Freud, S. (1963). Introductory lectures on psychoanalysis (1917). In *The standard edition of the complete psychological works of Sigmund Freud* (Vol. XVI).

González, F. J. (2020). Trump cards and Klein Bottles: On the collective of the individual. *Psychoanalytic Dialogues*, *30*(4), 383–398.

Grand, S., & Salberg, J. (Eds.). (2017). *Trans-generational trauma and the other: Dialogues across history and difference.* Taylor & Francis.

Gump, J. P. (2010). Reality matters: The shadow of trauma on African American subjectivity. *Psychoanalytic Psychology*, *27*(1), 42.

Harris, A. (2009). You must remember this. *Psychoanalytic Dialogues*, *19*(1), 2–21.

Harris, A. (2022). Discussion: "Interrogating race, shame and mutual vulnerability." *Psychoanalytic Dialogues*, *32*, 2.

Hart, A. H. (2006). Danger and safety: The analyst as analytic subject. In *International forum of psychoanalysis* (Vol. 15, No. 4, pp. 220–225). Taylor & Francis Group.

Hart, A. H. (2017). From multicultural competence to radical openness: A psycho-analytic engagement of otherness. *The American Psychoanalyst*, *51*(1), 12–27.

Hartman, S. (2020). Binded by the white: A discussion of "Fanon's vision of embodied racism for psychoanalytic theory and practice." *Psychoanalytic Dialogues*, *30*(3), 317–324.

Hoffman, I. (1998). *Ritual and spontaneity in the psychoanalytic process: A dialectical-constructivist view*. Analytic Press.

Knoblauch, S. H. (2020). Fanon's vision of embodied racism for psychoanalytic theory and practice. *Psychoanalytic Dialogues*, *30*(3), 299–316.

Jones, A. L. (2015). A psychoanalytic reader's commentary: On erasure and negation as a barrier to the future. *Psychoanalytic Dialogues*, *25*(6), 719–724.

Jones, A. L. (2020). A Black woman as an American analyst: Some observations from one woman's life over four decades. *Studies in Gender and Sexuality*, *21*(2), 77–84.

Layton, L. (2009). Who's responsible? Our mutual implication in each other's suffering. *Psychoanalytic Dialogues*, *19*(2), 105–120.

Layton, L., with Leavy-Sperounis, M. (2020). *Toward a social psychoanalysis: Culture, character, and normative unconscious processes*. Routledge.

Leary, K. (2000). Racial enactments in dynamic treatment. *Psychoanalytic Dialogues*, *10*(4), 639–653.

Levine, L. (2016). Mutual vulnerability: Intimacy, psychic collisions, and the shards of trauma. *Psychoanalytic Dialogues*, *26*(5), 571–579.

Levine, L. (2022). Interrogating race, shame and mutual vulnerability: "Overlapping and interlapping waves of relation." *Psychoanalytic Dialogues*, *32*, 2.

Mark, D. (2018). Forms of equality in relational psychoanalysis. In L. Aron, S. Grand, & J. A. Slochower (Eds.), *De-idealizing relational theory: A critique from within*. Routledge.

McGleughlin, J. (2020). The analyst's necessary nonsovereignty and the generative power of the negative. *Psychoanalytic Dialogues*, *30*(2), 123–138.

McKay, R. K. (2019). Bread and roses: Empathy and recognition. *Psychoanalytic Dialogues*, *29*(1), 75–91.

Nichols, B. K., & Connolly, M. L. (2020). *Transforming ghosts into ancestors: Unsilencing the psychological case for reparations to descendants of American slavery*. Other/Wise: Online Journal for the International Forum for Psychoanalytic Education.

Powell, D. R. (2018). Race, African Americans, and psychoanalysis: Collective silence in the therapeutic situation. *Journal of the American Psychoanalytic Association*, *66*(6), 1021–1049.

Rothberg, M. (2019). *The implicated subject: Beyond victims and perpetrators*. Stanford University Press.

Salberg, J., & Grand, S. (2017). *Wounds of history*. Routledge.

Sheehi, L. (2020). The reality principle: Fanonian undoing, unlearning, and decentering: A discussion of "Fanon's vision of embodied racism for psychoanalytic theory and practice." *Psychoanalytic Dialogues*, *30*(3), 325–330.

Silber, L. (2012). Ghostbusting transgenerational processes. *Psychoanalytic Dialogues*, *22*(1), 106–122.

Stephens, M. (2020). Getting next to ourselves: The interpersonal dimensions of double-consciousness. *Contemporary Psychoanalysis*, *56*(2–3), 201–225.

Stephens, M. (2022). Relational racialization and segregated whiteness: Discussion of Interrogating race, shame and mutual vulnerability: "Overlapping and interlapping waves of relation." *Psychoanalytic Dialogues*, *32*, 2.

Stern, D. B. (2009). Partners in thought: A clinical process theory of narrative. *The Psychoanalytic Quarterly*, *78*(3), 701–731.

Stern, D. B. (2013a). Field theory in psychoanalysis, Part 1: Harry Stack Sullivan and Madeleine and Willy Baranger. *Psychoanalytic Dialogues*, *23*(5), 487–501.

Stern, D. B. (2013b). Field theory in psychoanalysis, Part 2: Bionian field theory and contemporary interpersonal/relational psychoanalysis. *Psychoanalytic Dialogues*, *23*, 630–645.

Suchet, M. (2004). A relational encounter with race. *Psychoanalytic Dialogues*, *14*(4), 423–438.

Suchet, M. (2007). Unraveling whiteness. *Psychoanalytic Dialogues*, *17*(6), 867–886.

Tummala-Narra, P. (2015). Cultural competence as a core emphasis of psychoanalytic psychotherapy. *Psychoanalytic Psychology*, *32*(2), 275.

Vaughans, K. C. (2017). Repair and resilience in the transgenerational transmission of trauma. In J. Salberg & S. Grand (Eds.), *Wounds of history*. Routledge.

Vaughans, K. C. (2022). Commentary on Lauren Levine's "Interrogating race, shame and mutual vulnerability." *Psychoanalytic Dialogues*, *32*, 2.

White, C. J. (2015). Strangers in paradise: Trevor, Marley, and me: Reggae music and the foreigner other. *Psychoanalytic Dialogues*, *25*(2), 176–193.

White, K. P. (2002). Surviving hating and being hated: Some personal thoughts about racism from a psychoanalytic perspective. *Contemporary Psychoanalysis*, *38*(3), 401–422.

Winnicott, D. W. (1969). The use of an object. *International Journal of Psycho-Analysis*, *50*, 711–716.

Yi, K. Y. (1998). Transference and race: An intersubjective conceptualization. *Psychoanalytic Psychology*, *15*(2), 245.

# Index

For Product Safety Concerns and Information please contact our EU
representative  GPSR@taylorandfrancis.com
Taylor & Francis Verlag GmbH, Kaufingerstraße 24, 80331 München, Germany